# MASTERING CHAOS

## The Leadership Insights Triology

## ROBBIN LAIRD

Second Line of Defense

# CONTENTS

# MASTERING CHAOS



## Part One
## SETTING THE STAGE



## Part Two
## SHAPING AN APPROACH FOR CHAOS MANAGEMENT



## Part Three
## FURTHER THOUGHTS ON LEADERSHIP FOR MASTERING CHAOS

# FOREWORD

# INTRODUCTION

This omnibus edition combines three complementary works addressing the communication crisis that defines contemporary professional life: *Public Speaking for Professionals: How to Engage and Convince Your Audience*, *Listen to Lead: How Empathy and Better Conversations Transform Your Work and Life*, and *Mastering Chaos: Shaping a Way Ahead for Chaos Management*. Together, these volumes constitute not merely a skills-development curriculum but a sophisticated analytical framework for understanding and navigating the communicative challenges inherent in fragmented, complex organizational environments.

## THE FRAGMENTATION DIAGNOSIS

These works share a common analytical foundation: modern professional communication occurs within a fundamentally fragmented landscape. This fragmentation operates at multiple levels simultaneously. Social media and algorithmic content curation have created informational echo chambers that reinforce existing beliefs while eliminating meaningful encounters with opposing perspectives. Organizations mirror this dynamic internally, as functional specializations, professional vocabularies, and hierarchical divisions transform departments into isolated tribes that share physical space but inhabit different cognitive worlds.

The implications are profound. Traditional communication models assumed speakers and audiences shared basic frames of reference. In today's fragmented landscape, no such shared foundation exists. Speakers face audiences with divergent cultural backgrounds, professional vocabularies, and informational contexts. Leaders confront teams whose members literally perceive different organizational realities. Even the definition of "the problem" becomes contested, as different stakeholders see different facets of complex situations through their distinct lenses. Effective communication thus requires not just message clarity but the capacity to bridge fundamental divides in worldview and understanding.

## SPEAKING AND LISTENING AS COMPLEMENTARY DISCIPLINES

What makes this series distinctive is its recognition that the fragmentation crisis requires addressing both outward communication—the ability to craft and deliver compelling messages—and inward reception —the disciplined capacity to genuinely understand perspectives different from one's own. *Public Speaking for Professionals* addresses the former; *Listen to Lead* addresses the latter. The sequence is deliberate: professionals must first develop the confidence and technical capability to speak effectively before they can productively integrate the insights gained through empathetic listening.

*Public Speaking for Professionals* grounds itself in a fundamental truth: public speaking is not an optional communication channel but a vital tool for career advancement, leadership, and influence. In democratic societies and professional organizations alike, the ability to articulate ideas clearly and defend them persuasively determines whose perspectives shape decisions, whose expertise gains recognition, and whose careers advance. The volume systematically dismantles the barriers— primarily fear and lack of structured approach—that prevent professionals from developing this capability.

The book's treatment of stage fright exemplifies its practical orientation. Rather than offering platitudes about "just being yourself," it explains the psychological and evolutionary roots of performance anxiety, then provides concrete techniques—power posing, breathing exercises, personalized confidence rituals—for managing it. The emphasis on personalization reflects understanding that professionals operate in diverse contexts requiring different approaches; there is no single formula, but rather a toolkit from which individuals construct methods suited to their circumstances.

Similarly, the approach to speech construction balances structure with adaptability. The "elevator speech" concept, a concise, compelling core message—provides the necessary anchor, while the "speech blueprint" offers organizational scaffolding. Yet throughout, the work stresses the importance of reading and responding to audience cues, adapting presentations in real time to maintain engagement. This reflects a broader principle that effectiveness comes not from rigid adherence to plans but from disciplined improvisation grounded in thorough preparation.

The book's treatment of visual aids, time management, and handling unexpected challenges similarly prioritizes practical wisdom over theoretical purity. It acknowledges that public speaking is inherently unpredictable and provides guidance not for eliminating uncertainty but for maintaining composure and effectiveness within it.

## EMPATHY AS OPERATIONAL CAPABILITY

*Listen to Lead* builds on this foundation by reframing empathy from a soft interpersonal skill to a core operational capability required for effective leadership in complex, fragmented environments. This reframing proves crucial for professionals operating in high-stakes, information-intensive contexts where failure to understand diverse perspectives can have serious consequences.

The volume defines empathy not as sympathetic "feeling for" others at a distance, but as the disciplined practice of understanding others' experiences, constraints, and reasoning well enough that one can articulate their position in ways they would recognize. This definition transforms empathy from a personality trait into a learnable competency with specific component skills: active listening, perspective-taking, suspension of premature judgment, and integration of divergent viewpoints.

The work grounds this framework in neuroscience, explaining that empathy relies on plastic neural systems that strengthen or weaken through use, much as muscles respond to exercise. This biological foundation counters dismissive views of empathy as mere sentiment by anchoring it in fundamental human cognitive architecture. For professionals steeped in technical and analytical cultures, this provides permission to treat empathy as serious operational capacity rather than optional personal quality.

The central argument holds that most contemporary failures in leadership and teamwork are fundamentally communicative. Organizations possess tremendous technical expertise and strategic sophistication, yet fail because information doesn't flow, cross-functional collaboration breaks down, and critical warnings never surface. These failures trace not to insufficient analysis but to insufficient listening—the erosion of capacity to engage in genuine conversation across differences.

The prescribed solution centers on recovering "lost arts" of listening and conversation. Listening, properly understood, is not passive reception but active, cognitively demanding work: quieting internal monologue, suspending categorization, tolerating ambiguity, and offering generative attention that helps speakers clarify their own thinking. Conversation, similarly, is not serial monologue or adversarial debate but collaborative exploration—a process through which participants think better together than individually.

## FROM THEORY TO PRACTICE: CONCRETE DISCIPLINES

What distinguishes both volumes from typical communication guides is their emphasis on specific, repeatable practices rather than abstract principles. *Public Speaking for Professionals* provides structured approaches to crafting elevator speeches, developing speech blueprints, using the "rule of three" for memorable organization, and creating effective calls to action. It offers detailed guidance on managing time through techniques like time blocking and strategic pausing, and on integrating visual aids seamlessly into presentations.

*Listen to Lead* similarly emphasizes daily disciplines: the three-second pause before responding to ensure genuine processing; asking clarifying questions before asserting views; reflective listening that summarizes and checks understanding; and conversational architecture that protects attention through device-free sessions and formats prioritizing inclusive dialogue. These are not one-time workshop exercises but habits to be practiced until they become institutional norms.

The application to conflict resolution exemplifies this practical orientation. The work argues that organizational conflicts typically begin as listening failures, not irreconcilable interest differences. Parties retreat to positions, interpret disagreement as threat, and stop engaging genuinely. The empathetic approach requires articulating opposing positions to satisfaction before responding, shifting from assertion to inquiry about underlying concerns, and allowing conversations to develop rather than rushing to closure. Examples from defense and industrial contexts demonstrate how this approach unlocks previously invisible synthesis options by converting adversarial bargaining into collaborative problem-solving.

## CHAOS MANAGEMENT AND ADAPTIVE ORGANIZATIONS

*Mastering Chaos* extends the framework from managing discrete communication events to building adaptive organizational capabilities. Many institutions still treat disruption as temporary deviation from equilibrium, using linear "identify–analyze–solve–return to normal" models. In reality, compressed time cycles and ubiquitous complexity have made chaos a persistent operating condition, invalidating such approaches.

Empathetic communication becomes foundational to "chaos management" because only leaders and organizations that integrate multiple conflicting perspectives can construct understanding rich enough to guide wise action under uncertainty. The concept of "genuine projects"—initiatives addressing real, widely felt challenges that require diverse capabilities—provides the mechanism. By pulling people from different organizational tribes into concrete shared work, these projects convert abstract unity appeals into lived collaboration experiences, building trust through accomplishment rather than rhetoric.

This organizational vision parallels broader trends in operational transformation. Just as modern military operations have shifted from hierarchical "kill chains" to networked "kill webs," effective organizational communication requires moving from top-down message broadcasting to distributed conversational networks that surface and synthesize dispersed knowledge. In both cases, the fundamental challenge is accessing and integrating intelligence distributed across specialized functions, ranks, and cultures.

## COMMUNICATION AS TRANSFORMATION

This three-volume series represents far more than a communication skills curriculum. It constitutes a sophisticated framework for understanding and navigating the fundamental challenges of professional effectiveness in an age of fragmentation. By addressing both the technical capabilities required for effective speaking and the disciplined practices necessary for genuine listening, the series provides complementary approaches to a central problem: how to bridge divides, integrate diverse perspectives, and enable collective intelligence to function when traditional foundations of shared understanding have eroded.

The framework's power lies in its grounding in field research and practical experience with leaders confronting real stakes in defense, government, and corporate contexts. The emphasis on concrete practices over abstract principles, on adaptation over rigid formulas, and on building institutional habits through daily disciplines reflects this operational orientation.

For professionals navigating fragmented organizations, leading across cultural and functional boundaries, or simply seeking more effective ways to contribute and advance, these volumes offer essential guidance. They demonstrate that the communication crisis characterizing contemporary professional life need not be inevitable, but can be addressed through disciplined development of both speaking and listening capabilities. In doing so, they provide not just techniques for better presentations or meetings, but a pathway toward more adaptive, resilient, and effective professional practice in an age that demands it.

# PUBLIC SPEAKING FOR PROFESSIONALS

## How to Engage and Convince Your Audience

# PREFACE

When I arrived at Columbia University to begin my PhD, I also found myself teaching part time at a high school in Queens. Convincing a classroom of students with very different language skills and cultural backgrounds to stay with you for an hour is one of the most honest apprenticeships in public speaking you can have. You quickly learn that if you cannot interest them, you cannot teach them; and if you cannot teach them, you will not reach them at all.

Those early years shaped how I think about speaking. As a graduate student and then a university teacher, I discovered that standing in front of a diverse room is not a performance tacked onto "real" professional work. It is a core discipline. Speaking clearly and with conviction is one of the ways you earn the right to be taken seriously by people older, more established, or more powerful than you are or being able to work with younger generations who literally were born into a different digital and communications world then you were.

Over time I also learned a crucial lesson: whatever most excites you about your subject is the heart of your message. If you bury that energy under elaborate argument, overstuffed slides, or bureaucratic language, you lose both yourself and your audience. Your first task is not to display how much you know. Your first task is to show why this topic matters to you, and why it should matter to them.

When I later moved to Washington, DC and worked across research organizations and government agencies, I met a very different communication culture: the language of bureaucratese. Much of that discourse is designed to avoid commitment, to sound "sound" without saying anything that might obligate someone to act.

I have never aspired to that kind of soundness. The approach in this book grows instead from a different conviction: your professional voice should help shape a way ahead, not merely signal that you belong to the club.

That is why this book emphasizes authenticity and clarity. Audiences, whether in government, business, education, or the military, are not just evaluating your data. They are deciding whether you are someone worth listening to now or in the future. They want to know what you actually think, what genuinely interests you, and how your perspective might help them solve problems they care about.

Very often you will be asked to speak on a topic defined by others: a company initiative, a government policy, a project status, or a technical development. You may not control the assignment, but you can control how you inhabit it. The question to ask yourself is not "How do I cover every slide they sent me?" but "What do I find most interesting, most consequential, or most troubling about this subject?" Build your talk around that, and let supporting detail serve the core, not replace it.

The simple, frequently forgotten truth is that speaking is not writing. A speech is not an article read out loud, and it is not a book compressed into 30 minutes. You do not gain credibility by filling every second of your allotted time or by overwhelming the room with a blizzard of points. Decide on one central idea you want this audience to remember a year from now, write it down in one clear sentence, and shape everything else around it. You can always direct people to your reports, articles, or books for depth.

In an age where nearly every audience is equipped with cell phones, you are competing not just with other speakers but with the entire digital world. Your goal is not to win a contest for attention in the moment, but to earn a place in the much smaller mental list of people whose work they want to follow. You want them to leave thinking, "I need to keep track of this person," not "I hope I never have to sit through that again."

In that sense, you are inseparable from your message. If you fail to convey why you care, your message will not land, no matter how "important" it is on paper.

Success in public speaking is within reach if you are clear about your core message, disciplined about how long you speak, and willing to strip away the self-created "word salad" that so often passes for expertise.

Clear speaking drives clear thinking; clear thinking, sustained over time, is one of the paths to genuine leadership in your profession.

This book is written to help you build that path.

# INTRODUCTION

Public speaking is not just about standing up and delivering a talk it is about shaping how you think, how you connect, and how you lead in a world that is fragmenting and accelerating around you.

Early in my professional career, I stood before a room full of professionals, ready to share insights on a topic I cared deeply about. My heart raced; my mind worked overtime to keep fear at bay. What changed the moment was not a perfectly crafted sentence, but the decision to focus on the message and the people in front of me rather than on my own anxiety. As I watched the faces in the room shift from polite attention to genuine engagement, I learned something that has stayed with me across four decades public speaking, done well, is one of the most powerful disciplines for clarifying your own thinking and influencing the world around you.

Over the years, speaking has never been my only job. I have been a teacher, researcher, analyst, interviewer, author, and sometime trouble-maker in bureaucratic systems.

But in every role, the ability to stand up in front of other human beings and say something clear, honest, and worth their time has been central to my professional life. Speaking has been my most demanding classroom.

It has forced me to make my arguments simpler and more precise than they sounded in my head. It has exposed the gaps in my reasoning that dense prose could hide. It has taught me, again and again, that if you cannot explain an idea to a mixed room of busy people, you probably do not yet understand it yourself.

This book grows out of that very practical realization. Public speaking is not an ornament you add once you are already successful; it is one of the core tools through which you become the kind of professional who can adapt, influence, and continue to grow across very different roles and stages of life.

Learning to speak well is really about working on your mental furniture for thinking, writing, and communication. It gives you a portable skill set you can carry into classrooms, boardrooms, media interviews, multinational meetings, and informal conversations in hangars, wardrooms, and conference coffee breaks.

But the environment in which we now speak is fundamentally different from the one in which I began. We live in what I have elsewhere called the anarchy of the moment a world where events move faster than our institutions, where information floods us through multiple channels, and where the shared public spaces that once anchored democratic debate are eroding. You see it in tribalized social media feeds, in the collapse of a consensual national culture, and in the way audiences come to a room already living inside very different informational universes. You see it in the compression of time leaders no longer have weeks to react; they are pushed to respond within hours, sometimes minutes, under the scrutiny of cameras and phones.

In such a world, public speaking becomes even more important and more difficult. You are no longer addressing a relatively homogeneous audience that shares your references, your language, or your assumptions about reality. You are speaking across tribes, professions, and generational codes. You may be using English with people for whom it is a second or third language or with native speakers whose cultural experience of "English" bears little resemblance to your own. Signals are easily misread, metaphors misfire, and words that sound simple in one context carry very different weight in another.

That is why this book treats public speaking as more than a bag of tricks for slides and stage fright. It is an introduction to a discipline that will underwrite everything else you do as a professional in this age of fragmentation.

When you learn to shape and deliver a clear message, you are also learning to think under pressure. When you learn to read a room and adjust as you go, you are practicing the early stages of empathy. When you learn to hold your ground in a tough Q&A or recover from a failure at the podium, you are rehearsing small versions of what senior leaders must do in crises and chaotic environments.

This volume is the first in a series on Personal Professional Development Insights. Each book addresses a different layer of what it takes to grow as a professional and as a leader in this turbulent era. This one, *Public Speaking for Professionals,* focuses on your personal platform your voice, your confidence, and your ability to craft and deliver messages that people can hear and act upon.

The second volume, *Listen to Lead,* goes deeper into empathy, listening, and the art of genuine conversation in an age where we are more connected than ever yet often unable to understand one another.

The third, *Mastering Chaos,* addresses how organizations and leaders can build the adaptive capacity to operate effectively in an environment of perpetual disruption.

You should think of this book, then, as your entry ramp into that broader journey. Here we start with the basics that sound simple but are rarely mastered. Why public speaking matters so much for your professional development and your ability to shape a more flexible way ahead for your life. How English, as a diverse and global language, makes clarity both more challenging and more essential. How to build a foundation of confidence, not by pretending fear does not exist but by learning to manage it. How to structure your message so that non-specialists can follow your logic. How to actually engage an audience, not just talk at them. How to manage time, pacing, and unexpected disruptions in the room. How to develop a speaking style that is honest, distinctive, and suited to who you are, rather than an imitation of someone else's mannerisms.

As you work through these chapters, I encourage you to treat every speaking opportunity not as a test you either "pass" or "fail," but as an experiment. Each talk is a chance to clarify your thinking, to test how your ideas land with real people, and to learn something about your own reactions under pressure. Pay attention to what captures your audience's energy and what loses it. Notice the moments when you find yourself listening while you speak noticing a question behind a question, a hesitation in the room, or a line of thought you had not anticipated. Those are the moments where this book begins to intersect with the themes developed in the later volumes on empathy and chaos.

You do not need to aspire to political office or a CEO role to take this seriously. Whatever your profession, if you want to influence decisions, shape debate, or simply keep learning from the people around you, you will have to stand up and speak. You will have to do it to peers, to superiors, to subordinates, to strangers. You will sometimes have to do it in situations where you do not control the setting, the technology, or the mood in the room. You will occasionally have to do it when the stakes are high and the time is short. You cannot control all those conditions. You can control how prepared you are to meet them.

By the end of this book, you should be able to:

- Understand why public speaking is a core enabling skill for your long-term professional development, not a marginal elective.
- Build practical habits that help you manage fear, sharpen your message, and engage diverse audiences.
- See speaking as part of a larger discipline of listening, learning, and leading that you can deepen through the companion volumes on empathy and chaos management.

This is not a book about becoming a performer who dazzles and disappears. It is about becoming a professional whose voice carries weight because it is clear, grounded, and connected to real work and real people.

The stage, whether literal or virtual, is not a place apart from your life; it is one of the places where your life's work will be tested and made visible.

My aim is to help you step onto that stage with enough skill, structure, and self-knowledge that you can not only engage and convince your audience, but also grow, over time, into the kind of leader our turbulent era requires.

# 1

## WHY MASTERING PUBLIC SPEAKING IS SO IMPORTANT FOR PROFESSIONAL DEVLEOPMENT

I did not set out to become "a public speaker." I set out to think for a living, to write, to teach, to work with organizations wrestling with hard problems. Speaking came with the territory. Only later did I realize that learning to speak well was not an accessory to that work it was one of the core disciplines that made every other part of my professional life possible.

In most jobs, there is a path you can see from the start. You enter a profession, climb a ladder, and eventually retire from a role whose contours were visible early on.

My own life has been less a ladder and more an odyssey. I have taught in a high school in Queens, lectured at universities, worked in research institutes and government agencies, interviewed military leaders, written books, and built a platform that straddles several worlds. Across all of that, one skill has remained constant: the ability to stand up in front of diverse audiences and say something clear, honest, and worth their time.

Speaking has never been my main activity in a narrow sense. But mastering it has been essential to every role I have played. Public speaking has taught me how to organize my thinking, how to test ideas in front of skeptical professionals, how to engage people from different cultures and backgrounds, and how to keep learning long after most people would have settled into routines. It has given me the tools to remain professionally alive, rather than simply "finishing" a career.

This book begins from a simple conviction: if you can think clearly, speak clearly, and connect with others under pressure, you have built a core platform for professional development that will serve you in ways you cannot yet imagine.

## PUBLIC SPEAKING AS MENTAL FURNITURE

When I was a young college student, I thought public speaking was a class you took to learn a few tricks about how to present an argument to an audience. I did not yet see that speaking would become one of the main ways I worked on my mental furniture the arrangement of ideas, assumptions, and habits that shape how I think and act.

Speaking forces you to simplify and clarify. You cannot hide behind dense prose or jargon when you have a limited amount of time and a room full of people whose attention can wander at any moment. You have to decide what matters. You have to test whether your logic chain holds when it is exposed to the air. You have to answer the unspoken question every listener brings: "Why should I care about this?"

That discipline is brutal in the best sense. It reveals vagueness and self-deception. It shows you where you do not yet understand your own argument. It also shows you, often to your surprise, which of your ideas actually resonate with others. Each talk becomes a form of field testing for your thinking.

This is why I say that learning public speaking is about working your mental furniture for thinking, writing, and communication. When you strengthen one leg of that triangle, the others benefit. A talk that lands often becomes a clearer article. A conversation in a hangar or a conference hallway sharpens a chapter in a book. The process is circular and reinforcing.

If you want to remain adaptable over a long professional life, you need that kind of ongoing intellectual gymnasium. Public speaking provides it.

# FROM ONE JOB TO AN ODYSSEY

In my own case, speaking changed the very shape of my professional journey. As a graduate student and then a young university teacher, the ability to hold the attention of a classroom of diverse students was not optional. In a high school in Queens, where many students came from different language backgrounds, every successful class was a small victory in communication. Convincing those students to listen to you, guiding them through a learning experience, was ground truth in public speaking.

Later, as I moved into research organizations and government work in Washington, I encountered a different challenge: the great evil of communicating in bureaucratese. Washington discourse is often rooted in trying to say as little as possible. The goal is to sound "sound," to use a term the British apply to insiders who speak the group language that avoids commitment while signaling membership in the club.

I have never aspired to that kind of soundness. My public speaking has been designed instead to shape a way ahead for professionals who want to be authentic, who want to think about real problems, and who are willing to say something that actually commits them. That choice has had consequences. It has sometimes made life more difficult in bureaucratic settings. But it has also opened doors to conversations, collaborations, and roles that would never have appeared had I confined myself to safe language.

For many people, whatever job they start with is simply an entry point. Through public speaking, you can shape a brand or identity that becomes visible beyond your immediate role. Inside a firm, your ability to articulate ideas clearly can make you the person people seek out when real decisions are on the table. With customers, speaking can separate you from competitors who hide behind slides and jargon. Over time, it can give you the option to launch your own company, consultancy, or platform.

Public speaking is one of the key venues through which your professional identity becomes legible to the world.

# WHY IT MATTERS MORE IN THE
# ANARCHY OF THE MOMENT

All of this would be true in any era. But we are not living in any era. We are living in a time I have elsewhere called the anarchy of the moment a condition in which events move faster than the institutions designed to manage them, information floods through multiple channels, and shared frameworks for understanding reality are eroding.

Social media has accelerated tribalism. Different groups live in different informational universes, each with its own language, assumptions, and "facts." The consensual culture that once made it possible to assume a shared set of references in a national audience has fractured. Internationally, English has become a global language, but it is not a single, common language. It is a family of dialects, accents, and usage patterns that reflect different histories and power relations.

In this environment, public speaking is both more difficult and more essential.

It is more difficult because you cannot assume that your audience shares your cultural references, your metaphors, or even your default meanings for key words. A story that resonates in Washington may be opaque in Canberra or Paris. A term that seems neutral in one setting may be loaded in another. When you speak, you are not just conveying information; you are negotiating meaning across divides.

It is more essential because fragmented societies and organizations still need people who can articulate problems clearly, frame choices honestly, and help groups move from confusion to some kind of shared understanding. Speeches alone will not fix tribalism. But the disciplines you learn in speaking clear thinking under time pressure, the ability to read a room, the willingness to adjust based on feedback are exactly the disciplines leaders need when the environment will not sit still.

If you want to be effective in this anarchy of the moment, you cannot avoid learning how to speak. You must learn to do so in ways that are sensitive to language diversity, cultural fracture, and the collapsing attention span of over-stimulated audiences. That is hard work. It is also an opportunity. Those who can do it will be rare and valuable.

## ETHICS AND THE PUBLIC SQUARE

There is another dimension to why mastering public speaking matters for your development: the ethical one. In a democratic culture, public debate remains one of the few means we have to test ideas, hold power accountable, and chart the way ahead together. The 19th-century philosopher John Stuart Mill argued that any worthwhile opinion must be able to stand up to public scrutiny and debate. I would add: that presumes there are people capable of articulating those opinions in public, and of withstanding the discomfort that comes with doing so.

If you care about the direction of your profession, your organization, or your society, you cannot confine your convictions to private conversations. At some point, you will need to speak. That may be in a formal setting a hearing, a board meeting, a town hall or in a more intimate one a staff gathering, a classroom, a media interview. In each case, your ability to make a case clearly and honestly will affect whether your ideas remain abstractions or begin to shape reality.

Mastering public speaking is therefore not just a career play. It is part of your contribution to the public square, however narrowly or broadly you define that square. It is one way you exercise responsibility in decision-making and accountability in democratic cultures.

## THE LINK TO EMPATHY AND CHAOS MANAGEMENT

This book is the first in a series on Personal Professional Development Insights. Although it focuses on public speaking, it is not isolated from the themes of the other volumes. It is, rather, the entry point.

In this volume, you work on yourself: your clarity of thought, your confidence, your ability to structure messages, and your capacity to engage real audiences.

In the second volume, *Listen to Lead*, you deepen the relational side of that work. You move from speaking to listening, from presentation to conversation, from monologue to the shared work of understanding.

You learn how empathy, in a fragmented communication environment, becomes a core leadership competence.

In the third volume, *Mastering Chaos*, you extend these personal and relational skills to the organizational level. You explore how to build intellectual flexibility, institutional resilience, and social cohesion in institutions that must operate under conditions of perpetual disruption.

Seen together, these books trace a path from personal mastery to relational mastery to organizational mastery. Public speaking sits at the beginning because it trains several capabilities that recur all along that path:

- The ability to simplify complexity without falsifying it.
- The ability to stay present when you feel exposed.
- The ability to notice and respond to other people's reactions in real time.
- The willingness to treat every performance as part of a longer learning process.

As you read, I invite you to hold that larger arc in mind. You are not learning public speaking so that you can fill up time at conferences. You are learning it so that you can become the kind of professional who can think clearly, connect across differences, and lead others through the anarchy of the moment.

## WHAT THIS CHAPTER ASKS OF YOU

Before we turn to the practical work of dealing with language diversity, building confidence, structuring your message, and engaging audiences, take a moment to consider your own starting point.

Ask yourself:

- How has speaking, so far, shaped your opportunities or limited them?
- Where do you feel most uncomfortable when you have to speak in front of others?

- What kinds of audiences do you most want to reach in the next chapter of your professional life?
- What would become possible for you if you could think and speak clearly under pressure?

Your honest answers to these questions will do more for your development than any list of tips. They will help you see public speaking not as a hurdle to clear, but as a discipline to embrace a discipline that can carry you from your current role into futures you cannot yet fully see.

The chapters that follow will stay close to practice. We will talk about English as a diverse language, building a foundation of confidence, crafting and structuring your message, and engaging your audience effectively. But beneath each practical technique lies the larger stakes introduced here: your ability to think, connect, and lead in a world where none of those can be taken for granted.

# THE CHALLENGE OF ENGLISH AS A DIVERSE LANGUAGE

One of the great illusions of our time is that because "everyone" uses English, we therefore share a common language. In reality, English has become a sprawling family of dialects, idioms, and usage patterns shaped by different histories, cultures, and power relations. What you intend to say in your version of English is not necessarily what someone else hears in theirs.

If you speak only inside your own tribe, this illusion may never be challenged. The moment you step into international settings, cross-cultural groups, or even mixed American audiences shaped by different media ecosystems, the illusion collapses. You discover that words you thought were simple are not simple at all, that references you assumed were universal land with a thud, and that jokes you considered harmless can be puzzling or offensive.

For a professional speaker, this is not a marginal inconvenience. It is a central fact of your operating environment.

## ONE LANGUAGE, MANY WORLDS

I have been part of organizations on three continents and have often addressed audiences whose first language is not English or who use an

English that is decidedly not American. As George Bernard Shaw quipped, England and America are two countries separated by a common language. I would add Australia, and I would extend the list to any place where English operates as a second or third language layered over local tongues and cultures.

When you speak to an audience that shares your cultural experience and version of English, you tend to rely on shared references. You use idioms, jokes, and examples that come naturally to you and that you assume they will recognize. When you move abroad or into more diverse settings, that assumption fails. The stories that once carried your message now require explanation. The metaphors you use may have no resonance. Even the rhythm of your speech, the speed at which you move, and the way you signal transitions can feel off to listeners who learned English differently.

This is not simply a matter of politeness. It is a substantive challenge. If your listeners cannot map your words onto their lived experience, they cannot engage your ideas. No amount of charisma will fix that.

The most practical adjustment is often the simplest. When addressing heterogeneous or foreign audiences, it is useful to prepare a single page or handout that identifies the five key points you will make, in straightforward language, stripped of culture-bound references. That page becomes an anchor for people whose ears may struggle to keep up with your accent, whose own English may be inflected by different educational systems, and whose mental dictionary may not match your own. It is one way of acknowledging that English, in this room, is not one language but many.

## SPEAKING AS JOINT INVENTION

This challenge is not just a constraint; it is an opportunity. When you address a mixed audience in English, you have the chance to co-invent language with them. You are not merely transmitting a pre-packaged thought; you are negotiating meanings that can work across backgrounds. That is one of the most creative aspects of public speaking.

Some of my most rewarding experiences have been talks where the core subject was familiar to me, but the room combined different professions, cultures, or nationalities. In those settings, the task is not to repeat what I have already written. It is to discover, with the audience, a way of framing the problem that makes sense from their vantage point. For me, public speaking in such contexts is not about hearing what I have thought; it is about finding out what I am thinking now and into the future, in dialogue with them.

Practically, this means limiting your speaking time and using it to express a few clear ideas that invite response rather than exhaust it. If you do that, the audience will help you think. Their questions, comments, and puzzled looks often reveal aspects you have overlooked or assumptions that no longer hold. Their reactions may show you where your analysis is going astray or where new connections are possible.

When you view speaking this way, English as a diverse language becomes less a barrier and more a field for joint exploration. You come with a provisional map; they show you where it does and does not fit their terrain.

## ACCENTS, ASSUMPTIONS, AND MISREAD SIGNALS

Language difference is not only about vocabulary. It is about accents, tones, and the learned expectations people bring to each. Your accent is a challenge; theirs is a challenge. Both can become barriers to common understanding if you are not attentive.

If your English is native and confident, you may unconsciously equate fluency with comprehension. You assume that if people nod, they have followed you. In reality, many are working hard just to track your words; their cognitive bandwidth for processing meaning is narrower than you think. Conversely, when you listen to someone with a strong accent or non-standard grammar, you may underestimate their insight because you are distracted by form.

As a speaker, you cannot solve every asymmetry, but you can increase your awareness. Slow down slightly when you introduce core concepts. Avoid stacking clause onto clause in long, ornate sentences. Use fewer idioms. Periodically restate key ideas in simple language. If possible, build in short pauses where people can ask clarifying ques-tions rather than waiting until the end when confusion has already hardened into disengagement.

For critical terms, it can be useful to define what you mean explic-itly. The word "strategy," for example, means very different things to a military officer, a corporate planner, and a political operative. "Secu-rity" carries different connotations in different societies. If you assume your default meaning is obvious, you will talk past people who are interpreting those words through different histories.

This is tedious work. It is also deeply connected to the empathy developed in *Listen to Lead* and the pattern recognition needed in *Mastering Chaos*. You are practicing the habit of asking, implicitly: "What do these words mean from their side of the table?" That is not a linguistic trick; it is a leadership discipline.

## TRIBALISM AT HOME

The challenge of English as a diverse language is not confined to international settings. As I have argued elsewhere, the digital informa-tion age has fragmented the American audience as well. Social media has accelerated tribalism, carving the public into sub-cultures whose members consume different media, use different vocabularies, and inhabit different moral universes.

When you address a larger American audience, you cannot assume a shared common experience or a common language of the American people. A story that resonates on one side of a political divide can be heard as a provocation on the other. Cultural references that feel neutral to you may signal allegiance to a particular tribe. Words like "freedom," "equity," or "security" may arrive pre-loaded with partisan meanings you did not intend.

This is not an argument for censoring yourself or for seeking some bland middle ground where all content is smoothed into nothingness. It is an argument for conscious craft. If you want to bring people together, even temporarily, you must think about how your language will be heard across tribes, not just within your own.

That is one of the ethical tasks of public speaking in a democratic setting. Tribalism, by its nature, is hostile to speakers who seek common ground, rather than simply arousing their own base. Yet if no one attempts to speak across tribes, public debate collapses into parallel monologues and mutual incomprehension.

In that sense, the difficulty of speaking to a fractured national audience is not just a technical problem; it is part of the challenge of maintaining any kind of shared public space. The work you do on your language is part of the work of sustaining a workable political community.

## EARLY WARNINGS FROM THE INFORMATION SOCIETY

The seeds of our current communication landscape were visible decades ago. In the mid-1990s, at a UNESCO conference in Barcelona on the emerging information society, I argued that new communication technologies would aggravate two social problems: the collapse of a consensual culture and the accentuation of socioeconomic divisions. At the time, most discussion focused on access and inequality. I suggested that the first issue, the loss of a common cultural framework, was in many ways more problematic.

The question I posed then remains urgent now: in post-modern societies, how are consensuses put together so that there is responsibility in decision-making? Responsibility is crucial for accountability, especially in democratic cultures. Without some capacity to form shared understandings, it becomes very hard even to define a nation-state, let alone govern it.

Today we can see that the internet, social media, and global information flows have indeed both connected and fragmented us. They provide unprecedented inclusion and expanded professional communities. They also foster echo chambers, filter bubbles, and the tribalization of language. The reality of the digital age has reached exactly into the heart of public speaking. It has expanded your potential audience while making it much harder to assume anything about what that audience shares.

The warnings from that earlier era were not about technology per se. They were about what happens when communication systems outpace the institutions and habits that once underpinned a shared public sphere. We are now living in that world. As a speaker, you operate on that fault line.

# THE ALCHEMY OF LANGUAGE CHOICE

Given all this, how should you approach language when you prepare to speak?

- First, accept that there is no neutral language. Every word choice carries echoes of past uses, power relations, and cultural codes. You cannot control all of that, but you can choose deliberately rather than lazily.
- Second, think concretely about who will be in the room or on the call. What languages do they speak at home? What professional dialects do they inhabit? What media ecosystems have shaped their assumptions? You do not need to become an expert in all of that, but you do need to honor its existence.
- Third, shape your core message in a way that could make sense across those differences. That does not mean diluting your argument. It means choosing examples, metaphors, and structures that give people multiple ways into the idea. Sometimes this involves pairing a local example with a global one, or a story from one domain (say, military operations) with a parallel in another (say, corporate strategy).
- Fourth, be explicit about your own standpoint. A simple acknowledgment that "I am speaking from an American defense-analysis background" or "I am approaching this as someone who has spent decades in X context" can reduce misinterpretation. It signals that you are aware of your lens and open to others.
- Finally, remain curious about how your language actually lands. After a talk, ask people from different backgrounds what they heard, what confused them, and what felt foreign.

Their answers are data. Over time, that feedback becomes one of your most valuable teachers.

# FROM LANGUAGE TO LEADERSHIP

At first glance, this chapter is about a technical problem: how to cope with English as a diverse, global, and tribalized language. At a deeper level, it is about the beginnings of empathy and the foundations of adaptive leadership.

When you work this hard on your words, you are doing more than polishing a performance. You are training yourself to think about others' perspectives, constraints, and histories. You are learning to anticipate misunderstanding without becoming paralyzed by it. You are practicing how to build bridges in environments where common ground cannot be assumed.

Those are exactly the capacities that *Listen to Lead* will deepen as it takes you deeper into listening, conversation, and conflict in an age of fragmentation. They are also capacities that *Mastering Chaos* will scale up to the organizational level as it examines how institutions can maintain social cohesion and effective coordination under pressure.

For now, the most important thing is simple. When you prepare to speak, treat language not as a transparent conduit for your thoughts but as a living field in which meanings must be negotiated. That is where the real work of connection begins.

# BUILDING A FOUNDATION OF CONFIDENCE

Most people think of confidence in public speaking as a personality trait you either possess or lack. In reality, what looks like confidence is usually a set of trained habits: how you interpret your own bodily reactions, how you manage your attention, and how you respond when things do not go as planned. These habits can be learned, refined, and integrated into how you operate more broadly as a professional.

In this chapter, we are not aiming for swagger. We are aiming for something much more useful: the ability to remain present when you feel exposed. That ability is fundamental not only to good speaking but to leadership in any high-pressure environment. The same skills that help you stand calmly in front of an audience will help you think in a crisis, sit through a difficult conversation, or hold your ground when decisions must be made under uncertainty.

The fear of public speaking is rarely about standing up and talking. Often it is buried in the belief that you must lecture the audience perfectly, that any mistake will expose you, and that your safest option is to hide behind slides, scripts, or jargon. Many speakers use complexity as camouflage. They read a paper for forty minutes, burying both themselves and the audience in dense language, and then wonder why no one remembers what they said.

In what follows, we will treat confidence as a trainable discipline: a way of managing your body, your mind, and your habits so that you can show up as a real person in front of real people.

# UNDERSTANDING THE ROOTS OF STAGE FRIGHT

Stage fright is a universal human experience. It is not a sign that something is wrong with you; it is a sign that your nervous system is working as designed. When you step in front of a group and become the focus of attention, your body interprets that exposure as a potential threat. Your heart rate increases, your breathing changes, your thoughts accelerate. You are experiencing the same fight-or-flight systems that helped our ancestors survive.

The problem is not the existence of this response. The problem is how we interpret it. Many speakers experience the physical signs of arousal and conclude, "I am not ready," or "I am going to fail." They then try to fight the sensations directly, which usually makes them worse. Others attempt to suppress their anxiety by numbing themselves to the audience, which leads to flat, disconnected delivery.

A more useful approach is to recognize stage fright as energy that can be directed rather than an enemy to be eliminated. You can learn to interpret the physical sensations as preparation rather than catastrophe. Your heart is beating faster because your body is mobilizing resources. Your heightened awareness can be turned outward, toward the audience, instead of inward, toward self-criticism.

From a leadership perspective, this reframing is crucial. The environments described in *Mastering Chaos* are full of situations in which leaders feel pressure, ambiguity, and scrutiny. They cannot wait for calm to act. They must learn to function with elevated arousal without letting it drive them into paralysis or panic. Public speaking gives you repeated, contained opportunities to practice this.

To start, notice your own patterns. Before you speak, where does the fear show up in your body? What thoughts tend to accompany it? How do you usually respond, by rushing, by avoiding eye contact, by clinging to your notes? Write those patterns down. Naming them is the first step toward changing them.

## POWER POSING FOR PRE-SPEECH CONFIDENCE

One of the simplest tools for reshaping your internal state is how you use your body. The concept of "power posing" became widely known through research suggesting that expansive postures can influence hormone levels and feelings of power. Debates about the exact physiological mechanisms continue, but the practical observation remains sound: when you stand in a physically open, grounded posture, you tend to feel more capable and present.

For speakers, the value of power posing lies less in changing testosterone and cortisol and more in interrupting the collapse inward that fear often triggers. When you are nervous, you tend to shrink—shoulders hunched, arms folded, gaze down. Your body signals retreat; your mind follows. By deliberately choosing a posture that takes up space, you send a different signal up the chain.

Before you speak, find a private space, a hallway, a restroom stall, an empty corner. Plant your feet shoulder-width apart, let your shoulders drop back, lift your chest slightly, and place your hands on your hips or relaxed at your sides. Breathe slowly. Hold this posture for a minute or two. As you do so, visualize yourself standing calmly in front of your audience, speaking clearly and responding to them with ease.

This is not about pretending to be someone you are not. It is about reminding your body of what it feels like to be fully present, and letting that physical memory influence your mental state. Over time, you can build a small ritual around this, combining posture with a brief breathing practice or a simple phrase you say to yourself. The goal is to create a reliable bridge into a more grounded state.

Think of this as training in emotional regulation. Leaders in chaotic environments rarely have the luxury of ideal conditions. They walk into rooms where the stakes are high and their own feelings are mixed. The ability to adjust your internal posture deliberately, rather than being at the mercy of circumstances, is part of adaptive leadership. Public speaking gives you a regular, low-risk arena to practice.

# BREATHING TECHNIQUES TO CALM NERVES

Breathing is another powerful lever. When you are anxious, your breathing becomes shallow and fast. That, in turn, signals to your body that the threat level is rising, amplifying the cycle. By consciously slowing and deepening your breath, you can intervene in that loop.

Diaphragmatic breathing, where you breathe deeply into your abdomen rather than lifting your chest, is particularly effective. A simple exercise is the 4-7-8 pattern: inhale gently through your nose for a count of four, hold your breath for a count of seven, then exhale slowly through your mouth for a count of eight. Repeat this several times. The extended exhale helps activate the parasympathetic nervous system, which promotes calm and focus.

Another useful pattern is box breathing, often used by military and emergency personnel: inhale for four counts, hold for four, exhale for four, hold again for four. This rhythmic pattern can steady your mind and body when they want to scatter.

You do not need to perform these exercises in a dramatic way. You can stand backstage or sit in your chair before being introduced and quietly work through a few cycles. The point is not to eliminate all activation, but to bring it into a range where you can think and choose rather than react.

In the later work of *Mastering Chaos*, you will encounter leaders who must make decisions in fast-moving, high-stakes situations with incomplete information. Many of them have developed some form of breathing practice, not because they are speakers, but because they are humans under pressure. Learning these techniques now, in the comparatively benign setting of a presentation, means you are already building that capacity.

# OVERCOMING THE SPOTLIGHT EFFECT

Another source of anxiety is the "spotlight effect": the belief that everyone is scrutinizing you, noticing every flaw, and judging you harshly. In reality, your audience members are usually thinking about themselves, their own concerns, deadlines, and preoccupations. They notice you mostly in terms of whether you are helping or wasting their time.

Recognizing the spotlight effect does not mean pretending you are invisible. It means recalibrating your sense of proportion. You are important to the session; you are not the center of the universe. This realization can be liberating. If you make a mistake, it is unlikely to become the defining event of anyone's life, including your own.

One practical way to reduce the spotlight effect is to shift your focus outward. Before you speak, instead of ruminating on how you will appear, spend a few minutes thinking about what the audience needs. Why are they here? What pressures are they under? What would make this hour genuinely useful to them? When you orient your attention toward service rather than self-protection, your anxiety often diminishes. You have a job to do, and you are there to do it.

This outward orientation is also foundational for empathy. In *Listen to Lead*, we will explore empathy as the disciplined practice of understanding others' experience, perspectives, and reasoning. The first step in that discipline is to release the assumption that everyone is as obsessed with you as you are. When you speak with the audience's needs in mind, you are already training that shift.

## PERSONALIZING YOUR CONFIDENCE RITUALS

Confidence rituals are the small, repeatable actions you use to get yourself into a state where you can perform at your best. They can be physical (a stretch, a particular way of standing), cognitive (a short phrase you repeat to yourself), or practical (reviewing one note card with your core message).

The key is that they are yours. Borrowing someone else's ritual is a fine starting point, but over time you will discover which combinations of posture, breathing, words, and small actions actually help you. Some speakers listen to a specific song before going on stage. Others take a brief walk outside. Some review a list of past successful talks to remind themselves that they have done this before. Others write down their worst fear and then the realistic consequences if it actually happened, which usually reveals how much they have exaggerated the stakes.

Design a pre-speech routine that takes no more than five to ten minutes and that you can perform in most environments. Test it. Adjust it. The point is not superstition; it is familiarity. A well-practiced ritual sends your brain a message: "We have been here before. We know how to do this."

Confidence rituals also build a habit of intentional entry into important moments. Leadership is full of such moments: difficult conversations, crucial briefings, negotiation sessions, crisis calls at three in the morning. If you have a set of small practices that help you arrive mentally and physically, you will be better able to respond thoughtfully when the unexpected happens.

## EMBRACING MISTAKES AS LEARNING OPPORTUNITIES

No amount of preparation will prevent mistakes. You will occasionally forget a point, misstate a fact, lose your place, or encounter technology that fails at the worst possible time. The difference between a speaker who grows and one who retreats lies in how they interpret and respond to those moments.

If you treat every mistake as evidence that you should never speak again, you will shrink your world. If you treat mistakes as data, you will expand it.

After each talk, take a few minutes to reflect. What went well? Where did you feel most connected to the audience? Where did you feel yourself tighten or disconnect? If something went wrong, what exactly happened, and how did you respond? What could you do differently next time, not to guarantee perfection, but to increase your resilience?

This reflective loop, action, review, adjustment, is the same loop that adaptive organizations use to learn from experience. It is central to the kind of chaos management described in the third volume of this series. By applying it to your speaking now, you are aligning your personal habits with the patterns of effective learning at larger scales.

It can also be useful to solicit feedback, selectively. Ask a trusted colleague who was present for one concrete observation about what was most effective in your talk, and one suggestion for improvement.

Ignore vague generalities; look for specific moments. Over time, you will begin to see patterns. Some will confirm your own sense; some will surprise you. Both are useful.

## CONFIDENCE AS A LEADERSHIP DISCIPLINE

By now, you can see that confidence in public speaking is not merely about feeling good on stage. It is about building the capacity to show up fully in situations where you are visible, exposed, and accountable.

When you:

- Understand your own fear response and choose how to interpret it
- Use your body and breath to stabilize yourself under pressure
- Release the illusion that you are under a merciless spotlight
- Develop personal rituals that help you enter challenging moments
- Treat mistakes as information rather than as verdicts

you are doing more than becoming a better speaker. You are developing the emotional regulation and self-knowledge that underpin adaptive leadership.

The chapters that follow will build on this foundation. You will learn how to craft and structure your message, how to engage your audience effectively, and how to manage time and unexpected events. As you practice those skills, remember that each presentation is not just about that one room. It is part of a longer training program you are running on yourself.

In *Listen to Lead*, we will turn from managing your internal state to managing the relationship between you and others through empathy and conversation. In *Mastering Chaos*, we will see how all of these capacities scale into organizational life. For now, your task is concrete: keep stepping into opportunities to speak, keep practicing these confidence tools, and keep noticing what you learn about yourself when you do.

● 4

# CRAFTING AND STRUCTURING YOUR MESSAGE

Clarity is the most generous thing you can offer an audience. In a world saturated with information and starved of attention, people do not need more data points. They need someone to help them see what matters, in what order, and why. Crafting and structuring your message is how you do that.

This chapter is not about turning you into a rhetorical technician. It is about training you to think in ways that other people can follow under real-world conditions: limited time, competing demands, and fragmented backgrounds. When you discipline yourself to express one core idea, support it with a few well-chosen points, and connect those points through story and structure, you are doing more than organizing a talk. You are practicing the kind of sense-making leaders must provide when the environment will not sit still.

In later volumes in this series, this discipline will appear in different forms. In *Listen to Lead*, it will show up as the ability to frame issues in ways that invite genuine conversation rather than defensive reactions. In *Mastering Chaos*, it will show up as the ability to distinguish complicated from complex problems and to express the difference in language that helps organizations act. Here, we start with your next presentation.

# START WITH ONE CORE IDEA

Most talks fail not because the speaker lacks content, but because the speaker tries to deliver too much of it. The result is a verbal data dump. Listeners leave with a vague sense that something was important but no clear idea of what to do with it. Their mental shelves are already crowded; you have added another box without a label.

The antidote is ruthless simplicity. Before you open your laptop or think about slides, ask yourself: if my audience remembered only one idea from this talk six months from now, what would I want it to be? Write that idea in a single sentence, in plain language. That sentence becomes your north star.

Everything else you include should serve that one idea. Supporting points, stories, statistics, and examples are there to strengthen and illuminate it, not to compete with it. If a favourite anecdote does not reinforce your core idea, cut it or save it for another occasion. Discipline is painful in the short term; it pays off in attention and impact.

This habit is not just about presentations. It is a way of thinking. When you force yourself to compress your argument into one sentence, you discover what you actually believe. You also make it much easier for others to test, challenge, and refine that belief with you—which is exactly what empathy and adaptive leadership require.

There is a second benefit to this discipline that emerges slowly over time. When you consistently deliver one clear idea per talk, people begin to trust your judgment about what deserves attention. They know you have done the work of filtering. That trust becomes a kind of professional capital. You are not the person who buries important insights under mountains of supporting detail; you are the person who identifies what truly matters and says it clearly enough that others can carry it forward.

# THE ELEVATOR SPEECH TRICK

A useful tool for clarifying your core idea is the "elevator speech" trick: imagine you meet someone in an elevator on their way to a meeting and they ask, "What are you talking about today?" You have thirty seconds before the doors open. What do you say?

A good elevator speech has three elements:

- Context: the situation or problem space ("Right now, our teams are drowning in information but starving for clarity about priorities").
- Core idea: what you want them to grasp ("I'm going to show a simple way to frame our decisions so we can move faster without losing coherence").
- Why it matters: the consequence of ignoring or acting on it ("If we get this right, we can stop re-litigating the same issues and focus on execution").

You do not need to recite this speech in your talk. The benefit lies in the preparation. If you cannot explain your topic in thirty seconds to an intelligent colleague, you are probably not ready to hold a room for thirty minutes. The elevator test is a kindness you perform for your audience in advance.

The elevator speech also reveals gaps in your own understanding. When you try to compress a complex topic into thirty seconds, you quickly discover whether you grasp the core mechanism or whether you are relying on jargon to hide uncertainty. Jargon works in written reports where readers can pause and look things up. In a brief spoken exchange, it signals that you have not yet done the intellectual work of simplification. The elevator speech forces that work to happen before you step in front of an audience.

Later, when you move into the relational space of *Listen to Lead,* this same skill will help you frame issues in conversations. When you can state a concern briefly and clearly, others are more willing to tell you how they see it. When you wander through a thicket of half-formed thoughts, they often shut down. The discipline you build here—compressing ideas without distorting them—becomes essential when the stakes involve human relationships rather than conference attendance.

# DEVELOPING A SPEECH BLUEPRINT

Once you have your core idea and a clear way to state it, you need a blueprint: a simple outline that organizes your material into a sequence listeners can follow. A blueprint is not a script; it is a skeleton. It tells you how you will begin, what main points you will cover in what order, and how you will end.

One of the classic patterns is: Opening with hook and context (why this matters now); three main points that are distinct but related, each reinforcing the core idea; and conclusion that restates the core idea, names implications, and offers next steps or questions.

Within each main point, you can use a mini-structure: statement, explanation, example. For instance, if your core idea is that clear speaking sharpens thought, one main point might be that speaking forces you to simplify. You would then explain how that works and give a concrete story from your own experience that illustrates it.

This may sound basic, but under pressure basic structures save you. When you have a blueprint, you can recover from disruptions, questions, or glitches without losing the thread. You know where you are in the arc and what remains. That is exactly the kind of mental map leaders need in chaotic environments, where plans are constantly being interrupted and re-stitched.

The blueprint also gives you freedom within constraints. Because you know the overall structure, you can adapt individual sections to the energy in the room without losing coherence. If one example falls flat, you can shift to another without derailing the entire talk. If a question opens up an unexpected but valuable line of discussion, you can follow it briefly and then return to your blueprint. Paradoxically, the more tightly you structure the talk in advance, the more flexibility you have in the moment.

There is also a deeper reason blueprints matter. When you present complex ideas without a clear structure, audiences spend cognitive energy trying to figure out where you are going instead of engaging with what you are actually saying. That is wasted attention. The blueprint lets them relax into the content because they trust you have a destination in mind. They do not need to second-guess your next move; they can focus on evaluating your argument.

# STORYTELLING AS A STRUCTURAL TOOL

Stories are not decorative extras tacked onto a "serious" argument. They are one of the primary ways human beings process information, especially under complexity. A well-chosen story provides context, emotion, and memory hooks for your ideas. It shows what your abstractions look like in real life.

In your own career, you already have stories: the high school classroom in Queens where you had to hold the attention of students with different language backgrounds, the first time a talk shifted a room's thinking, the disastrous presentation that taught you what not to do. When you place these stories at strategic points in your blueprint, you give the audience a way to feel the problem and its solution, not just to understand them intellectually.

The key is to use stories as structural elements, not as digressions. Ask: what does this story demonstrate about my core idea? Where in the arc will it be most useful? Does it replace a long abstract explanation I would otherwise be tempted to give?

Stories also create identification. When you share a moment of confusion, failure, or breakthrough, audiences recognize their own experience. That recognition builds trust. It signals that you understand the territory because you have been there yourself, not because you read about it in a management book. This is particularly important when you are asking people to change their behavior or adopt a new framework. Change requires trust, and trust often begins with shared experience.

The danger with stories is that they can overwhelm the argument if not disciplined. A compelling narrative can take on a life of its own, pulling the talk in directions that do not serve the core idea. This is why the structural question matters: does this story reinforce what I am trying to say, or does it distract from it? If the story is too good but off-topic, save it for another occasion. The blueprint exists to protect your core idea from your own enthusiasm.

In *Listen to Lead*, you will see how stories also function as vehicles for empathy. When you listen to others' stories and share your own judiciously, you create space for mutual recognition. In *Mastering Chaos*, you will see how stories of past crises and adaptations become part of institutional memory. Here, you are learning to deploy story in the service of clarity.

# USING THE RULE OF THREE FOR CLARITY

There is a reason so many effective messages come in threes. The human mind seems to find three points easy to hold and compare. Fewer may feel too thin; more often feels like a list. Three gives you enough room to show pattern and variation without overwhelming.

You can apply the rule of three at several levels: three main points in the talk; three sub-points within a main point; three examples that illustrate a pattern; or three short phrases that summarize a conclusion.

For instance, if your core idea is that public speaking is foundational for professional development, your three main points might be: it sharpens your thinking, it expands your opportunities, and it prepares you for leadership in crises. Each can then be developed with its own statement, explanation, and example.

The goal is not to force everything into threes artificially, but to use the pattern as a restraint against over-stuffing. When you find yourself with six or seven "main" points, ask which three truly matter for this audience at this time. The rest can be supporting detail or material for another day.

This discipline in structuring information is central to chaos management. When leaders try to respond to complex situations with endless lists of priorities, organizations freeze. When they identify a small number of real priorities and explain them clearly, people can act. The rule of three is not just a rhetorical device; it is a cognitive tool that acknowledges human limitations and works within them rather than pretending they do not exist.

There is also something aesthetically satisfying about three. Two feels incomplete, like a comparison waiting for resolution. Four begins to blur into a list where individual elements lose distinctness. Three offers a sense of completeness without excess. This is not mysticism; it is pattern recognition shaped by thousands of years of oral tradition. The pattern persists because it works.

# CREATING POWERFUL CALLS TO ACTION

A talk without any implied or explicit action is an interesting noise that fades quickly. That action does not always have to be dramatic. It may be as simple as "think differently about this issue," "ask this new question in your next meeting," or "try this specific technique."

A call to action answers the question: "What now?" It connects your core idea to the listener's world in a concrete way. It can operate at several levels:

Individual: "At your next presentation, choose one core idea and build around it."

Relational: "In your next difficult conversation, try articulating the other person's position before stating your own."

Organizational: "Over the next quarter, examine where your processes assume stability and where you need adaptive capacity."

You do not need to announce these levels explicitly in every talk, but being aware of them will sharpen your calls. The important thing is that the action be realistic and meaningful. Asking people to "change everything" leads to nothing. Asking them to do one specific thing differently tomorrow has a chance of success.

The call to action is where your credibility meets the audience's agency. If you have built trust through the talk, by being clear, by offering useful frameworks, by sharing genuine experience, then people are willing to consider changing their behavior. But they need to know what that change looks like in practical terms. Vague exhortations about "thinking differently" or "being more adaptive" do not translate into Monday morning. Specific, bounded actions do.

This is also where you discover whether you actually believe what you are saying. If you cannot identify a concrete action that follows from your argument, you may be trafficking in abstractions rather than actionable insight. The call to action is a reality check. It forces you to connect ideas to behavior, which is ultimately what leadership requires.

In the larger arc of this series, calls to action are what turn ideas into practice. *Listen to Lead* will ask you to adopt new habits of listening and conversation. *Mastering Chaos* will offer a 12–24 month agenda for organizational change. The small calls you make in your talks are training for making larger, more consequential ones later.

## TAILORING CONTENT FOR DIVERSE AUDIENCES

No structure exists in a vacuum. The same core idea will need to be framed differently for a room full of engineers, a mixed civilian-military audience, a group of corporate executives, or a cohort of young professionals. The basic blueprint can remain, but the examples, metaphors, and emphasis must shift.

Before you finalize your message, ask: Who is in the room? What do they already know? What are they responsible for? What pressures are they under? What language do they use about this topic? What are they likely skeptical about? What are they hoping for?

For a military audience, you might draw on operational examples and focus on decision-making under pressure. For a corporate audience, you might emphasize market disruption and organizational resilience. For young professionals, you might highlight how speaking sharpens their "mental furniture" and opens unforeseen career paths.

This tailoring is more than marketing. It is early work in cultural empathy. You are not changing your core convictions for each group; you are translating them into terms that respect their reality. That is exactly what leaders must do when they move across units, professions, or nations.

The danger is over-tailoring, where you dilute the message to avoid any potential friction. Tailoring means choosing examples and language that connect with the audience's experience; it does not mean telling people only what they want to hear. If your core idea challenges prevailing assumptions—and the best ideas often do—then you still need to deliver that challenge. You simply frame it in ways that give people a path to engage with it rather than reject it reflexively.

There is also a practical limit to how much tailoring you can do. If you are speaking to a genuinely mixed audience, different professional backgrounds, different levels of authority, different national contexts, you cannot optimize for everyone. In those cases, choose examples that transcend specific contexts or offer multiple entry points. Acknowledge the diversity in the room explicitly, and use it as an asset rather than trying to paper over it. The most valuable conversations often happen precisely because people from different worlds are in the same space, trying to make sense of a shared problem.

## A TOOL FOR LEADING IN CHAOS

By now, the pattern should be clear. The tools in this chapter are not just about making clean slides or pleasing conference organizers. They are tools for thinking and leading:

Choosing a core idea forces you to decide what truly matters. The elevator speech trick trains you to express complex issues succinctly. Blueprints and the rule of three give you mental scaffolding that holds under pressure. Stories make abstractions real and memorable. Calls to action connect ideas to behavior. Tailoring content builds empathy and bridge-building instinct.

In a world defined by speed, fragmentation, and uncertainty, people are hungry for this kind of structured sense-making. They may not use that term; they will say instead that you are "clear," "helpful," or "easy to follow." Those are not superficial compliments. They are signals that you are providing something rare: order without rigidity.

The skills you develop here scale in unexpected ways. When you learn to compress a talk into one core idea, you are also learning how to brief senior leaders who have ninety seconds between crises. When you build a blueprint that survives disruptions, you are practicing the mental discipline required to lead through operational chaos. When you tailor content for diverse audiences, you are developing the cultural fluency that alliance management demands.

None of this happens automatically. It requires repeated practice, honest feedback, and willingness to revise. You will give talks that miss the mark. You will choose examples that confuse rather than clarify.

You will discover halfway through a presentation that your core idea was not actually core. These failures are not signs you should stop; they are the raw material of improvement. Every failed talk teaches you something about structure, about audiences, or about your own thinking that you could not have learned any other way.

The next chapter will build on this by focusing on how you engage the audience in the moment, how you open, how you read the room, and how you adjust. As you move through it, remember that every talk you give is practice in the larger disciplines this series explores: empathy that listens, and leadership that can navigate chaos without collapsing into it. The message you craft is only the beginning. How you deliver it, how you respond when it meets resistance, and how you adapt when circumstances shift and that is where the real work of leadership begins.

# ENGAGING YOUR AUDIENCE EFFECTIVELY

You can stand in front of a room with a well-structured talk and still fail if you do not genuinely engage the people in front of you. Engagement is not decoration added after the "real" content. It is the way you discover, in real time, whether your ideas are landing and how your audience is making sense of them. It is also your first serious laboratory for empathy and adaptive thinking.

In earlier chapters, you learned to clarify your message and manage your own nerves. Now we turn to the other side of the relationship: the people listening. Every decision you make about how to open, where to pause, when to invite questions, and how to use humor is a decision about how you will connect with your listeners' concerns, attention span, and emotional state. You are not just transmitting information; you are sharing the work of meaning-making with the room.

This is exactly the discipline that later volumes deepen. *Listen to Lead* will explore empathy and conversation as leadership practices in a fragmented age. *Mastering Chaos* will show how leaders use those same skills under pressure, when the environment is shifting faster than their plans.

In this chapter, you are beginning that journey at a very practical level. Each technique you use to engage an audience is a small exercise in reading others, adjusting your maps, and building temporary but real social cohesion in the room.

As you work through these pages, notice two things.

First, which engagement moves feel natural to you, and which feel forced. That tells you something about your current habits and comfort zones.

Second, notice how your own thinking changes when you are truly in contact with your audience rather than performing at them. That is the beginning of adaptive leadership.

## CRAFT YOUR ICEBREAKER

Your first words set the tone for everything that follows. A good icebreaker does more than warm up the room; it signals that you understand who is in front of you and why they have given you their time. When you open with something that resonates with their reality, a shared challenge, a vivid story, a surprising question, you are making a simple promise: "I see you, and this will be about something that matters to you."

Think of the icebreaker as your first act of practical empathy. You are answering, before they ask it, the quiet question in every audience member's mind: "Why should I listen to you?" You do not answer with a recitation of your credentials. You answer by showing that you have paid attention to their world. That habit of attention is the same habit you will need later when you are leading teams divided by function, generation, or political tribe.

When you prepare your opening, ask yourself three questions: what do they care about, what are they worried about, and what are they tired of hearing? Then craft something that meets them where they actually are, not where you wish they were.

The best icebreakers often come from the edges of your preparation rather than its center. Perhaps you noticed something unexpected during your research, a tension everyone acknowledges but no one addresses directly, or a question people keep asking that reveals an underlying anxiety. Surface that. Or tell a compact story from your own experience that illustrates why this topic has stakes for real people, not just theoretical importance. The goal is not cleverness; it is connection.

Consider the difference between generic and specific openings. A generic opening sounds like this: "Today we're going to talk about the challenges of change management." That could apply to any organization, any situation. A specific opening acknowledges what is actually happening: "Three months ago, your division merged with another team that does things completely differently, and I've heard that some of you are wondering whether anyone is paying attention to how hard that is." The second version tells people you have done your homework and that you understand the texture of their daily reality.

Another effective approach is to begin with a question that frames the stakes. Not a rhetorical softball like "Who wants to be more effective?" but something that requires actual thought: "When you're in a meeting where you know the decision being made is wrong, but you're not sure you have the standing to say so, what runs through your mind?" That question invites people to retrieve a specific memory, which means they are already engaged before you say another word.

One warning: do not begin with an apology or a hedge. "I know you're all busy" or "I'm not sure this will be interesting" signals that you are uncertain about the value of what you are about to say. If you do not believe your message matters, your audience will not either. Start with confidence grounded in your understanding of their needs, not in your opinion of yourself.

The icebreaker is also where you establish the contract for the session. Will this be formal or conversational? Will you invite interruptions or hold questions until the end? Will there be participation exercises or sustained listening? You signal these things not just through explicit instructions but through tone, pacing, and stance.

If you want a collaborative atmosphere, your opening should feel like the beginning of a conversation, not a lecture. If you need people to track with a complex argument before they react, your opening should prepare them for sustained attention without making them feel like passive receptacles.

# EYE CONTACT: MAKING A CONNECTION

Eye contact is one of the simplest ways to turn a monologue into a relationship. When you look directly at individual people, for a complete sentence or two, you are not just projecting confidence. You are signaling a willingness to be in contact and to let your audience know that their reactions matter to you.

This shift from scanning the back wall to meeting actual eyes can be uncomfortable at first, especially if you are used to hiding in your notes or your slides. But discomfort here is instructive. If you cannot tolerate the vulnerability of real eye contact in a controlled speaking situation, you will struggle when you must hold someone's gaze in a difficult conversation or a crisis meeting.

Treat eye contact as training in presence. Pick one person, deliver a thought to them; then shift to another. Notice how your language and pace change when you are talking to people rather than to "the audience." That is the same shift you will make later when you move from talking at your organization to listening and responding to it.

Some practical mechanics: hold eye contact for the duration of a complete thought, usually one to two sentences. Do not dart around the room; that reads as nervousness. Do not lock onto one friendly face for the entire talk; that excludes everyone else. Instead, work systematically through different sections of the room, making genuine contact with individuals. People in the back matter as much as people in the front. Those sitting silently matter as much as those nodding visibly.

You will know you are doing this well when you start to see individual reactions rather than a collective blur. One person furrows their brow when you mention a deadline; another leans forward when you describe a solution. These are data, and they should influence what you do next. Eye contact is not just about being seen by them; it is about seeing them.

There is a cultural dimension to eye contact that deserves attention. In some cultures, sustained direct eye contact is a sign of respect and engagement. In others, it can be interpreted as aggression or disrespect, particularly across hierarchies or between strangers. If you are speaking to a culturally diverse audience, modulate your approach. Make eye contact, but do not insist on holding someone's gaze if they look away. The goal is connection, not dominance.

Another dimension: virtual presentations. On video calls, "eye contact" means looking at the camera, not at the faces on your screen. This feels counterintuitive because you want to see people's reactions, but looking at the screen makes you appear to be looking downward or away from the audience. Practice alternating: look at the camera when you are making a key point, then glance at the screen to check reactions, then back to the camera. This rhythm approximates in-person eye contact and helps maintain connection across the digital barrier.

## THE POWER OF RHETORICAL QUESTIONS

Rhetorical questions are not just devices for variety; they are invitations to think. A well-placed question forces your audience to pause, turn inward for a moment, and test your claims against their own experience. In doing so, they become active participants in the talk rather than passive recipients.

This is where engagement intersects with adaptive thinking. When you ask, "What do you think is the real obstacle here?" or "Have you ever found yourself in this situation?", you are momentarily handing part of the cognitive work to the room. You are acknowledging that they bring knowledge and perspective you do not have. That stance, treating others as thinking partners rather than targets of persuasion, is central to the kind of leadership you will need in chaotic environments, where no single person sees the whole picture.

Use rhetorical questions sparingly but deliberately. Aim them at the key junctions in your argument, where you want people to test assumptions and re-frame the problem with you, not simply accept your solution.

Timing matters. After you pose a rhetorical question, give people a beat of silence to actually consider it. Do not rush to answer your own question or fill the pause with nervous chatter. That silence is where the thinking happens. In a culture obsessed with continuous information flow, a well-placed pause can be more powerful than another slide or another statistic.

One caution: rhetorical questions lose their power if they are too easy or too predictable. "Who wants to be more effective?" is not a real invitation to think; it is empty rhetoric. Better: "When was the last time you changed your mind about something important at work and what made that possible?" That question has texture. It asks people to retrieve a specific memory and examine the conditions that enabled learning. The answers they generate, even silently, will prime them to engage more deeply with what you say next.

Rhetorical questions also serve a diagnostic function. Watch how people respond. If most of the room is nodding or making eye contact, you have touched something familiar. If people look confused or skeptical, you may have revealed an assumption that does not match their experience. That feedback can guide your next move. Perhaps you need to provide more context, or acknowledge a competing perspective, or simply spend more time on this point before moving forward.

The best rhetorical questions are the ones that people continue thinking about after you have moved on. They plant a seed that grows as the talk unfolds. You might ask early in the session, "What would it look like if this problem actually got solved?" and then return to that question implicitly as you work through your material. By the end, people should be able to answer the question more fully than they could at the beginning—not because you gave them the answer, but because you gave them a framework to construct it themselves.

## USING HUMOR TO BREAK DOWN BARRIERS

Humor, when used thoughtfully, can dissolve tension, open closed faces, and remind everyone in the room that they are dealing with a human being, not a machine dispensing bullet points. The goal is not to become a comedian; it is to make it easier for people to relate to you and to each other.

Humor, however, exposes your judgment. The wrong joke can reinforce division, make some people invisible, or signal that you have not understood the sensitivities in the room. In a fragmented environment, where audiences may differ sharply in culture, age, or politics, you cannot assume that what you find funny will land the same way everywhere. That is why humor is also a test of your situational awareness and empathy.

As a rule, aim humor at yourself, at shared absurdities, or at the complexities of the situation, not at particular groups or individuals. Use it to lower defenses, not to score points. When in doubt, leave it out. The deeper lesson is not about jokes; it is about learning to sense what a given audience can carry in that moment.

Self-deprecating humor can be particularly effective because it demonstrates that you do not take yourself too seriously. It creates permission for others to be imperfect and human as well. But there is a line: if you undermine your own credibility too much, people will wonder why they should listen to you. The balance is to show that you are aware of your limitations without suggesting that you have no business being in front of them.

Observational humor about the shared situation works well because it acknowledges a common reality. If you are speaking at 8 a.m. after a late reception the night before, a brief acknowledgment of collective fatigue can create solidarity. If everyone is frustrated by a system that is not working, naming that frustration with a light touch can release tension and build trust. You are showing that you see what they see.

What to avoid: humor that depends on insider knowledge that not everyone shares, humor that punches down at people with less power or status, and humor that turns serious issues into punchlines. If your audience includes people who have been historically marginalized, be especially careful. What reads as playful teasing to some may read as dismissal or hostility to others. This is not about political correctness; it is about basic competence in reading a room.

Humor also serves as a pressure valve. If you are delivering difficult news, confronting uncomfortable truths, or asking people to change long-standing habits, occasional moments of levity can make the message more bearable. People can only absorb so much intensity before they shut down. A well-timed moment of lightness signals that you are not asking them to be grim and serious every second, and it creates space for them to metabolize what you are saying.

## INTERACTIVE EXERCISES TO FOSTER ENGAGEMENT

Interactive exercises, polls, brief pair discussions, quick written reflections, change the energy of a session. They break the pattern of one-way speech and signal that you expect the audience to think and contribute. Done well, they also give you valuable information about how people are understanding the issue.

From a leadership perspective, these small exercises are prototypes of collaborative sensemaking. When you ask people to turn to a neighbor and discuss a question, you are not just "keeping them busy." You are creating a miniature network where different perspectives collide and new ideas can emerge. When you then harvest a few of those insights in the room, you are practicing how to surface distributed intelligence, exactly what leaders must do in complex, rapidly changing environments.

The key is to design interactions that are tightly linked to your core message and respectful of people's time. One incisive question and two minutes of paired conversation can be more powerful than a sprawling group exercise. Afterward, take a moment to adjust your talk based on what you heard. That small act of adaptation tells the room that their input was not cosmetic; it mattered.

Practical formats that work well: Think-pair-share, where individuals reflect silently for 30 seconds, discuss with a partner for two minutes, then a few pairs share with the room. Quick polls using raised hands or mobile devices to gauge opinion or experience on a key question. Brief written reflection, where people jot down one concern or one implication before you move to the next section. Structured small-group discussions if you have more time, with clear prompts and a tight reporting process.

What makes these exercises valuable is not the format but your willingness to let what you learn actually shape what happens next. If people reveal a widespread misconception, address it on the spot. If they surface an objection you had not considered, acknowledge it and work through it. If their insights are more sophisticated than you expected, adjust your level of detail accordingly. This responsiveness is what transforms an exercise from a gimmick into genuine engagement.

One mistake to avoid: do not use interactive exercises as filler when your content runs short, or as a way to kill time. People sense when participation is perfunctory. Use interaction only when it serves a clear purpose, to surface assumptions, test understanding, build investment in a solution, or integrate diverse perspectives. Every minute you ask people to spend on an activity should yield something they could not have gained from simply listening.

Consider also the logistical challenges of interaction in different settings. In a large auditorium, paired discussions work better than whole-room conversations. In a virtual session, chat functions and breakout rooms can substitute for in-person interaction, but you need to build in more time for transitions. In a workshop with twenty people, you can create richer exchanges by forming small groups of four or five. The format should match the context, not the other way around.

## READING AND REACTING TO AUDIENCE CUES

Finally, engagement depends on whether you can read what is actually happening in front of you and react without losing your thread. People's posture, facial expressions, note-taking, and even fidgeting are data. They tell you when you have lost the room, when you have hit a nerve, and when you have found a live connection.

Instead of fearing these cues, cultivate the habit of noticing them. If you see confusion, pause and restate. If energy drops, shorten your next segment or move to a concrete example. If discussion flares around a particular point, consider spending more time there and trimming something less essential later. Each small adjustment is an exercise in acting on a provisional map, one of the central demands of leadership in chaotic settings, where no plan survives contact with reality unchanged.

You do not need to narrate every adjustment. You simply need to let what you see influence what you do. Over time, this habit, of letting reality in, even when you are "in performance", will serve you far beyond the podium.

What are you looking for specifically? Arms crossed and faces closed suggest defensiveness or skepticism, you may need to slow down and address unstated objections. People leaning forward and making eye contact suggest strong interest, you can go deeper on that point. Widespread note-taking means they are tracking with you; scattered attention (phones, side conversations) means you have lost them. Furrowed brows suggest confusion; head nods suggest agreement. None of these cues is definitive on its own, but patterns across the room are reliable signals.

The difficult part is not seeing these cues. Most people notice them at some level but knowing what to do in response while maintaining forward momentum.

This is where preparation matters. If you know your material well enough that you are not enslaved to your script, you have the cognitive bandwidth to notice and adjust. If you have thought through which sections are essential and which are flexible, you can make real-time trade-offs without panic.

Consider building in explicit check-ins as well. Mid-way through a longer talk, you might pause and ask: "Are we on the same page so far, or should I clarify something before we move on?" That simple question gives people permission to surface confusion and gives you information about whether your message is landing. It also models intellectual humility that you are willing to acknowledge that communication is a two-way process and that you do not have perfect insight into their understanding.

Some speakers worry that adjusting on the fly will make them appear unprepared or uncertain. The opposite is true. Rigidly adhering to your plan when it is clearly not working makes you look oblivious. Adapting to what you see demonstrates competence and respect. It shows that you care more about whether your message lands than about executing your script perfectly.

There is also a feedback loop at work here. The more you practice reading and responding to audience cues, the better you become at anticipating them. You start to sense where confusion is likely to arise, where people will want more detail, where skepticism will surface. That anticipatory skill makes your preparation more efficient and your delivery more fluid. You are not reacting to surprises; you are navigating a landscape you have learned to read.

## MOVING FORWARD

By now, you can see that "engagement" is not about entertaining people so they will tolerate your content. It is about treating your audience as participants in a shared thinking process. When you look at them, ask them questions, invite their contributions, use humor carefully, and adjust to their cues, you are doing the early work of leadership and not just speaking.

Each technique in this chapter serves a dual purpose. On the surface, it helps you deliver a more effective presentation. At a deeper level, it trains habits of attention, adaptation, and collaboration that will define your leadership capacity later. The speaker who can read a room and adjust without losing the thread is practicing the same skills that a leader needs when navigating organizational change, managing conflict, or responding to unexpected crises.

Notice which techniques come naturally to you and which require deliberate effort. That asymmetry is information. If eye contact feels effortless but interactive exercises make you nervous, you may be more comfortable with individual connection than with distributed sensemaking. If humor flows easily but adjusting your plan on the fly feels risky, you may prize control over responsiveness. None of these patterns is inherently good or bad, but they reveal your default settings and defaults can be overridden with practice.

The most important shift is internal. Can you move from treating the audience as a problem to be managed, a source of potential disruption or judgment, to treating them as a resource to be engaged? When people ask challenging questions, surface unexpected objections, or reveal gaps in your argument, are you threatened or curious? That stance makes all the difference. Threat narrows your focus and triggers defensive routines. Curiosity opens your focus and invites learning.

In the next chapters, you will apply these same habits to how you use time and pacing, and to how you handle the inevitable surprises that occur when human beings gather.

Later, if you choose to continue into *Listen to Lead*, you will deepen the listening side of this equation, learning how to create space for voices that are usually silenced, how to navigate conversations fractured by ideology or identity, and how to build understanding across positions that seem irreconcilable.

And in *Mastering Chaos,* you will see how this kind of engagement scales to organizations under pressure, where the environment is shifting faster than plans can accommodate and where leaders must continuously adapt their maps to emerging realities.

For now, the most important thing is simple: every time you stand up to speak, treat the people in front of you as partners in understanding, not as targets. That is how speakers become adaptive leaders. It begins with small acts, holding someone's gaze, pausing after a question, adjusting your plan when you see confusion.

Over time, those acts accumulate into a different way of being in relationship with others. You learn to trust that the people you are addressing have insights you need, that their resistance often contains valuable information, and that the work of making meaning is genuinely shared.

This chapter has given you practical tools for engagement, but the deeper lesson is about stance. Engagement is not a set of techniques you apply to get people to listen.

It is a commitment to being in genuine contact, to letting what you see change what you do, to treating every speaking opportunity as a laboratory for learning about others and yourself. That commitment, more than any particular skill, is what separates speakers who inform from leaders who transform.

6

# MANAGING TIME AND PACING

In an age when attention is fragmented and calendars are over-loaded, how you use time in a talk is as important as what you say. People do not experience your presentation as a word count; they experience it as a sequence of moments: when you began, when you lost them, when you brought them back, when you finished. Managing time and pacing is the art of shaping those moments so that your audience can stay with you and leave with something usable.

This is also rehearsal for a larger challenge. In the "anarchy of the moment" that defines our era, leaders rarely enjoy leisurely deliberation. They are forced to think and decide under temporal compression: crises that unfold over hours, not weeks; decisions that must be made before complete information is available. Learning to structure a 15–30 minute talk so that it breathes, moves, and lands is small-scale practice in operating under those constraints.

The temporal dimension of leadership has become more acute as the pace of change accelerates. What military thinkers call the "OODA loop" — Observe, Orient, Decide, Act — compresses in chaotic environments. Adversaries exploit delays. Opportunities vanish. Windows close. The organization that masters tempo often masters the situation. Your talk is a microcosm of this dynamic. How you compress, expand, allocate, and adjust time within your presentation mirrors how you will handle temporal pressure in operational settings.

In this chapter, we will look at how to allocate time across your talk, how to pace your delivery, how to handle overruns, and how to adapt when the clock changes unexpectedly. These are not just presentational tricks. They are ways of disciplining your thinking so that you can stay effective when the clock is unforgiving.

## TIME BLOCKING FOR BALANCED DELIVERY

Many speakers pour most of their energy into the beginning of a talk and run out of time at the end, rushing through key points or skipping the conclusion entirely. The result is a lopsided experience: an elaborate runway and an abrupt landing. Listeners leave without a clear sense of what to remember or what to do.

A simple remedy is to block your time deliberately before you prepare your details. Suppose you have 20 minutes. You might allocate it as follows:

- 3 minutes for opening (hook + context)
- 4 minutes for Point 1
- 4 minutes for Point 2
- 4 minutes for Point 3
- 3 minutes for conclusion and call to action
- 2 minutes of embedded flex (small pauses, transitions, a quick question)

You can adjust the numbers to fit your slot, but the principle stands: decide in advance how much time each segment deserves based on its importance, not based on how long you feel like talking about it in the moment.

This is an exercise in priority-setting. When you force yourself to assign minutes to ideas, you surface what you actually value. You may discover, for instance, that you want to allocate more time to an example than to a theoretical explanation, or to audience interaction than to a dense list. Those decisions tell you something about your own instincts and about what you believe will help this audience most.

Time blocking also forces you to confront scarcity. In organizational life, leaders constantly face resource constraints—not enough people, not enough budget, not enough runway before a deadline. Time is the ultimate non-renewable resource. You cannot manufacture more of it, borrow it from tomorrow, or redistribute it from someone else's surplus. The discipline of allocating scarce minutes to competing priorities in your talk is exactly the discipline required to allocate scarce hours to competing operational demands.

Consider the alternative. Speakers who do not block time in advance tend to drift. They begin with enthusiasm, expand on whatever feels interesting in the moment, and suddenly realize they have consumed 15 of their 20 minutes on the opening and first point. The remaining content gets compressed, quality degrades, and the conclusion, the place where meaning crystallizes, becomes an afterthought. This pattern mirrors how organizations misallocate resources when leaders do not impose structure on their own attention.

In organizational life, the same discipline applies. Leaders who cannot allocate time and who let meetings drift, crises expand, and routines consume every available slot signal that priorities are fuzzy. Practicing time blocking in your talks helps you build the habit of aligning time with what matters. Each minute you assign to a segment is a vote for its importance. Where you invest time reveals where you invest belief.


## TECHNIQUES FOR HANDLING OVERRUNS

No plan survives first contact with the clock. Introductions run long. Technology takes an extra five minutes to cooperate. A previous session eats into your slot. Or you simply underestimate how long it takes to say what you want to say. The question is not whether you will ever run over; the question is how you respond when you do.

One of the most practical things you can do is to design your talk with "shedding points" built in: elements that can be dropped cleanly without breaking the structure. That might mean:

- Having one example per main point, with a second in
  reserve that you can cut if time tightens.
- Designing your third main point so that it can be condensed
  into one strong sentence if needed.
- Preparing a short version of your conclusion that still
  restates the core idea and call to action.

This concept of shedding points comes directly from crisis management doctrine. Military planners build flexibility into operations by identifying which objectives are essential and which are desirable. When circumstances change, enemy contact, weather, equipment failure, commanders preserve the essential and abandon the desirable without hesitation. Your talk operates on the same principle. Identify in advance what you can afford to lose.

If you realize you are behind schedule, do not panic and start talking faster. Speeding up usually makes you less clear, increases your audience's cognitive load, and can signal anxiety. Instead, quietly decide what you will drop or compress, then deliver the remaining material at a normal pace. Your audience will appreciate clarity more than completeness.

Talking faster under time pressure is a natural reflex, but it compounds the problem. When you accelerate, listeners must work harder to process your words. Comprehension drops. Retention suffers. And because your own stress becomes audible, the audience begins to feel anxious on your behalf. The room's energy shifts from engaged to uncomfortable. Far better to make a clean cut and maintain composure.

You can also practice "time checks in motion." Glance at the clock or a discreet timer at natural transition points. If you see that you are halfway through your time but still in your first point, that is a signal to accelerate your progression, not your words. Move to the next section and save the details for Q&A or follow-up materials.

From a chaos-management perspective, this is about preserving optionality. When circumstances change, you do not try to force the original plan through reality; you adapt the plan while preserving its core intent. Learning to do this calmly in a talk trains the reflex you will need when a crisis compresses your strategic timeline. The leader who cannot adjust gracefully when time evaporates is the same leader who will freeze or flail when operational reality diverges from the pre-brief.

# PAUSING FOR IMPACT

In a world of noise and distraction, silence can be one of your most powerful tools. Many speakers, especially when nervous, rush to fill every second with sound. They fear that if they pause, they will lose the room. In practice, the opposite is often true. A well-timed pause gives the audience space to absorb, to think, and to feel.

Pauses serve several purposes:

- They signal importance: when you pause after a critical sentence, you tell people, "That was worth a moment's thought."
- They give people time to catch up, especially if English is not their first language or if the material is complex.
- They allow you to check the room: faces, posture, note-taking.
- They give you a moment to breathe and reset.

You can build pauses into your blueprint by marking places where you will deliberately slow down. After stating your core idea for the first time, pause. After a story's punchline that illustrates a key point, pause. After posing a rhetorical question, let a few seconds of silence pass before you continue.

This may feel uncomfortable, especially if you are used to equating fluency with speed. But remember that your audience experiences time differently than you do. What feels like a long silence to you may feel like a welcome moment of relief to them. Cognitive science tells us that human working memory needs processing time to transfer information into longer-term storage. A pause is not dead air; it is the moment when learning happens.

At a deeper level, the willingness to pause is also a mark of leadership. Leaders who cannot tolerate silence tend to rush decisions, shut down dissent, and confuse motion with progress. They fear that stillness reveals weakness, so they maintain constant activity. But the best leaders know when to stop talking and create space for others to think, react, or respond. Public speaking gives you daily chances to practice that pause. Each time you resist the urge to fill silence, you strengthen your capacity to sit with uncertainty in higher-stakes settings.

Consider what happens in operational environments when leaders cannot pause. Decisions get made prematurely. Subordinates withhold information because they sense the boss does not want to hear complications. Plans proceed on momentum rather than merit. The organization develops a culture of "ready, fire, aim." In contrast, leaders who can pause, who can absorb information, let silence work, and then act deliberately, create conditions for better judgment throughout the organization. Your comfort with pauses in a presentation is a leading indicator of your comfort with pauses under pressure.

## PRACTICING WITH A TIMER

The simplest way to get better at time management is to practice with a timer. Many speakers run through their talk "in their head" and assume that the timing will work out. It rarely does. Thinking speed and speaking speed are not the same, and both are slower than we imagine when adrenaline is flowing.

Choose whatever device you like, a kitchen timer, a phone, a small countdown clock, and rehearse your talk at least once at near-full delivery. Note how long it actually takes. If a 20-minute talk consistently runs to 28, you have a reality check. You can then adjust content, pacing, or both before you face a live audience.

As you practice, pay attention not only to total duration but to where time accumulates. Do you linger too long in the opening? Do you get lost in digressions around your second point? Do you spend three minutes on housekeeping that could be done in thirty seconds? These observations will help you refine both structure and discipline.

Practicing with a timer also reveals emotional patterns. You may notice that certain sections expand because you feel passionate about them, while others contract because you are less confident. Those distortions are diagnostic. They show you where your enthusiasm overtakes your judgment and where your uncertainty creates vagueness. Once you see these patterns, you can correct them: trim the passion, strengthen the uncertain sections, and bring the whole talk into balance.

Practicing with a timer is not about turning you into a robot. It is about aligning your internal sense of time with external reality. This alignment is crucial far beyond the podium. In chaotic environments, organizations suffer when leaders misjudge how long things take: to implement changes, to respond to threats, to build capabilities. Leaders who think a policy shift can be executed in three months when it actually requires nine create cascading failures. Leaders who believe they have weeks to respond when they actually have days lose the initiative. The more accurate your temporal intuition, the better your decisions. And that intuition is built through repetition, feedback, and adjustment which is exactly what rehearsing with a timer provides.

## ADAPTING TO UNEXPECTED CHANGES

Even with careful planning, things will change. You may be told, moments before you begin, that your 30-minute slot is now 15. A key participant may arrive late or leave early. A discussion may erupt that you did not plan for. A technical failure may force you to speak without slides.

In such cases, your composure and flexibility matter more than your original plan. The audience will remember how you handled the disruption as much as what you said.

If your time is suddenly cut, resist the urge to apologize extensively or complain. Instead, briefly acknowledge the change, state your core idea, and promise to focus on the most important points. Then do it. Deliver a concentrated version of your talk, and offer supplementary material (handouts, links, follow-up conversations) for those who want more.

This is where your time-blocking and shedding-point preparation pays off. If you have already identified what is essential versus desirable, cutting on the fly becomes manageable. You can drop the second example, compress the third point, and still deliver a coherent message. The audience may not get everything you planned, but they will get something usable and they will see a leader who adapts without panic.

If an unexpected conversation takes off, perhaps someone asks a question that reveals a live fault line in the group, consider whether engaging that issue may be more valuable than finishing your prepared outline. Sometimes, the real work of the session happens in those unplanned exchanges. Your job is to decide, in the moment, whether to follow that energy or gently park it and return to your structure.

This is the same judgment leaders must exercise in chaotic situations: when to stick to the plan, when to pivot, and how to do either without losing the group. Plans exist to provide coherence, but rigidity in the face of changing reality is not discipline. Rather, it is obstinacy. The art lies in sensing when the situation has shifted enough to warrant adjustment and making that shift decisively. Your talk becomes a microcosm of that larger dance.

Military history offers countless examples of this tension. Commanders who cling to pre-battle plans as conditions evolve often lose engagements they should have won. Commanders who abandon structure at the first sign of friction create chaos. The effective ones from Nelson at Trafalgar to Mattis in Fallujah balance commitment to intent with responsiveness to reality. They know what is negotiable and what is not. Public speaking trains that same balance in miniature.

## PACING AS RESPECT

Underlying all of these techniques is a simple principle: how you handle time is a form of respect. When you start on time, you signal that you value the audience's schedule. When you finish on time or slightly early you signal that you are disciplined and that you trust your content enough not to drag it out. When you pace your delivery so that people can follow without strain, you demonstrate that you care whether they can actually use what you are offering.

Respect is also the foundation of the empathy we will explore in *Listen to Lead.* You cannot listen deeply to people you secretly hold in contempt. Likewise, you cannot pace a talk well if you are indifferent to the cognitive and emotional burden you are placing on your listeners. Time is one of the ways that indifference or care shows up.

From the perspective of *Mastering Chaos,* pacing is how leaders help others cope with temporal compression. You cannot slow the external world, but you can shape the tempo inside the room: slowing down for decision points, creating breathing space in the midst of pressure, and ending decisively rather than drifting.

Organizations inherit the temporal habits of their leaders. If you habitually run meetings over, show up late, or let agendas drift, the people around you learn that time is fungible and deadlines are soft. If you start and end punctually, use time intentionally, and respect others' schedules, the organization develops a culture of temporal discipline. This discipline becomes operational advantage when speed matters and when a competitor moves first, when a crisis demands rapid response, when an opportunity window closes faster than expected.

## BRINGING IT TOGETHER

Managing time and pacing may sound like a technical topic. In practice, it touches the heart of how you think, how you treat others, and how you operate under pressure.

When you:

- Block time deliberately
- Design your talk with shedding points and flex
- Use pauses instead of constant speed
- Practice with a timer to align perception and reality
- Adapt calmly to changes in the schedule

you are not just becoming a more polished presenter. You are training yourself to live and lead inside the temporal realities of our era.

The skills you develop in managing a talk's tempo translate directly to operational leadership. The discipline of allocating scarce minutes becomes the discipline of allocating scarce resources. The reflex to shed non-essential content under time pressure becomes the reflex to prioritize ruthlessly when crises compress decision cycles. The willingness to pause becomes the capacity to create space for judgment when everyone else is rushing. These are not metaphors. They are the same cognitive and emotional muscles exercised in different contexts.

The next chapter will focus on handling unexpected situations, tough questions, distractions, technical failures, the small "chaos drills" embedded in every public appearance. As you move into that terrain, remember that your work on time and pacing is not separate from your work on confidence and structure. Together, they form the backbone of your personal readiness to operate in the anarchy of the moment.

(7)

# HANDLING UNEXPECTED SITUATIONS

No matter how carefully you prepare, reality will refuse to follow your script. A question comes out of nowhere. The projector dies. Phones ring, people walk in late, someone in the front row challenges your premise. These moments feel uncomfortable, but they are not anomalies. They are features of the environment in which you will live your professional life.

In miniature, each unexpected situation in a talk is a drill in chaos management. You are forced to act on incomplete information, under time pressure, with other people watching. You cannot consult all your notes or hold a committee meeting. You must decide: do I answer this now, park it, redirect, or change tack entirely? The way you handle these moments says as much about you as a leader as the most polished part of your prepared remarks.

This chapter will explore strategies for handling tough questions, using humor to defuse tension, preparing backup points, navigating technical difficulties, and turning distractions into opportunities. As you work through them, keep in mind: you are practicing, in a controlled setting, the same cognitive and emotional skills you will need in much larger, messier contexts.

# STRATEGIES FOR HANDLING TOUGH QUESTIONS

Tough questions are not attacks by definition. They may be clumsily phrased, loaded with frustration, or misinformed, but they often signal genuine concern or curiosity. How you respond determines whether the room becomes more open or more defensive.

When you receive a tough question, your first task is not to answer it. Your first task is to understand it. That requires listening, even when your heart rate spikes. The temptation to begin formulating your response while the questioner is still speaking is nearly universal among presenters. Resist it. The split second you spend truly hearing the question will often reveal nuances that a premature answer would miss entirely.

A simple sequence can help:

- Pause and breathe. Take a brief breath before you speak. This prevents reflexive defensiveness and gives you a split second to think. The pause also signals to the audience that you are treating the question seriously, not reflexively batting it away.
- Clarify. Restate the question in your own words: “If I understand you correctly, you are asking....This ensures you are addressing the real issue and shows respect. Often, the act of restating will prompt the questioner to refine their concern, giving you even better information to work with.
- Acknowledge. Recognize the concern behind the question: That is a fair concern or I can see why that would worry you. This does not mean you agree; it means you have heard. In highly charged environments, acknowledgment alone can lower the temperature enough for genuine dialogue to occur.
- Respond honestly. Answer as directly as you can. If you don't know, say so and commit to finding out. If the issue is complex, give the core of your answer and offer to follow up

in more detail later. Audiences can tolerate uncertainty far better than evasion. A simple I don't have that data with me, but l will get it to you by end of day builds more credibility than a vague non-answer delivered with false confidence.

- Re-anchor. Briefly connect your reply back to your core idea so the talk does not fragment. This prevents the Q&A from becoming a series of disconnected tangents. For example: So to tie that back to the main point, this is why distributed decision-making becomes critical in environments where... You are not dismissing the question; you are integrating it into the larger narrative.

This approach aligns with the listening practices developed in *Listen to Lead:* articulation, inquiry, attention, and patience. In many organizations, conflict escalates not because questions are unanswerable, but because people feel dismissed. When you treat tough questions as opportunities to deepen understanding rather than as threats to your authority, you model a different way of operating.

From a chaos perspective, tough questions are also signals. They reveal where your framing has not landed, where there are hidden constraints or unspoken anxieties. Ignoring those signals in a small room is a rehearsal for ignoring them in a large system and with predictable consequences. In complex systems, the weak signals you dismiss today often become the cascading failures of tomorrow. Learning to attend to difficult questions in a presentation is practice for attending to difficult truths in an organization.

## USING HUMOR TO DEFUSE TENSION

Humor, used well, can release tension, humanize you, and allow a room to reset after a sharp exchange or an awkward moment. Used poorly, it can deepen divisions, belittle questioners, or signal that you are not taking real concerns seriously.

The distinction matters because humor operates on multiple levels simultaneously. It can bond a group or fracture it. It can demonstrate confidence or betray anxiety. It can open space for difficult truths or close off serious inquiry. Which of these outcomes you produce depends largely on where you aim the humor and what you do with the space it creates.

When dealing with unexpected situations, a few principles are worth keeping:

- Aim humor at yourself or at the situation, not at individuals or groups. Self-deprecation, in moderation, shows that you do not take yourself too seriously even when you take the topic seriously. It creates permission for others to relax without feeling that you are trivializing the work.
- Avoid sarcasm directed at questioners. It may win a laugh from some, but it often silences others who now fear being made an example. The immediate laughter you gain is paid for in longer-term caution and withdrawal from the audience.
- Use humor to create space, not to dodge substance. A light remark can ease the room, but it should be followed by a genuine answer if a real issue is on the table. The pattern should be: humor to reset the emotional temperature, then a substantive response to the underlying concern.

For example, if the projector fails just as you begin, you might say, This is a brutal way to test whether my ideas make sense without slides and pause for the chuckle, and then continue with your core message. You acknowledge the problem, bring the group into the moment, and move forward. What you have done is normalize the disruption without letting it become the focus of the session.

In *Listen to Lead,* we will see how shared laughter can reinforce social cohesion when it is inclusive, not at someone’s expense. In *Mastering Chaos,* you will see that leaders who can carry a sense of proportion and even humor into crisis settings often help their organizations stay flexible rather than brittle. The small acts of humor you practice here are early steps in that direction.

# PREPARING BACKUP POINTS

You cannot predict every unexpected turn, but you can prepare additional material that gives you options. Backup points are short, self-contained ideas or examples you can deploy when needed:

- A second example ready if the first does not resonate with this audience. What works for engineers may fall flat with finance professionals, and vice versa. Having an alternative in reserve allows you to pivot without losing momentum.
- A concrete illustration you can use if someone challenges your abstraction. Abstract arguments are powerful, but they can feel distant. A well-chosen concrete case can ground your point in something tangible and immediately recognizable.
- A brief alternative angle for a key point, in case your initial explanation fails. Sometimes a concept clicks when approached from a different direction. If your first explanation produces blank stares, having a second pathway ready prevents you from simply repeating yourself louder.

These backups are not extra content you must cram into your allotted time. They are reserves. You may use them or not, depending on what happens. Think of them as the intellectual equivalent of a spare tire: you hope not to need it, but you are vastly better off having it available.

From a cognitive standpoint, preparing backups trains you to think in flexible modules rather than in one brittle script. You begin to see your material as a set of building blocks that can be recombined to meet different situations. This is precisely the mindset leaders need when circumstances change rapidly. They do not start from zero each time; they draw from a repertoire and adapt it.

Backup points also make you less anxious. Knowing that you have additional ways to approach a topic reduces the sense that everything depends on one perfect explanation. That reduction in anxiety translates directly into greater presence and adaptability in the moment.

# NAVIGATING TECHNICAL DIFFICULTIES

Technical difficulties are no longer the exception; they are a regular part of modern presentations. Slides freeze, audio fails, connections drop. If your entire talk depends on a fragile chain of devices, you are building on sand.

The problem is not technology itself but over-reliance on it. Slides, videos, and live demos can enhance a presentation, but they should never become its foundation. Your core message must be able to survive the total loss of every technological support system. If it cannot, you do not yet have a talk; you have a dependency.

A few practices help:

- Always have at your disposal a minimalist version of your talk. This could be a single page with your core idea, main points, and key examples. If the slides disappear, you can still deliver a coherent message. Some of the most effective presentations ever given have been delivered without any visual aids at all.
- Test equipment early when possible. This reduces surprises but will never eliminate them entirely. Cables fail, formats become incompatible, network bandwidth evaporates. You test to catch what you can, knowing that something else will break anyway.
- Decide in advance how you will proceed if visuals fail. Will you describe key diagrams verbally? Will you switch to a more conversational format? The time to think about this is before it happens. Having a pre-decision reduces cognitive load in the moment of failure.

When something breaks during the session, your demeanor matters more than the technology. If you remain calm, acknowledge the issue briefly, and move on, the audience will usually come with you. If you panic, apologize repeatedly, or fixate on the glitch, you amplify its impact. The audience takes its cues from you. Treat the failure as a minor inconvenience, and they will too. Treat it as a catastrophe, and the session collapses.

This is a small-scale analogue of what organizations face when critical systems fail. Leaders who have practiced staying focused on core intent and communicating the essential message or decision even when tools collapse are better prepared when the stakes are higher. The presentation that continues smoothly despite technical failure is a rehearsal for the operation that continues effectively despite infrastructure loss.

## TURNING DISTRACTIONS INTO OPPORTUNITIES

Distractions come in many forms: late arrivals, phones, side conversations, noise from outside, an emotional reaction in the room. You cannot control all of them. You can decide whether to fight them, ignore them, or incorporate them.

Sometimes, the best course is to ignore. A single phone vibrating does not require a public scolding. Over-reacting can draw more attention to the distraction than the distraction itself. You want the audience focused on your message, not on your irritation.

At other times, gentle acknowledgement helps. If a loud noise interrupts you, pausing until it passes shows that you are aware and respectful of the audience's divided attention. The pause says: I know you can't hear me right now, so l will wait rather than compete. That brief act of respect often earns you more attention when you resume than you would have gotten by plowing through.

Occasionally, a distraction can be turned into a bridge. If a phone ringtone is unintentionally funny, a light remark and a smile can reset the room and allow you to continue. If someone's question or comment reveals an underlying concern shared by many, you can use that moment to address something more important than what you had planned for the next two minutes. The distraction becomes a gift: it surfaces an issue you needed to address anyway.

The key is to keep your core intent in mind. Ask yourself: in light of this distraction, what response best serves the purpose of this talk and this audience?

That question moves you from irritation to leadership. You are no longer merely defending your planned performance, you are stewarding the group's attention and energy toward something useful. The shift from *this is ruining my talk* to *how do I use this moment productively* is the shift from presenter to leader.

## MICRO-CHAOS DRILLS

Viewed through the right lens, every unexpected situation in a talk is a micro-chaos drill. You are practicing:

- Acting on provisional maps: responding before you have full information. You will never have complete clarity about why the question was asked, what the questioner really wants, or how others in the room are interpreting the exchange. You act anyway, using your best judgment with incomplete data.
- Preserving optionality: adjusting course without abandoning your core idea. The ability to change tactics while maintaining strategic direction is essential in fluid environments. Each unexpected moment in a presentation is a chance to practice that balance.
- Maintaining social cohesion: handling tension in ways that keep the group connected rather than split. The way you respond to a tough question or a disruption either builds trust or erodes it, brings people together or drives them apart. You are managing not just content but relationships.
- Regulating your own emotions so that you can think clearly. When your heart rate spikes and your defenses rise, your capacity for nuanced thinking drops. Learning to notice that response and modulate it is a skill you will need repeatedly.

These are the same capacities *Mastering Chaos* will describe at organizational scale. The difference is one of magnitude, not of kind. The stakes in a single talk are lower, but the patterns are the same. The executive who freezes when a board member asks an uncomfortable question is exhibiting the same failure mode as the junior analyst who panics when the projector dies. Conversely, the junior analyst who handles technical failure with composure is building the same skill set the executive needs when a critical initiative collapses.

That is why it is so important not to aim for flawlessly controlled presentations. If you script away every possibility of surprise, you also script away much of your learning. The goal is not to invite chaos for its own sake, but to treat its inevitable arrival as part of your training, rather than as a failure.

# BRINGING IT TOGETHER

By now, you have seen that the messy, unpredictable parts of public speaking are not defects to be eliminated; they are integral to the discipline. How you respond when the unexpected happens reveals and shapes who you are as a professional.

When you:

- Listen carefully to tough questions before answering
- Use humor to ease tension without dodging substance
- Prepare backup points that give you flexibility
- Stay focused when technology fails
- Treat distractions as manageable rather than catastrophic

you are doing more than coping. You are developing the habits of mind and presence that leaders draw on when the stakes are higher and the chaos is real.

In the next chapters, we will look at how you use visual aids and how you develop a unique speaking style. As you work on those topics, remember that style and tools sit on top of something more fundamental: your capacity to remain a thinking, listening, responsive human being when events do not go according to plan. That is what this chapter has begun to cultivate, and it is what the later books in this series will build on at greater scale.

# ENHANCING YOUR DELIVERY WITH VISUAL AIDS

Slides, charts, and images are not the message. They are tools for helping people see the message. When used well, visual aids create a shared mental map that allows diverse audiences to follow your thinking and remember what matters. When used poorly, they bury your ideas under clutter and distract from the human connection you are trying to build.

In an era of information overload, visual aids are everywhere. Most professionals have sat through countless slide decks crammed with text, graphs, and bullet points that seem designed to show how much the speaker knows rather than to help anyone understand. The result is not clarity; it is fatigue.

This chapter takes a different stance. We will treat visual aids as instruments of sense-making. They are ways of externalizing complex ideas so that people can see relationships, patterns, and choices. That is exactly the work leaders must do when they operate in the anarchy of the moment: help others visualize what is going on and where they might go. The skills you practice here, choosing what to show, how much to show, and how to talk about it, are the same skills you will use later when designing maps for teams and organizations.

Think about the last time you were in a room where someone tried to brief a crisis. The moment becomes clearer when someone draws on a whiteboard: arrows showing who reports to whom, boxes showing where resources are, lines showing what flows where. That rough diagram is not decoration. It is a shared reference point that lets the room argue productively about what to do next. Visual aids in your presentations should do the same work.

# THE ROLE OF CHARTS AND DIAGRAMS

Charts and diagrams are most valuable when they reveal a pattern that would be hard to grasp through words alone: a trend over time, a relationship between variables, a structure of an organization or system. They are least valuable when they replicate text you are already speaking.

Before adding any chart or diagram, ask:

- What problem does this picture help the audience solve?
- What relationship or pattern will they see that they could not see as clearly otherwise?
- Can I explain this visual in one or two simple sentences?

If you cannot answer these questions, the visual is likely decoration or a crutch.

For example, a simple line graph showing a change in response times before and after a process change can help people see the impact of that change at a glance. A diagram showing how information flows between units can reveal bottlenecks or gaps. A three-circle Venn diagram can illustrate the overlap between three key elements of your argument.

The key is to keep visuals as simple as the situation allows. Complexity belongs in your analysis; simplicity belongs in your slide. Leaders in chaotic environments must be able to move between those levels and doing complex thinking behind the scenes and presenting clear visuals that help others act.

Consider the difference between showing a table with fifty data points and showing a graph with a clear trend line. The table proves you have the data. The graph helps people understand what the data means. In fast-moving situations, understanding beats comprehensiveness. You can always provide the full dataset as a backup, but your visual should answer the question: "So what?"

Military briefings offer instructive examples here. The best ones use schematic representations, blue forces here, red forces there, arrows showing movement, that let commanders see the situation at a glance. The worst ones use dense PowerPoint slides filled with acronyms and nested bullet points that require translation. Your audience should not need a decoder ring to understand your visual.

## AVOIDING OVERLOAD: LESS IS MORE

The temptation to fill slides with information is strong. You want to demonstrate that you have done your homework. You worry that if you leave something out, someone will accuse you of ignoring it. So you add one more bullet, one more chart, one more line of text.

The result is cognitive overload. Audiences cannot read dense text and listen to you at the same time. They either tune you out and read, or watch you and ignore the slide, or give up on both. None of these outcomes serves your purpose.

A useful rule is: one slide, one idea. That does not mean every slide can only contain three words. It means that every slide should have a clear focal point or a single question it helps answer. If you find yourself cramming multiple unrelated points onto one screen, split them.

Consider adopting some simple constraints:

- Limit yourself to a small number of words per slide, especially in the main body.
- Use large, legible fonts and high contrast.
- Avoid complex backgrounds that compete with your content.
- Use color sparingly and consistently, to signal categories rather than to decorate.

These constraints force you to choose, and choosing is the essence of leadership in information-rich environments. In *Mastering Chaos*, we will talk about "signal versus noise" systems: mechanisms that help organizations distinguish what matters from what does not. Your slide deck can be an early, personal version of such a system.

Here is a practical test: show your slide to someone unfamiliar with your topic for five seconds, then hide it. Ask them what they remember. If they cannot tell you the main point, your slide has failed. This is not because your audience is inattentive. It is because human working memory is limited, and visual clutter exhausts it quickly.

Some speakers worry that simple slides will make them look unprepared or superficial. The opposite is true. Simple slides signal confidence. They say: I have thought deeply enough about this problem that I can distill it to what matters. Complexity in a slide often masks uncertainty in the speaker.

## INTEGRATING VISUALS SEAMLESSLY INTO YOUR SPEECH

Visual aids should feel like a natural extension of your spoken message, not interruptions or separate performances. When you move to a slide, the audience's attention shifts. If you ignore that shift by continuing to talk in the same way without reference to what they see, you create dissonance. If you overcompensate by reading the slide aloud, you bore them.

To integrate visuals well:

- Introduce each slide. Briefly tell the audience what the visual is about: "This chart shows how our response times changed after we shifted our process."
- Name the point. State the key takeaway before or after showing the detail: "The main thing to notice is that we cut our average time by 30 percent in the first six months, and then plateaued."
- Guide their eyes. Use words or a pointer to direct attention: "Look at the difference between the blue and red lines here."

- Return to you. Once the point is made, shift their focus back to you. The slide should support the moment, not own it.

Think of visuals as partners in a conversation between you and the audience. They speak when they have something important to contribute, then fall silent. If they are on screen while you are discussing a different topic, they are making noise.

This means you need to manage the rhythm of your presentation deliberately. Some speakers advance slides reflexively, as if the deck controls the pace. Resist that. Pause on a slide when the conversation around it deepens. Blank the screen when you want undivided attention on a story or a moment of reflection. The remote control is not just a navigation device; it is a tool for orchestrating attention.

In *Listen to Lead,* we will focus on how you orchestrate conversations: who speaks when, how you create space, how you move from one voice to another. Integrating visuals into your speaking is an early form of that orchestration. You are learning to conduct multiple streams of information, your words, their words, the images on screen, so that they harmonize rather than compete.

## ENGAGING VISUAL LEARNERS

People process information in different ways. Some gravitate to words; others to images or spatial relationships. Visual aids give you a way to include those who think best when they can "see" what is being discussed.

To engage visual learners:

- Use simple diagrams to show relationships: flows, hierarchies, feedback loops.
- Use icons or symbols consistently to represent recurring concepts.
- Use timelines to place events in sequence.
- Use maps when geography matters.

However, do not assume that "more pictures" automatically means better comprehension. The value lies in the match between visual and idea. Overly stylized graphics can be as confusing as dense text. Clip art that adds nothing but decoration wastes attention. Every visual element should earn its place by doing real work.

Remember also that in global and tribalized audiences, images carry cultural meanings. A color that signals success in one culture may signal warning in another. A symbol that is neutral in one context may be loaded in another. When in doubt, choose simplicity and universality over cleverness. A circle-and-arrow diagram transcends language barriers in ways that culturally specific metaphors do not.

The broader leadership lesson is that people differ in how they construct meaning. Leaders who can present ideas in multiple modes, spoken, written, visual, are more likely to reach those differences. Visual aids are one part of that flexibility. They are not a substitute for clear speaking or rigorous thinking, but they can make both more accessible to audiences who struggle with pure abstraction.

## USING PROPS TO ENHANCE YOUR MESSAGE

Props, physical objects you bring into the room, can be powerful when they are tightly connected to your message. A model, a tool, a simple object that embodies an abstract idea can make your point tangible. They also signal that this session is not just another slide show.

The same questions apply: What does this object help people understand that words alone would not? How will you introduce it and retire it without distraction?

Used sparingly, props can create memorable moments. For example, snapping a small stick to illustrate brittleness versus resilience, or laying out three physical items to represent your "three pillars," can lodge images in people's minds that persist long after they have forgotten your exact wording. A former Marine officer once used a length of rope in a briefing to demonstrate the concept of distributed operations, each strand weak alone, collectively strong, and years later, people still remembered that rope.

Be cautious, however, not to let props become gimmicks. If the room remembers the object but not the idea it was meant to carry, you have missed the point. The prop should clarify, not distract. It should disappear once it has done its work, not sit on the table demanding attention throughout the rest of your talk.

From a chaos-management perspective, props remind us that the world is not all screens and abstractions. Organizations operate in physical space, with real constraints and assets. A supply chain is not just lines on a flowchart; it involves containers, trucks, warehouses.

A communications network is not just boxes on a diagram; it involves cables, satellites, handsets. Leaders who can connect conceptual discussions back to tangible realities help others stay grounded when complexity threatens to become overwhelming.

## VISUALS AS SHARED MENTAL MAPS

The most important shift in thinking about visual aids is to see them as shared mental maps. When you put a chart, diagram, or image in front of a group, you are offering a provisional representation of reality: "This is how I see the landscape." The group then has something external to point at, question, correct, or refine.

This is immensely valuable. Without such externalizations, disagreements remain vague: "I don't see it that way." With a visual, people can say, "You've left out this factor," or "The feedback loop actually runs the other direction." The map becomes a site of collaborative sense-making.

In military operations, this function is explicit. A common operational picture, a shared map updated in real time, allows dispersed units to coordinate without constant radio chatter. Everyone can see where friendly forces are, where threats have been identified, where gaps exist. The map does not eliminate the need for judgment, but it gives judgment something to work with.

In *Mastering Chaos*, we will explore how organizations build such maps at scale: dashboards, system diagrams, scenario projections. Here, you are learning the basic craft at the individual level. Every time you design a visual, you are making choices about what to include, what to leave out, and how to frame relationships. Those choices shape how others will think about the issue.

Consider a simple organizational chart. If you draw it as a strict hierarchy with clear lines of authority, you communicate one kind of reality. If you draw it as overlapping circles showing collaborative relationships, you communicate another. Both may be technically accurate, but they invite different conversations. The visual is not neutral; it is an argument about how things work.

That is why ethical responsibility extends to your slides. Misleading charts, distorted axes, cherry-picked data, manipulative framing, do not just make for bad presentations. They erode trust and damage the shared capacity to reason together. In environments where rapid adaptation depends on collective sense-making, dishonest visuals are not merely unethical; they are operationally dangerous.

## BRINGING IT TOGETHER

Visual aids can amplify your message or obscure it. The difference lies in whether you treat them as decorations or as tools for shared understanding.

When you:

- Use charts and diagrams to reveal patterns rather than to show off data
- Embrace "less is more" to protect your audience from overload
- Integrate visuals seamlessly into your spoken narrative
- Design with visual learners and cultural differences in mind
- Use props carefully to make abstractions tangible
- Treat visuals as shared mental maps open to refinement

you are doing more than improving your slides. You are practicing the kind of clarity and collaborative sense-making that leaders must bring to fragmented, fast-moving environments.

The skills transfer directly. When you learn to simplify a complex idea into a single compelling visual, you are developing the same discipline required to brief a crisis team under time pressure. When you learn to guide an audience's attention between yourself and a slide, you are practicing the orchestration required to manage multiple information streams in an operations center. When you learn to create visuals that invite correction rather than passive acceptance, you are building the foundation for the collaborative leadership that chaos demands.

In the chapters ahead, we will turn to developing your unique speaking style and to the practices of continuous improvement and community. As you work on those areas, remember that visuals are not separate from your voice. They are part of how you make your thinking visible so that others can engage with it, challenge it, and build on it with you.

# DEVELOPING A UNIQUE SPEAKING STYLE

Style is often misunderstood as a layer of polish you apply after you have figured out your content, a set of gestures, vocal tricks, or "signature moves" that make you recognizable. In reality, your speaking style is the outward expression of how you think, how you relate to others, and how you handle yourself under pressure. It is not something you bolt on; it is something you uncover and refine through sustained practice and honest self-examination.

In a world where audiences are increasingly skeptical of canned performances and corporate scripts, authenticity has become non-negotiable. People may tolerate a certain amount of formality, but they are quick to sense when a speaker is pretending to be someone they are not. They notice the gap between what you say and how you say it, between the confidence you project and the uncertainty you feel. They are also quick to notice when someone is willing to show up as a person with real convictions and curiosity, someone capable of being wrong and learning in public. The former breeds distance and erodes credibility; the latter builds trust and opens genuine dialogue.

This chapter is about discovering and strengthening an authentic style that is both true to you and responsive to the demands of the environments you operate in. That style will become an asset not only on stage but in the conversations and crises explored in *Listen to Lead* and *Mastering Chaos*. It is the foundation of how you show up when the stakes are highest and the room is most difficult.

## DISCOVERING YOUR AUTHENTIC VOICE

Your authentic voice lies at the intersection of three things:

- What you care about: the subjects that animate you, the problems that refuse to leave your mind, the principles you are unwilling to compromise on even when doing so would be expedient.
- How you naturally think and speak when you forget to be self-conscious: the cadence, metaphors, and logical patterns that emerge when you are talking with someone you trust about something that matters.
- What your audiences genuinely find helpful and engaging: the moments when they lean forward, ask follow-up questions, or reference your ideas weeks later.

Many early speakers suppress that voice. They imitate others, famous politicians, professors, or senior colleagues, or they retreat into safe, bureaucratic language to avoid being judged. The result is a bland, generic style that offends no one and moves no one. It may get you through the talk, but it does not create the conditions for influence or trust.

To find your voice, start by paying attention to moments when you are most alive in conversation. When you talk with a trusted colleague about a subject that matters to you, how do you sound? Do you use vivid images or stark contrasts? Do you ask questions or make declarative statements? Do you use humor to lower defenses or stories to make abstractions concrete? Do you lean on narrative or on crisp argument? Those tendencies are clues to the natural architecture of your thought.

Next, notice which parts of your talks seem to connect most strongly. When do people lean forward, take notes, or follow up afterward? When do you see recognition in their faces or hear your phrases repeated back to you? Those reactions tell you what aspects of your natural style work for others, not just for you. Often, you will find that the moments you felt most "yourself" are the same moments the audience found most compelling. The challenge is not manufacturing those moments but learning to access them more consistently.

Your goal is not to freeze that style into a trademark performance. Audiences can smell the difference between someone who is being themselves and someone who is performing a version of themselves. The former invites engagement; the latter creates skepticism. Authenticity is not about oversharing or ignoring context. It is about aligning your words, tone, and presence with what you actually think and feel about the subject at hand.

Leaders who speak in their own voice, rather than in inherited formulas, create the conditions for the empathy and genuine conversation explored in *Listen to Lead*. People are more willing to speak honestly with someone who has been honest with them. They are more willing to admit uncertainty when they see that you can do the same. Style, in this sense, is not ornamental. It is the medium through which trust either forms or fails to form.

## BALANCING FORMALITY AND PERSONALITY

Different settings call for different degrees of formality. A briefing to a defense minister, a keynote at a corporate conference, and a workshop with junior staff each invite different expectations. Your challenge is to adapt your style to the room without losing yourself in the process. This is harder than it sounds because the pressures of formal settings often push you toward caution and blandness.

Think of formality and personality as two sliders you can adjust independently. At one extreme, you have full formality: scripted remarks, careful protocol, limited interaction, language scrubbed of ambiguity or color. At the other extreme, you have full informality: conversational tone, improvisation, frequent back-and-forth, comfort with messiness and digression. Most situations lie somewhere in between, and your judgment about where to position yourself will improve with experience.

When you shift toward greater formality, focus on tightening your structure, clarifying your language, and being precise in your claims. Use the discipline of formality to sharpen your thinking. But do not strip out all traces of your personality in pursuit of an imagined professional neutrality. Even in formal settings, small touches, an honest aside, a brief story, a moment of humor, a willingness to say "I was wrong about that", signal that a human being is speaking, not an institutional voice box. Those touches do not undermine authority; they reinforce it by demonstrating intellectual honesty.

When you shift toward greater informality, be careful not to drift into self-indulgence. It can be tempting to fill time with anecdotes, tangents, or in-group jokes that entertain you more than they serve the audience. Informality should invite participation and lower barriers to understanding, not become an excuse for lack of preparation or discipline. Your personality should serve the audience's understanding, not merely your own comfort or need for approval.

Over time, you will learn how to calibrate this balance instinctively. You will know when to tighten and when to loosen, when to hold protocol and when to break it for effect. That calibration is not just a stylistic issue; it is a leadership skill. Leaders who can move along this spectrum without losing their core voice are better equipped to operate across the variety of settings that modern professional life demands from crisis meetings to public testimony to private counsel.

## LEVERAGING PERSONAL STORIES

Your own experiences are a rich source of stories that can make your talks concrete and memorable. Used well, these stories reveal how you came to care about a topic, what you learned the hard way, and how your thinking has changed. They give audiences a way to connect with you beyond your role or title, and they make abstractions tangible by grounding them in lived reality.

The danger is turning stories into ego trips. A talk filled with "I, I, I" can quickly wear thin, especially if the stories serve mainly to establish your importance or settle old scores. The question to ask before including any personal story is: what is this in service of? If the story clarifies a concept, illustrates a principle, or acknowledges a mistake that others can learn from, it is likely worth telling. If it mainly flatters you or reinforces your status, leave it out.

When sharing personal stories in a fragmented and tribalized environment, be aware of perspective. Experiences that feel universal to you may not be universal at all. What seemed obvious from your vantage point may have looked entirely different to others in the same situation. Acknowledge the particularity of your background: "From where I sit, having spent decades in X, this is how it looked..." or "I came to this issue through Y, which shaped what I saw and what I missed." This honesty invites others to bring their own perspectives into the conversation, rather than implying that yours is the only possible frame.

Personal stories are also invitations to vulnerability. The most powerful ones are often the stories of failure, confusion, or change, the moments when you got something wrong and had to rethink your assumptions. These stories build credibility because they demonstrate intellectual humility and a willingness to learn. They also give permission to others to admit their own uncertainties and mistakes.

In *Listen to Lead,* we will look at how listening to others' stories is as important as telling your own. In *Mastering Chaos,* you will see how organizational narratives, shared stories about past crises and adaptations, shape what people believe is possible. The personal narratives you craft now are the seeds of those larger stories. They model the kind of honest, reflective account-giving that makes collective learning possible.

## CREATING MEMORABLE SOUND BITES

While you should avoid reducing complex issues to slogans, well-crafted phrases can help people remember key ideas long after your talk ends. A good sound bite captures the essence of a thought in language that is simple, vivid, and precise. It is not an advertising jingle designed to manipulate; it is a distillation that clarifies.

Such phrases are part of my work and have invented them to convey my thoughts to an audience such as "the anarchy of the moment," "working your mental furniture," "tribalization of the audience," "from crisis management to chaos management." These are not gimmicks; they are conceptual handles that help readers and listeners grasp patterns that would otherwise remain diffuse. They stick because they compress insight into memorable form.

To create sound bites that fit your style, start from the core idea you want people to remember. Ask yourself what is truly essential or the irreducible insight that everything else depends on. Then play with different ways of expressing it. Try metaphors that draw on physical experience or visual imagery. Try contrasts that sharpen the distinction you are making. Try short, declarative sentences that land with force. Test these formulations in conversation and notice which ones people repeat back to you or use in their own explanations.

The aim is not to pepper every sentence with quotable lines. That would feel forced and exhausting. It is to have a few key formulations that anchor your message and give people language to think with. These phrases often become reference points in later discussions, both for you and for others. They provide continuity across talks, articles, and books, creating a cumulative effect that reinforces your ideas over time.

From a leadership standpoint, such formulations are tools for building shared language. Organizations that navigate complexity well often have a small set of phrases that encode important distinctions or habits or ways of talking that capture hard-won lessons and guide decision-making. Your personal sound bites can contribute to that shared vocabulary, helping teams coordinate their thinking even when you are not in the room.

## BUILDING A SIGNATURE OPENING AND CLOSING

Openings and closings carry disproportionate weight in any talk. Your opening determines whether people will lean in or check out. Your closing determines what they take away and how they feel as they leave. While you should avoid rigid scripts that make you sound robotic, having a few signature patterns for beginnings and endings can anchor your style and reduce the cognitive load of preparation.

A strong opening often combines three elements: a concrete example, story, or image that grounds the talk in reality; a clear statement of why this topic matters now, not just in general; and a brief indication of where you are going, so people can track the argument as it unfolds.

For instance, you might begin with a short vignette from your own career, a moment of failure or surprise that crystalized a problem, then connect it to broader themes of fragmentation and adaptation, and finally outline the arc of the talk in two or three sentences.

The opening is also where you establish tone and relationship with the audience. Are you speaking as an expert with answers, or as someone wrestling with questions? Are you challenging their assumptions, or affirming what they already suspect? Are you formal or conversational? These choices should be intentional, not accidental. The opening is your chance to signal what kind of conversation this will be.

A strong closing often does four things: it restates the core idea in fresh language, so it does not feel like mere repetition; it names one or two key implications, showing why this matters beyond the immediate topic; it offers a concrete next step or question, giving people something to do or think about after they leave; and it ends on a note that matches the tone you intend, sober, hopeful, challenging, or reflective.

Over time, you will develop openings and closings that feel natural to you. You may find that you tend toward stories, or toward sharp questions, or toward succinct summaries. That pattern is part of your style, and you should lean into it rather than fighting it. The goal is to have enough structure that you do not waste time searching for a way to begin or end, but not so much structure that your talks sound formulaic.

In the broader arc of this series, openings and closings are training for how you frame and conclude conversations and meetings. Leaders who begin without clarity and end without synthesis create confusion and waste time. Leaders who can open and close well help others orient themselves in time and purpose, even when the middle is messy.

# EMPHASIZING AUTHENTICITY OVER PERFECTION

Perhaps the most important element of your style is how you relate to imperfection. If you aim for flawless performance, you will either freeze, become brittle, or retreat behind a polished mask that keeps audiences at a distance. If you accept that every talk will contain small errors, awkward moments, and missed opportunities and that these are occasions for learning rather than humiliation, you create room for growth and connection.

Authenticity does not mean spilling every thought or emotion. It does not mean treating the stage as therapy or using your audience as a confessional. It means aligning your external behavior with your internal commitments. If you say you value questions but respond defensively when challenged, your style is out of alignment. If you claim to care about listening but rush through Q&A to get to lunch, the mismatch will be obvious. Audiences may not articulate these disconnects, but they feel them, and trust erodes accordingly.

The work of *Listen to Lead* will push you further in this direction, asking you to let go of the illusion that you must always be the one with the answer. The work of *Mastering Chaos* will push you to admit uncertainty while still taking responsibility for decisions made in conditions of incomplete information. Your speaking style can prepare you for this by allowing yourself to say, when appropriate, "I don't know," "I was wrong about that," or "You have changed how I see this." These are not signs of weakness. They are signs of intellectual honesty and confidence in your own learning capacity.

Audiences generally do not demand perfection. They demand seriousness, presence, and respect. When you show that you are committed to the topic, that you have prepared, and that you are willing to engage honestly, including admitting limits to your knowledge, they forgive minor stumbles. They may even appreciate them as evidence that you are human. Over time, that pattern creates a reputation far more valuable than any performance: the reputation of being someone whose words can be trusted because they are connected to actual thought and actual character.

# STYLE AS LEADERSHIP PRACTICE

Developing your speaking style is not about branding in the narrow sense, about creating a marketable persona that you perform on demand. It is about cultivating a way of being in public that is sustainable, effective, and aligned with the kind of leader you wish to become. The choices you make about how to speak, what to emphasize, what to concede, how to treat disagreement, are choices about what kind of influence you want to have and what kind of community you want to build.

When you speak in a voice that reflects your real convictions, you invite others to do the same. When you balance formality with personality based on context, you demonstrate flexibility without opportunism. When you use personal stories that serve the audience rather than your ego, you model the vulnerability that makes collective learning possible. When you craft phrases that clarify rather than manipulate, you contribute to a shared language that can survive your absence. When you open and close in ways that orient and mobilize, you help others navigate complexity with you. When you choose authenticity over the appearance of perfection, you create space for others to be imperfect and honest as well.

You are doing more than becoming a more engaging presenter. You are rehearsing the stance you will take in the rooms that matter most: negotiating tables, crisis cells, strategic retreats, and difficult one-on-one conversations. The habits you build on stage, clarity under pressure, honesty about limits, responsiveness to challenge, are the same habits that define effective leadership in moments of high stakes and low visibility.

As you move into the final chapters of this book, treat your style as a living experiment. Keep what is true and helpful; discard what is false or performative. Let your speaking style become one coherent expression of the larger discipline you are building: the discipline of thinking, listening, and leading in the anarchy of the moment. That discipline is not about control. It is about presence, adaptability, and the capacity to remain yourself even when everything around you is shifting.

10

# CONTINUOUS IMPROVEMENT AND COMMUNITY BUILDING

Public speaking is not a talent you either possess or lack. It is a craft you develop over time through cycles of practice, reflection, and adjustment. The same holds true for leadership. The people who appear effortless on stage or in crisis rooms are usually those who have quietly done the work for years, treating each experience as part of an ongoing apprenticeship rather than as a one-off test.

This chapter examines how you can build a deliberate path of improvement as a speaker and how you can surround yourself with people who support that path. Continuous improvement and community are not optional extras. They are the mechanisms by which you translate one book, one course, or one good intention into a living discipline that can sustain you through the turbulence described in Listen to Lead and Mastering Chaos.

## SETTING ACHIEVABLE SPEAKING GOALS

Improvement requires direction. Without clear goals, you may speak often and still feel that nothing changes. Vague aspirations such "as I want to be a better speaker" rarely produce concrete progress. They substitute wish for work.

Start by setting specific, achievable goals for a defined period, such as the next three to six months. For example: deliver at least three talks or presentations, each to a different type of audience; practice one new technique per talk, whether a clearer core idea, a stronger opening, or more deliberate pauses; solicit feedback from at least two people after each talk on one particular aspect, such as clarity, engagement, or pacing; and record and review at least one talk to observe your own habits.

These goals give you something to aim at and something to measure. They also help you move from a passive stance —" I hope my next talk goes well" — to an active one: "Here is how I will use my next talk to learn."

Importantly, set goals that stretch you but do not overwhelm you. If you try to change everything at once, you will fragment your attention. Focus on one or two aspects per cycle. Over time, those small improvements accumulate into something that looks like mastery but is really just disciplined iteration.

The same logic holds for leadership development. Organizations that attempt to transform everything at once usually fail. Those that set clear, staged goals aligned with a longer-term vision have a better chance of adapting. You are practicing this sequencing on yourself, learning a pattern you will later apply at organizational scale.

## THE IMPORTANCE OF FEEDBACK LOOPS

Without feedback, your learning will be slow and distorted. You will overestimate how well some things worked and underestimate others. You may fix problems that did not exist and ignore ones that did. This is not a deficiency unique to you. It is a structural feature of human perception. We see what we expect to see and discount evidence that contradicts our self-image.

Feedback comes in several forms. Self-observation means watching or listening to recordings of your talks, noting where your energy rises or falls, where you rush, where you hesitate, and how your structure lands. Audience behavior involves noticing when people lean in, when they look confused, when they disengage, and when they return to engagement. Direct comments mean asking trusted colleagues or participants for specific observations, not general praise or criticism.

When seeking feedback, ask targeted questions rather than "How was it?" That question invites polite generalities. Try questions like: Was my main point clear, and if so, how would you state it? Where did you feel most engaged, and where did your attention drift? Was there anything that felt confusing or unnecessary? These questions invite concrete responses you can act on. They also model the kind of curiosity that underpins empathy and collaborative sense-making.

Feedback can sting, especially when you care about your work. The key is to treat it as information, not as a verdict on your worth. Separate your identity from any single performance. You are not "good" or "bad" on the basis of one talk. You are a practitioner on a path. Each performance is a data point, nothing more.

In *Mastering Chaos,* feedback loops become critical at organizational scale. Institutions that cannot see themselves clearly cannot adapt. Leaders who confuse their intentions with their impact lose touch with reality. By building honest feedback loops into your speaking practice now, you are preparing to design and live with such loops later as a leader. The habits of receptivity you develop as a speaker will serve you when you are responsible for entire systems.

## BUILDING A SUPPORTIVE PRACTICE NETWORK

You will improve faster if you are not alone. A practice network is a small group of people who share an interest in developing their speaking and leadership skills, who observe each other, offer feedback, and exchange opportunities. This is not networking in the transactional sense. It is community in the developmental sense.

This network does not need to be formal. It might be a few colleagues who commit to attend each other's talks; a small cross-functional group inside your organization that meets periodically to practice presentations and give feedback; or a circle of peers across institutions who share recordings and reflections. What matters is not the structure but the commitment: mutual honesty, psychological safety, and a shared understanding that everyone is experimenting.

The key is mutual commitment and psychological safety. Members agree to be honest, specific, and constructive. They understand that everyone is experimenting. They celebrate improvements and treat missteps as learning opportunities, not as failures to be punished or embarrassments to be concealed.

Such networks also expose you to different styles and contexts. Watching how others handle questions, structure messages, and connect with audiences expands your repertoire. You may discover approaches that you would never have invented alone. You see that there is no single "right" way to speak effectively, only a range of approaches that work for different people in different situations.

From the perspective of *Listen to Lead,* practice networks are spaces to practice listening as well as speaking. You learn to attend to others' intentions, not just their delivery. You develop the habit of asking what someone was trying to do before you critique how well they did it. From the perspective of *Mastering Chaos,* they are micro-communities that model the kind of trust and openness organizations will need to navigate disruption. If you cannot build that culture in a group of five, you will struggle to build it in a group of five hundred.

## LEARNING FROM REAL-LIFE SUCCESS STORIES

Stories of other speakers' journeys, what they struggled with, what changed, what practices helped them, can be both instructive and encouraging. They remind you that proficiency is built, not bestowed. They also remind you that the path is not linear. People who are excellent speakers today were often mediocre or poor speakers at some earlier point.

As you encounter speakers you admire, resist the temptation to simply label them "naturals." That label is lazy and misleading. It lets you off the hook by suggesting that excellence is beyond your reach. Instead, ask: How did they begin? What specific practices did they adopt? How did their style evolve over time? What failures or embarrassments did they endure and learn from?

You can gather such stories through conversations, biographies, or careful observation. Pay attention not only to grand figures but to people closer to your own context, colleagues or mentors whose progress you have actually seen. These stories are often more instructive than celebrity examples because the challenges and constraints are similar to yours.

Reflecting on these stories helps you contextualize your own path. You see that the fear you feel before a talk is not unique, that the mistakes you make are not fatal, and that the distance between where you are now and where you want to be can be covered through repeated, deliberate effort. You also see that excellence does not eliminate vulnerability. Many great speakers still feel nervous. They have simply learned to work with that nervousness rather than against it.

In the broader trilogy, stories play a diagnostic role. In Listen to Lead, other people's narratives reveal how fragmentation and echo chambers affect their lives. In *Mastering Chaos*, institutional stories reveal patterns of resilience or brittleness. Learning to pay attention to such stories now with regard to how they are constructed, what they emphasize, what they omit, sharpens your interpretive eye. You become better at reading the deeper patterns beneath surface events.

## UTILIZING ONLINE COMMUNITIES FOR GROWTH

In addition to in-person networks, online communities can play a significant role in your development. Digital platforms allow you to access talks from around the world, participate in discussion forums, and share your own content with wider audiences. Geography is no longer a constraint on who you can learn from or who can learn from you.

Used wisely, online spaces can offer exposure to diverse speaking styles and cultural approaches; opportunities to present in virtual formats, which have their own demands and conventions; and feedback from people outside your immediate circle, which can reveal blind spots your local network misses.

At the same time, online environments carry risks: superficial feedback that focuses on performance rather than substance, performative criticism designed to demonstrate the critic's cleverness rather than help the speaker improve, and the lure of chasing likes rather than substance. Platforms optimize for engagement, not for depth. What gets rewarded online is often what is most polarizing or entertaining, not what is most thoughtful or useful.

Approach online communities with clear intentions. Use them as laboratories for ideas and as sources of inspiration, not as the sole arbiters of your value. Participate selectively. Contribute where you can add value. Ignore the noise. Remember that the metrics of online success, views, likes, shares, are poor proxies for actual impact.

The themes of fragmentation and tribalism explored in *Listen to Lead* are particularly acute online. Engaging there gives you practice in communicating across echo chambers and in maintaining your voice without being captured by the dynamics of outrage and performance. It is a testing ground for the kind of communication that builds bridges rather than walls.

## COMMITTING TO LIFELONG LEARNING IN PUBLIC SPEAKING

Ultimately, the most important decision you can make about public speaking is to treat it as a lifelong practice rather than as a hurdle to clear. As your roles change, your audiences will change. The stakes of your talks will rise. The contexts in which you speak, from small teams to international forums, from classrooms to crisis briefings, will evolve. If you view speaking as something you "sorted out" early in your career, you will stagnate. If you view it as a craft you will be working on for as long as you are active professionally, you will keep finding new edges.

Lifelong learning in this domain might include periodically revisiting your core skills, clarity, structure, engagement, as your content becomes more complex; seeking out new kinds of audiences to stretch your adaptability; reflecting, every few years, on how your style has changed and what that says about your development; and connecting lessons from public speaking to other arenas such as negotiation, teaching, crisis communication, and organizational leadership.

This commitment links directly to the later volumes in the series. The more you work on your speaking, the more naturally you will move into the deeper work of *Listen to Lead*, empathy, listening, conversation, and the systemic work of *Mastering Chaos*, designing and leading institutions in turbulent times. Each book builds on the practices of the previous one. Public speaking is not separate from leadership. It is one of the fundamental disciplines through which leadership is exercised.

## PRACTICE AS THE BRIDGE TO THE NEXT STAGE

By this point in the book, you have encountered the major elements of effective public speaking: understanding your environment, building confidence, crafting your message, engaging your audience, managing time and surprises, using visuals, and developing your style. This chapter anchors all of that in a simple reality: nothing changes without practice, reflection, feedback, and community.

When you set concrete goals for your next few talks, build feedback loops that show you what actually happened in the room, surround yourself with people who will push and support you, learn from others' journeys rather than envying them, use online spaces with intention, and commit to continuing this work as long as you speak, you are doing more than improving a skill. You are building a personal learning system. That system is what will carry you into the kind of leadership described in the companion books.

Public speaking, treated this way, becomes more than a professional requirement. It becomes a lifelong discipline that keeps your thinking sharp, your relationships honest, and your capacity to navigate the anarchy of the moment alive. It is a practice that compounds. Every talk you give well makes the next one easier. Every piece of feedback you integrate expands your range. Every network connection you make opens new possibilities.

# 11

# FROM SPEAKER TO ADAPTIVE LEADER

Most people begin thinking about public speaking in narrow terms. They want to get through the talk without freezing, avoid embarrassing themselves, and perhaps earn a few compliments afterward.

By the time you reach this chapter, I hope you can see that speaking well is not about "getting through" anything. It is about becoming a different kind of professional someone who can think clearly under pressure, connect across differences, and help others navigate complexity and change. In short, public speaking is one of the most direct training grounds for becoming an adaptive leader.

Adaptive leadership does not start in a crisis room. It starts in smaller rooms, when you stand up in front of colleagues and try to make sense of something that is not yet fully clear even to you. You prepare your remarks, you choose a structure, you step into the space between your ideas and their reactions, and you adjust in real time. In those moments, you are already doing the work of adaptation. You are testing mental models, noticing where they fit and where they break, and modifying your approach based on what you learn. The podium becomes a laboratory where you practice exactly the habits leaders need in an environment defined by speed, fragmentation, and uncertainty.

Think about what you have practiced in the pages you have just read. You have learned to clarify what matters most in your message, to strip away jargon and clutter, and to build a simple, coherent structure around a single core idea. That discipline is the foundation of intellectual flexibility.

Leaders who can no longer hide behind dense PowerPoint decks or committee language must be able to express a position clearly enough that others can challenge it, improve it, or act on it. When you force yourself to speak in plain language, you are not dumbing down your thinking you are strengthening it. You are building the habit of working with ideas in forms that can survive contact with reality.

You have also practiced managing your own emotional state in the face of exposure. Stage fright, the spotlight effect, the fear of making a mistake these are miniature versions of what leaders feel when the stakes rise and the margin for error shrinks. When you learn to regulate your breathing, to use your body language intentionally, to reframe anxiety as energy, and to recover from missteps without collapsing, you are training emotional regulation under stress. You are teaching yourself that you can remain present even when you feel uncomfortable. That capacity does not magically appear later when you are dealing with crises or chaos it is forged in the modest but very real stresses of presentations, Q&A sessions, and difficult rooms.

Along the way, you have been asked to pay attention to the people in front of you. Effective speaking is never a one-way transmission. It is built on noticing your audience's cues, asking good questions, reading their faces and posture, and adjusting your pace, tone, and examples accordingly. These are the early muscles of empathy. When you learn to see your audience not as an undifferentiated mass but as a collection of individuals with their own knowledge, fears, hopes, and blind spots, you begin to think like a leader rather than a performer.

You stop asking "How do I get through my material?" and start asking "What does this group need from me right now, and how can we move forward together?" That shift from self-preoccupation to other-orientation is the doorway through which adaptive leadership walks.

You have also experimented, perhaps for the first time deliberately, with speaking across lines of difference. English as a diverse language, audiences shaped by different cultural references, the tribalization of public life these are not background inconveniences. They are central features of the world you are operating in.

Every time you work to make your message accessible to non-specialists, to non-native speakers, or to people whose political or generational assumptions differ from your own, you are doing more than being polite.

You are practicing how to create shared meaning where none can be taken for granted. Adaptive leaders are distinguished not by their ability to dominate their own tribe, but by their ability to build bridges across tribes and professions without dissolving what is essential to their own view.

Finally, throughout this book, speaking has been treated as a cycle rather than an event. You prepare, you deliver, you reflect, you adjust. You look honestly at what worked and what did not, you seek feedback that is useful rather than merely flattering or destructive, and you use each experience to refine your style and your substance.

That loop of action, reflection, and adaptation is the basic rhythm of leadership in any domain. Organizations that navigate uncertainty well are those whose leaders institutionalize that rhythm. Individuals who continue to grow long after their peers plateau do the same thing in their own professional lives. Public speaking gives you a concrete, repeatable arena where you can build that rhythm into your habits.

So where does this leave you? If you take seriously what you have practiced in these chapters, you are no longer "just" a presenter. You are someone who:

- Can think aloud in front of others without losing coherence.
- Can manage your own reactions well enough to stay present when you feel exposed.
- Can read a room and adjust without panic.

- Can cross linguistic, cultural, and professional boundaries with intention.
- Can treat each appearance not as a performance to be judged, but as part of a longer learning process.

That is a fair, working definition of an adaptive leader at the personal level.

The work does not stop here. This book has focused on you as an individual professional building your voice, your confidence, and your ability to engage and convince.

The next step is to deepen the relational side of that work your capacity to listen, to conduct genuine conversations, and to resolve conflicts in an age of fragmentation. That is the focus of the companion volume, *Listen to Lead*, which takes you further into empathy, listening, and the craft of conversation as the core practices of modern leadership.

And beyond that lies the challenge of leading organizations through what I have called the anarchy of the moment designing structures, cultures, and decision frameworks that can function when the environment will not sit still. That is the terrain of *Mastering Chaos*.

You can, of course, read those books independently. But if you have worked through this one, you have already begun the journey they describe. You have started to align your thinking, your speaking, and your presence in ways that make it possible to lead others, not just yourself.

The more you treat public speaking as an integral part of that larger journey, the more value you will gain from every speech, briefing, panel, or informal talk you give.

One final suggestion as you go forward. Before each future speaking engagement, ask yourself three questions:

- What idea or perspective do I most need to clarify for myself by speaking about it?
- How can I use this occasion to understand this audience better, not just to persuade them?

- What will I learn from this experience that I can carry into the next level of responsibility?

If you build the habit of answering those questions honestly, every time you speak, you will not only become a more effective communicator. You will steadily become the kind of adaptive leader our era demands someone whose words are anchored in thought, whose presence is grounded under pressure, and whose voice helps others find their own footing in a turbulent world.

## 12

# SUMMARY: PUBLIC SPEAKING
# FOR PROFESSIONALS

This book represents far more than a conventional guide to presentation skills. It presents a comprehensive framework that positions public speaking as a foundational professional discipline essential for navigating the complexity and fragmentation of contemporary organizational life.

Drawing on decades of my experience spanning academic teaching, government service, defense analysis, and international consulting, the work argues that the ability to communicate clearly and persuasively is not merely a useful skill but a core competency that enables professionals to shape outcomes, build coalitions, and lead effectively in what is characterized as the "anarchy of the moment."

## THE CENTRAL THESIS: SPEAKING
## AS STRATEGIC DISCIPLINE

The book's fundamental argument challenges the widespread perception of public speaking as a performance skill separate from substantive professional work. Instead, it positions communication as intellectual infrastructure, what I have termed "mental furniture" that shapes how professionals think, organize knowledge, and engage with complexity.

This reframing transforms public speaking from an anxiety-inducing ordeal into a disciplined practice that clarifies thought, tests ideas against diverse perspectives, and opens pathways for influence and leadership.

The approach emerges from a distinctive career trajectory that began in Queens high school classrooms, where engaging students from diverse linguistic and cultural backgrounds required authentic interest and clear conviction rather than academic posturing. This foundational experience, followed by university teaching and decades of work across defense and policy communities, demonstrated that whatever excites a speaker most about their subject must be the heart of their message. If that energy gets buried under elaborate arguments, overstuffed slides, or bureaucratic language, both speaker and audience are lost.

## WHY MASTERING PUBLIC SPEAKING MATTERS MORE THAN EVER

The opening chapter establishes why public speaking has become more critical in the current professional environment. We live in an age of increasing fragmentation, organizational silos, cultural divides, generational differences, and specialized professional languages that make genuine communication progressively more difficult. Traditional assumptions of shared context, common vocabulary, and aligned interests no longer hold. In this fractured landscape, the ability to bridge divides, translate across boundaries, and build understanding becomes decisive.

The book introduces the concept of "mental furniture" or the cognitive infrastructure that determines how professionals organize information, recognize patterns, and generate responses under pressure. Public speaking develops this infrastructure by forcing speakers to clarify core arguments, anticipate objections, structure information logically, and adapt to real-time feedback.

Unlike writing, which allows infinite revision, or private conversation, which permits casual imprecision, public speaking demands discipline in thought and expression while making that discipline visible to others.

This connects to professional development through the argument that career advancement increasingly depends on the ability to articulate vision, defend analysis against skepticism, and persuade diverse stakeholders with competing interests.

In organizations where formal authority is contested and collaboration across boundaries is essential, communication becomes a primary mechanism of influence. Those who can speak clearly and convincingly gain access to opportunities, shape institutional priorities, and build coalitions that enable substantive work.

The chapter also addresses ethics and the public square, emphasizing that public speaking carries moral responsibilities. When speakers address audiences, they shape what others believe, how they act, and which options they consider viable. This influence requires honesty about uncertainty, respect for opposing views, and commitment to argument grounded in evidence rather than manipulation. The text insists that effectiveness without ethics produces short-term gains at the cost of long-term credibility and institutional health.

Finally, the work links public speaking to empathy and whatI have called "chaos management" or the ability to operate effectively in conditions of persistent complexity rather than temporary disruption. Understanding and engaging diverse perspectives is not just morally preferable but operationally necessary when traditional planning assumptions no longer hold and success depends on synthesizing dispersed knowledge across organizational boundaries.

## THE CHALLENGE OF ENGLISH AS A DIVERSE LANGUAGE

Chapter two confronts a reality often ignored in public speaking guides: English is not a single language but a family of dialects, professional vocabularies, and cultural contexts that create profound communication challenges. Drawing on my international experience, the chapter shows how the same words carry different connotations across

English-speaking communities and how accent, idiom, and reference assumptions can create barriers even among native speakers.

The chapter introduces the concept of "speaking as joint invention," emphasizing that communication is not simply transmitting prepackaged content but actively constructing shared meaning with audiences. This requires reading audience cues, adjusting vocabulary and examples in real time, and recognizing when messages are not landing despite superficial indicators of understanding.

The work also addresses "tribalism at home" or the way professional communities, generational cohorts, political identities, and organizational cultures develop their own languages that facilitate in-group communication while excluding or alienating outsiders. Academic jargon, bureaucratic euphemisms, technical acronyms, and digital-native communication styles all serve this function. Effective speakers must navigate these tribal boundaries, translating their core message into terms that resonate with each specific audience without diluting substance.

The chapter concludes by arguing that language choice is not a neutral technical decision but a strategic one that signals identity, establishes authority, and shapes what kinds of conversations become possible. Choosing accessible language over specialized jargon is not "dumbing down" but demonstrating respect for audiences and commitment to genuine engagement rather than status signaling.

## BUILDING A FOUNDATION OF CONFIDENCE

The third chapter shifts to the practical and psychological dimensions of public speaking, beginning with the near-universal experience of stage fright. Rather than dismissing anxiety as weakness or offering superficial reassurance, the work explores the roots of performance anxiety in our evolutionary wiring and social psychology. The fear of judgment, the spotlight effect (our tendency to overestimate how much others notice our mistakes), and the physiological stress response all combine to make public speaking genuinely difficult.

However, the chapter reframes this challenge as manageable through specific techniques and disciplined practice. Power posing, adopting expansive, confident physical postures before speaking, is introduced as a method to influence psychological state and hormonal responses. While acknowledging ongoing scientific debate about mechanism, the text emphasizes that embodied confidence practices consistently improve speaker self-perception and audience response.

Breathing techniques receive detailed attention as practical tools for calming nerves and managing physical stress responses. Controlled breathing activates the parasympathetic nervous system, counteracting fight-or-flight reactions and creating space for clearer thinking. The chapter provides specific exercises that speakers can use in the moments before taking the stage.

Overcoming the spotlight effect requires cognitive reframing, recognizing that audiences are generally sympathetic rather than hypercritical, that minor mistakes are quickly forgotten, and that perceived disasters are rarely as catastrophic as they feel in the moment. Examples from speaking disasters illustrate that recovery and authenticity often matter more than flawless performance.

The chapter emphasizes personalizing confidence rituals rather than adopting generic formulas. Some speakers benefit from visualization, others from physical movement, still others from reviewing core points or connecting with individual audience members before beginning. The goal is discovering what works for each individual and making it a consistent part of preparation routines.

Crucially, the work argues for embracing mistakes as learning opportunities rather than evidence of inadequacy. Every speaking experience, successful or failed, provides data about what works with particular audiences, which content engages, and how to improve. This learning orientation transforms anxiety from a barrier into motivation for continuous development.

The chapter concludes by positioning confidence as a leadership discipline rather than innate personality trait. Leaders must communicate under pressure, often with incomplete information and uncertain outcomes. Developing speaking confidence builds the psychological resilience necessary for broader leadership responsibilities.

# CRAFTING AND STRUCTURING YOUR MESSAGE

Chapter four addresses content development and message architecture or how to transform complex knowledge into clear, actionable communication. The work begins with a deceptively simple rule: start with one core idea. Most ineffective presentations fail not because speakers lack knowledge but because they try to communicate everything at once, overwhelming audiences with complexity rather than focusing on what matters most.

The "elevator speech trick" provides a forcing function for clarification. If speakers cannot explain their central argument in 90 seconds, they do not yet understand it well enough to present it effectively. This exercise requires identifying the essential insight, benefit, or call to action that justifies audience attention, then building everything else around that core.

The chapter introduces a speech blueprint approach that structures presentations around problem, solution, and implications rather than chronological narratives or comprehensive literature reviews. This problem-centered structure immediately engages audience interest by establishing relevance before providing answers.

Storytelling emerges as a structural tool rather than mere ornamentation. The argument is made that humans process information through narrative. We remember stories, identify with characters, and understand causation through plot. Effective speakers embed their key points in concrete examples, case studies, and personal experiences that make abstract arguments tangible and memorable.

The "rule of three" receives attention as a cognitive architecture principle. Ideas grouped in threes are easier to remember, create satisfying rhythm, and feel complete without overwhelming. Whether organizing main points, supporting evidence, or recommended actions, structuring around three elements improves both speaker control and audience retention.

Creating powerful calls to action transforms presentations from information dumps into catalysts for change. The work emphasizes that every professional presentation should answer the implicit audience question: "So what should I do now?" Vague exhortations to "think about" or "consider" waste the opportunity created by successful engagement. Specific, actionable recommendations that audience members can implement immediately create both value and credibility.

Tailoring content for diverse audiences requires understanding not just what speakers want to say but what specific audiences need to hear and how they process information. Technical experts need detail and precision; senior leaders need strategic implications; operational personnel need practical application. The same core insight may require entirely different presentations depending on audience expertise, authority, and interests.

The chapter concludes by connecting message structure to chaos management. In complex, rapidly changing environments, clear communication becomes a tool for creating shared understanding across organizational boundaries, enabling diverse specialists to coordinate effectively despite lacking complete information or aligned incentives.

## ENGAGING YOUR AUDIENCE EFFECTIVELY

Chapter five focuses on techniques for creating and maintaining audience engagement throughout presentations. The work emphasizes that engagement is not a natural consequence of good content but an active process requiring deliberate choices and continuous attention to audience response.

Crafting effective icebreakers sets the tone for everything that follows. Rather than generic jokes or forced enthusiasm, good openings establish relevance, create curiosity, or make personal connections. Opening with provocative questions, surprising statistics, or brief stories immediately signals why topics matter to specific audiences.

Eye contact receives extended treatment as the primary mechanism for making individual connections within group presentations. Rather than scanning the room or staring at notes, effective speakers make sustained eye contact with specific individuals, creating moments of direct communication that make entire audiences feel personally engaged.

Rhetorical questions provide a tool for intellectual engagement without requiring actual audience participation. Well-crafted questions prompt internal reflection, highlight tensions between conflicting values, or prepare audiences for surprising information. However, the text warns against overuse, rhetorical questions lose power when they become predictable formulas rather than genuine invitations to think.

Using humor to break down barriers requires understanding that humor's primary function in professional presentations is not entertainment but creating psychological safety and building connection. Self-deprecating humor that acknowledges challenges, observational humor that recognizes shared experiences, and playful analogies that make abstract concepts concrete all serve this function. However, humor that punches down, relies on stereotypes, or trivializes serious subjects undermines speaker credibility.

Interactive exercises represent the most powerful engagement technique when appropriately deployed. Rather than passive information reception, exercises require audiences to actively process content, apply concepts to their own situations, and reveal their thinking. This generates immediate feedback for speakers while creating investment in outcomes.

Reading and reacting to audience cues closes the engagement loop. The work describes the constant feedback process during presentations, audience body language, facial expressions, side conversations, device usage, and questions all signal comprehension, interest, confusion, or resistance. Skilled speakers adjust pacing, revisit unclear points, or pivot to more relevant examples based on these real-time signals rather than rigidly following prepared scripts.

The chapter emphasizes that engagement techniques must be authentic rather than manipulative. Audiences quickly detect when questions are rhetorical traps, when humor is forced, or when interaction is performance rather than genuine interest in their perspectives. Sustainable engagement requires respecting audience intelligence and valuing their contributions.

# MANAGING TIME AND PACING

Chapter six addresses the temporal dimension of public speaking or how to structure time effectively, maintain appropriate pacing, and handle the common challenge of finishing on schedule while covering essential content.

Time-blocking is introduced as a preparation technique, allocating specific time periods to each section of presentations and building in buffers for questions, interaction, or unexpected complexity. This prevents the common failure mode where speakers spend too much time on introductory material, then rush through key points when time runs short.

Strategic pausing emerges as one of the most underutilized tools in public speaking. The argument is made that many speakers fear silence, filling every moment with words even when pauses would improve comprehension and emphasis. Deliberate pauses after key points give audiences time to process information, signal importance, and create natural transitions between topics.

The chapter provides guidance on adjusting pace based on content complexity and audience familiarity. Technical material for non-specialist audiences requires slower pacing and more repetition than updates for expert colleagues. Similarly, counterintuitive arguments or policy recommendations that challenge conventional wisdom need more time for audiences to wrestle with implications.

The work also addresses the challenge of staying within time limits, particularly when questions or discussion reveal audience interest in particular topics. A distinction is drawn between discipline (covering planned content regardless of engagement signals) and responsiveness (adjusting to audience needs even when that means leaving some material unaddressed). Professional judgment requires balancing these competing demands based on setting, audience, and objectives.

# HANDLING UNEXPECTED SITUATIONS

Chapter seven prepares speakers for the inevitable complications that arise despite careful preparation. Technical failures, difficult questions, hostile audience members, and personal mistakes all test speaker competence and confidence.

The chapter begins with technical preparation or testing equipment in advance, having backup plans for failed technology, and knowing how to proceed without slides if necessary. The text emphasizes that over-reliance on technology creates vulnerability; effective speakers must be able to deliver their core message without visual aids or with improvised alternatives.

Handling difficult questions receives extensive attention. Distinctions are drawn between genuine clarification requests, challenges to analysis, attempts to redirect the conversation toward questioner priorities, and hostile questions designed to embarrass or discredit. Each requires different responses: genuine questions deserve direct answers; analytical challenges merit respectful engagement with evidence; redirect attempts need acknowledgment while maintaining focus; hostile questions require calm reframing that addresses underlying substance while refusing personal attacks.

The chapter provides specific techniques for managing questions speakers cannot answer. Rather than bluffing or becoming defensive, the recommendation is to honestly acknowledge limits while offering to follow up with additional information or connecting questioners with appropriate resources. This honesty builds rather than undermines credibility.

Dealing with humor or humor-based recovery from mistakes represents another dimension of handling unexpected situations. When speakers stumble over words, display the wrong slide, or make factual errors, genuine recovery comes from acknowledging the problem without dwelling on it, making light of the situation when appropriate, and moving forward with renewed focus.

The chapter concludes by arguing that unexpected situations often provide the most valuable learning opportunities. Reflecting on what went wrong and how speakers responded, then incorporating those lessons into future preparation, transforms disasters into development experiences.

# ENHANCING YOUR DELIVERY WITH VISUAL AIDS

Chapter eight examines how to use slides, props, and other visual elements to support rather than overwhelm messages. The work begins by challenging the default assumption that professional presentations require PowerPoint decks, arguing that visual aids should enhance communication rather than serve as speaker notes or demonstrate software proficiency.

The chapter introduces principles of effective slide design: minimal text, high-contrast visuals, clear data visualization, and strategic use of images that reinforce rather than distract from key points. The emphasis is placed on the principle that slides should direct audience attention rather than divide it. When audience members are reading dense text on slides, they are not listening to speakers' words.

Data visualization receives particular attention, with guidance on choosing appropriate chart types, avoiding misleading representations, and presenting quantitative information that audiences can quickly comprehend and remember. The goal is making data meaningful rather than impressive or showing patterns and relationships that support arguments rather than overwhelming audiences with raw numbers.

The chapter discusses minimalism in presentation design, arguing that less is consistently more. Each element on a slide should serve a specific communication purpose. Decorative backgrounds, multiple fonts, excessive animation, and cluttered layouts all detract from clarity. Professional design means focusing audience attention on what matters most.

The work also addresses the strategic choice of when to use no visual aids at all. In some settings, small group discussions, one-on-one briefings, or intimate speaking situations, visual aids create barriers rather than enhancing communication. The best presenters know when to rely entirely on direct engagement without technological mediation.

The chapter concludes with guidance on integrating visual aids seamlessly into presentations. This means knowing slides well enough to avoid reading from them, using them as prompts rather than scripts, and maintaining primary connection with audiences rather than with technology.

## DEVELOPING A UNIQUE SPEAKING STYLE

Chapter nine addresses the longer-term project of developing an authentic, distinctive voice that reflects professional identity and values. The work argues against imitating famous speakers or adopting generic presentation formulas, emphasizing instead that effective style emerges from understanding individual strengths, interests, and communication preferences.

The chapter explores how personal storytelling serves as both content and style development. Sharing experiences from professional journeys, lessons learned from failures, and insights from unexpected sources makes presentations memorable while revealing distinctive perspectives. Authenticity in storytelling creates connection that polished performance cannot replicate.

Style development is iterative rather than fixed. Speaking voices will evolve as practitioners gain experience, work with different audiences, and encounter new subject matter. Rather than seeking a permanent "brand," the focus should be on continuous refinement of how speakers engage specific audiences with specific content.

The chapter concludes by connecting individual style to professional positioning. Speaking style signals competence, authority, and trustworthiness. Strategic choices about tone, language, and delivery communicate professional identity as effectively as explicit arguments.

## CONTINUOUS IMPROVEMENT AND COMMUNITY BUILDING

Chapter ten addresses the long-term practice of developing speaking skills through deliberate learning and community engagement. The argument is made that public speaking, like any complex skill, requires sustained practice, structured feedback, and community support rather than isolated preparation for individual presentations.

The chapter emphasizes feedback loops as essential for improvement. Recording presentations and watching them critically, seeking honest evaluation from trusted colleagues, and analyzing which techniques work with which audiences all generate actionable insights. However, feedback must be processed selectively, not every critique represents valid improvement opportunity, and excessive self-criticism can undermine confidence.

The work also addresses the value of teaching and mentoring others as accelerators for individual development. Explaining speaking techniques to novices forces clarity about what works and why. Coaching others reveals dimensions of effective communication that practitioners may execute intuitively without conscious awareness.

The chapter concludes by arguing that continuous improvement requires patience and perspective. Skill development occurs incrementally through accumulated experience rather than sudden breakthroughs. Comparing current performance to past performance rather than to accomplished speakers maintains motivation and recognizes genuine progress.

# FROM SPEAKER TO ADAPTIVE LEADER

The final chapter integrates public speaking into broader leadership development, arguing that the disciplines cultivated through effective speaking create capacities essential for leadership in complex organizations.

The work emphasizes that leadership increasingly requires operating across boundaries, functional specialties, organizational cultures, geographic locations, and generational cohorts. The translation skills developed through public speaking, understanding diverse perspectives, adapting messages to different audiences, building connection through authentic engagement, directly enable this boundary-spanning work.

The chapter introduces "chaos management" as a conceptual framework for contemporary leadership. Traditional leadership models assume relatively stable environments where leaders can plan comprehensively, execute methodically, and return to equilibrium after disruptions. However, compressed time cycles, interconnected global systems, and rapid technological change have made chaos the persistent operating condition rather than exceptional crisis.

Leadership in chaotic environments requires different competencies: comfort with ambiguity, ability to make decisions with incomplete information, capacity to synthesize contradictory perspectives, and skill at building adaptive organizations rather than perfecting bureaucratic procedures. Public speaking develops these capacities by forcing leaders to engage complexity, test ideas publicly, and learn from diverse reactions.

The communication framework is connected to broader analytical work on military transformation. Just as modern warfare requires shifting from hierarchical "kill chains" to networked "kill webs" that leverage distributed intelligence, contemporary organizations need distributed conversational networks rather than top-down message broadcasting. Leaders who can facilitate these networks—not by controlling information flow but by enabling effective exchange across boundaries—create adaptive organizational capabilities.

The chapter discusses empathy as foundational to adaptive leadership. Understanding how different stakeholders perceive challenges, what constraints they face, and what motivates their positions enables leaders to construct strategies that integrate rather than override diverse perspectives. This empathetic engagement requires disciplined listening, genuine curiosity, and willingness to be changed by learning, dispositions cultivated through public speaking practice that values audience response.

The concept of "genuine projects" is introduced or concrete initiatives addressing widely felt challenges that require diverse capabilities. These projects convert abstract unity rhetoric into lived collaboration experiences, building trust through shared accomplishment rather than relationship-building exercises.

Leaders who can articulate compelling visions for such projects, recruit diverse participants, and sustain momentum through transparent communication create the organizational adaptation that formal restructuring cannot achieve.

The chapter concludes by arguing that communication capabilities, both speaking and listening, are not soft skills subordinate to technical expertise but foundational competencies determining professional effectiveness. In fragmented organizations where formal authority is contested and success requires voluntary collaboration, the ability to engage diverse stakeholders, build shared understanding, and mobilize collective action becomes the decisive leadership capacity.

# CONCLUSION: A FRAMEWORK FOR PROFESSIONAL DEVELOPMENT

This book offers a sophisticated, experience-grounded framework for understanding public speaking as central to professional effectiveness rather than peripheral performance skill. The approach challenges conventional presentation guides by integrating speaking discipline with broader professional development, ethical responsibility, and leadership capacity.

The book's distinctive contributions include: repositioning public speaking as cognitive infrastructure that shapes how professionals organize knowledge and respond to complexity; addressing the linguistic and cultural fragmentation that makes communication increasingly difficult; providing practical techniques grounded in decades of field experience across diverse professional contexts; connecting individual speaking competence to organizational adaptation and leadership effectiveness; and situating communication skills within an ethical framework emphasizing respect, honesty, and commitment to genuine dialogue.

For professionals navigating fragmented organizations, leading across cultural boundaries, or simply seeking more effective ways to contribute and advance, this book provides both immediate practical guidance and a long-term development framework. It demonstrates that the communication challenges facing contemporary professionals are not inevitable but can be addressed through disciplined development of speaking capabilities that serve substantive work rather than replacing it.

In doing so, it offers not just techniques for better presentations but a pathway toward more effective, resilient, and ethically grounded professional practice in an age that demands it.

# BIBLIOGRAPHY


OUPblog. "The Origins of Performance Anxiety." Oxford University Press Blog. Accessed January 2026. https://blog.oup.com.

Elsesser, Kim. "The Debate on Power Posing Continues: Here's Where We Stand." Forbes. October 2, 2020. https://www.forbes.com.

"Breathing Exercises Guaranteed to Calm Nerves – Use These Strategies Before Any Public Speech." Speaking Coach. Accessed January 2026. https://www.speaking.coach.

"Spotlight Effect and Social Anxiety: What Is the Spotlight Effect?" Verywell Mind. Accessed January 2026. https://www.verywellmind.com.

"Your Professional Elevator Pitch." Public Relations Society of America (PRSA). Accessed January 2026. https://www.prsa.org.

Dlugán, Andrew. "Speech Preparation: Speech Outline Examples." Six Minutes. Accessed January 2026. https://sixminutes.dlugan.com.

Divecha, Shivani. "7 Storytelling Techniques Used by the Most Inspiring TED Presenters." Medium. Accessed January 2026. https://medium.com.

"Examples of the Rule of Three." Presentation Magazine. Accessed January 2026. https://www.presentationmagazine.com.

"12 Ice Breakers for Presentations: Engage with Icebreakers." Prezentium. Accessed January 2026. https://prezentium.com.

"Senior Leader Communication Skills: Studying Barack Obama's Public Speaking." Speak by Design. Accessed January 2026. https://www.speakbydesign.com.

"Rhetorical Question in 'The Letter from Birmingham Jail': Analytical Essay." EduBirdie. Accessed January 2026. https://edubirdie.com.

Haskell, Isaac. "Rhetorical Analysis: Ellen DeGeneres and Comedy." Medium. Accessed January 2026. https://medium.com.

"Creating a Timeline for Speeches." Communication Center, James Madison University. Accessed January 2026. https://www.jmu.edu.

"The Benefits of Time-Blocking, and Some Tips to Get You Started." Toscah. Accessed January 2026. https://dev.toscahhht.

"Master the Positive Power of the Pause in Presentations." Benjamin Ball Associates. Accessed January 2026. https://benjaminball.com.

Tomich, Janice. "Three Relaxation Techniques to Manage Your Fear of Public Speaking That Actually Work." Janice Tomich, Presentation Skills. Accessed January 2026. https://janicetomich.com.

"How Politicians Get Away with Dodging the Question." NPR. Accessed January 2026. https://www.npr.org.

"Humour Is a Powerful Public Speaking Tool: Here's How to Use It Effectively." Soft Skill Success. Accessed January 2026. https://www.softskillsuccess.ie.

"Technical Issues During Sessions: What Can Happen, and How to Prepare." Sessionize Playbook. Accessed January 2026. https://sessionize.com.

"7 Tips for Designing and Delivering PowerPoint Presentations." MTSS, The College of New Jersey. Accessed January 2026. https://mtss.tcnj.edu.

"The Importance of Data Visualisation in Presentations and How to Use It Effectively." DeckSherpa. Accessed January 2026. https://decksherpa.com.

"The Power of Minimalism in Presentation Design." Accessed January 2026. (Publisher and URL not fully specified in original notes.)

"Visual Learning: Effective Strategies and Best Practices." Instructure. Accessed January 2026. https://www.instructure.com.

"The Importance of Personal Storytelling." openpress.usask.ca. Accessed January 2026. https://openpress.usask.ca.

"5 Strategies to Make Your TED Talk Go Viral." Fearless Presentations. Accessed January 2026. https://www.fearlesspresentations.com.

"6 Key Business Storytelling Strategies from Oprah Winfrey." aclasses.org. Accessed January 2026. https://aclasses.org.

"How to Craft a Memorable Sound Bite." Doole Communications. Accessed January 2026. https://www.doolecommunications.com.

"11 SMART Goals Examples for Your Public Speaking Skills." Develop Good Habits. Accessed January 2026. https://www.developgoodhabits.com.

"Pathways Learning Experience: Paths and Projects." Toastmasters International. Accessed January 2026. https://www.toastmasters.org.

"Feedback Loops: The Driving Force Behind Continuous Improvement." Mavim Blog. Accessed January 2026. https://blog.mavim.com.

"Toastmasters International – Home." Toastmasters International. Accessed January 2026. https://www.toastmasters.org.

# LISTEN TO LEAD

## How Empathy and Better Conversations Transform Your Work and Life

# INTRODUCTION

Years ago, I met a leader whose presence was as commanding as it was comforting. He had the rare ability to make each person feel heard and understood. In meetings where tensions ran high, he defused conflicts with a simple nod or a well-timed question. What struck me most was not merely what he said, but how he listened.

He possessed an almost uncanny ability to hear not just words, but the unspoken concerns beneath them. He could sit in silence while others spoke, his attention so complete that people found themselves articulating thoughts they hadn't known they possessed.

His secret?

Empathy, manifested through the lost art of genuine listening and the patient cultivation of meaningful conversation.

This encounter planted the seed for this book, but the soil in which it has grown is the profound crisis of communication I have witnessed accelerate over four decades of working with leaders, organizations, and diverse communities across the globe. We live in an age of unprecedented connectivity, yet we are simultaneously experiencing an epidemic of disconnection. The art of listening has atrophied in our social media era, where individuals increasingly inhabit isolated worlds or cluster within echo chambers of those who think exactly as they do.

This fragmentation poses perhaps the greatest challenge to effective leadership and organizational adaptation in our time.

The central premise of this book is both simple and profound: empathy in communication empowers individuals and paves the way to effective leadership.

But empathy requires more than good intentions or surface-level acknowledgment. It demands the cultivation of two practices that have become endangered in modern discourse: genuine listening and the art of conversation. By truly understanding others through active listening and engaging them through meaningful dialogue, you can foster profound personal and professional growth and build the adaptive organizations that our complex world demands.

Consider the landscape of contemporary communication. We live in an age where people scroll through feeds of content algorithmically designed to reinforce their existing beliefs. We "like" and "share" without truly engaging. We respond to headlines without reading articles. We participate in comment threads that generate heat but rarely light.

The result is a society increasingly segregated into tribes of the like-minded, where the ability to understand perspectives different from our own has dangerously diminished. We mistake exposure for engagement, and volume for dialogue.

This communication crisis extends far beyond personal relationships. It permeates our organizations, communities, and institutions. Leaders today face the challenge of bringing together diverse teams whose members may inhabit entirely different informational universes.

Building adaptive organizations, those capable of responding effectively to rapid change and complex challenges, requires something more fundamental than new technologies or management systems. It requires the ability to bridge divides, to connect people across differences, and to forge genuine projects that bring diverse perspectives together toward common purpose.

Building this bridging capacity demands empathy, but empathy of a particular kind. It is not merely the capacity to feel what others feel, though that matters. It is the disciplined practice of seeking to understand experiences, perspectives, and reasoning different from your own. It is the willingness to sit with discomfort, to question your own assumptions, and to recognize that the person across from you possesses insights you lack. This kind of empathy cannot be cultivated through reading alone or through abstract commitment. It requires the practice of listening.

Yet listening has become a lost art. In conversations, we often wait to speak rather than seeking to understand. We formulate our responses while others are still talking, mentally rehearsing our points rather than absorbing theirs. We interrupt, redirect, and hijack conversations to return to our own priorities. We listen for what we expect to hear rather than remaining open to being surprised.

This failure of listening is not merely a personal failing: it is a leadership catastrophe. A leader who cannot listen cannot learn. A leader who cannot learn cannot adapt. And organizations that cannot adapt do not survive, notably in the age of the anarchy of the moment in which we live. In an age where we need to learn and practice the art of chaos management.

The art of conversation has similarly atrophied in our age. A true conversation is not a sequential exchange of monologues or a debate to be won. It is a collaborative exploration, a shared journey toward understanding. Good conversations have rhythm and flow. They build energy rather than dissipate it. They open possibilities rather than close them down. A skilled conversationalist knows how to ask questions that invite reflection, to offer observations that spark insight, to create space for others to think aloud, and to weave together diverse contributions into something larger than any individual could create alone.

A good leader understands that the quality of conversation within an organization directly determines its capacity for innovation and adaptation. When conversations are shallow, defensive, or dominated by hierarchy, organizations become brittle. Information flows poorly. Problems are hidden or ignored. Innovation stagnates.

But when leaders cultivate genuine dialogue, conversation characterized by authentic curiosity, respectful challenge, and collaborative exploration, organizations become resilient and creative. People bring their full intelligence and commitment to their work. Problems surface early. Novel solutions emerge from unexpected combinations of perspectives.

Throughout my career spanning more than forty years, I have worked with varied audiences, discussing complex subjects and witnessing firsthand the power of empathy in communication. I have observed transformational leaders in military settings, corporate environments, government agencies, and non-profit organizations. What distinguishes the most effective among them is not superior technical knowledge or strategic brilliance, though these matter. It is their capacity to listen deeply, to engage others in genuine conversation, and to build bridges across the divides that fragment organizations and communities.

I have seen how empathy can break down barriers that seemed insurmountable. I have watched leaders transform hostile groups into collaborative teams by the simple practice of ensuring every voice was heard and understood. I have observed organizations revitalize themselves when leaders created space for honest conversation about challenges everyone knew existed but no one felt safe to name. These experiences have convinced me that empathy, manifested through listening and conversation, is not a "soft skill" peripheral to leadership effectiveness. It is the foundational capacity upon which all other leadership capabilities rest.

In our fast-paced and often fragmented world, empathy is more critical than ever. But cultivating empathy requires more than commitment or good intentions. It requires practice in specific disciplines that our current communication environment actively undermines. We must deliberately cultivate the capacity to listen, not just to words but to meanings, concerns, and possibilities. We must practice the art of conversation, learning to ask better questions, to create space for reflection, to build understanding across difference, and to forge shared purpose from diverse perspectives.

Building adaptive organizations in this environment means creating cultures where listening and genuine conversation are valued and practiced. It means moving beyond the illusion that broadcasting messages through multiple channels constitutes communication. It means recognizing that the silos and echo chambers that fragment society also fragment our organizations, and that breaking down these barriers requires patient, empathetic bridge-building.

This bridge-building is not about pretending differences don't exist or papering over genuine conflicts. It is about creating conditions where people with different perspectives, experiences, and priorities can engage each other productively. It requires leaders who can facilitate difficult conversations, who can help groups move beyond positional bargaining to collaborative problem-solving, and who can identify and pursue genuine projects that unite people across their differences.

The genuine projects that bring people together share certain characteristics. They address real challenges that multiple stakeholders care about. They require diverse perspectives and capabilities to succeed. They create opportunities for people to experience working together effectively, building trust through shared accomplishment rather than abstract appeals to unity. Identifying and catalyzing such projects is a crucial leadership skill, one that depends fundamentally on the empathetic understanding of what matters to different groups and individuals.

This book is organized to guide you through the different facets of empathetic communication, with particular attention to listening and conversation as foundational practices. We will begin by exploring what empathy truly means and why it is vital in our current context. We will then delve into practical strategies for cultivating empathy in your interactions, with specific chapters devoted to the disciplines of listening and the art of conversation. Each chapter will build on the last, providing you with a toolkit for enhancing your communication and leadership abilities.

You will learn techniques for breaking through the barriers that prevent genuine understanding. You will discover how to create conditions for productive conversation even among groups with deep disagreements. You will explore strategies for building adaptive organizations capable of learning and evolving in response to complex challenges. Throughout, the focus will be on practical approaches grounded in real-world experience across diverse contexts.

Now, I invite you to reflect on your current communication style.

- How often do you find yourself truly listening to others, giving them your complete attention without mentally preparing your response?
- When was the last time you had a conversation that genuinely changed your thinking or opened new possibilities?
- How effectively do you bridge divides in your organization or community, connecting people who might otherwise remain isolated in their separate spheres?

Consider the potential benefits of enhancing your empathy skills through dedicated practice in listening and conversation. Imagine the connections you could forge and the conflicts you could resolve. Picture the adaptive, innovative organization you could help build. Envision the leader you could become, not through dominating discourse but through facilitating genuine dialogue, not through having all the answers but through asking the questions that help others discover solutions.

By the end of this book, you can expect to improve your communication skills significantly. You will enhance your leadership abilities and gain a deeper understanding of empathy's role in various contexts. Whether you are leading a team, managing clients, navigating organizational change, or simply looking to improve your personal relationships, this journey holds the potential to transform your interactions. You will develop specific capabilities in listening and conversation that will serve you throughout your career and life.

As we embark on this journey together, I encourage you to envision a future where empathy is at the core of your communication. Imagine organizations where genuine conversation replaces superficial exchange, where listening is valued as highly as speaking, where bridges are built across divides rather than walls erected to reinforce them. Imagine a world where understanding and connection are the norms, not the exceptions. This vision is not just inspirational; it is achievable and urgently necessary.

In this book, you will find narratives that illustrate empathy's impact and data that underscores its importance. You will also encounter challenges that encourage you to apply what you learn, particularly in developing your listening capacity and conversational skills. By the time you finish, you will have embarked on a transformative journey, one that empowers you to lead with empathy and communicate with purpose in an age that desperately needs these capacities.

Empathy is not just a skill; it is a pathway to leadership and a key to unlocking human potential. But empathy without the practices of listening and genuine conversation remains abstract and ineffective. Together, these form the foundation for building the adaptive organizations and connected communities our complex, fragmented world requires. Let us begin this journey together, and together, we will forge a new way forward.

**1**

# THE CAULDRON FORESEEN

In 1996, while technology enthusiasts and policy makers gathered in Madrid under UNESCO's auspices to celebrate the coming "information society," I offered a warning in my contribution to the symposium on "Copyright and Communication in the Information Society" which warned of a possible downside of the new information society, namely fragmentation, polarization, and institutional strain that now define our networked world.[*]

While other participants debated bandwidth requirements, copyright provisions, and the technical specifications of information superhighways, I insisted on asking a more fundamental question: What happens to political community, democratic discourse, and shared public space when communication networks reconfigure society faster than institutions can adapt? My answer was that we risked creating a "cauldron of change" producing fragmentation rather than connection reads today less like speculation and more like documentation of our lived reality.

---

[*]  Moufida Goucha, ed., *What Kind of Security?* (Paris: UNESCO Publishing, 1998).

# THE MADRID MOMENT: OPTIMISM MEETS CAUTION

The 1996 Madrid conference captured a particular historical moment when the promise of digital networks seemed boundless. Participants spoke enthusiastically of "learning without frontiers," new "islands of prosperity," and the "equitable dissemination of knowledge." The prevailing mood assumed that with proper legal frameworks, updated copyright laws, technical protection measures, collective rights management, the information society would deliver unprecedented democratic participation and economic opportunity.

Positioned as the lead substantive contribution in the conference's first panel on global infrastructure, my chapter, "The United States or the Untied States?" reframed the entire discussion. Where others focused on cables, protocols, bandwidth, and regulatory convergence, I insisted that the real infrastructure of the information society was institutional and political. The critical questions were not technical but social: whose voices would be amplified, who would benefit from these new networks, and what would happen to democratic deliberation when communication was reorganized around personalized choice rather than shared public forums.

My analysis centered on a United States undergoing multiple simultaneous transformations: no longer a bounded nation-state but a "global entity," with traditional cultural frameworks obsolete and the economic base shifted to globally engaged networks. I described America not as a model for others to follow but as a case study in institutional stress, where new information technologies were catalyzing changes that political systems could not manage. This "cauldron of change" was blurring the line between inside and outside, fragmenting the public into specialized niches, and making it increasingly difficult to define who "the people" were or how democratic authority could be maintained.

# AGAINST TECHNOLOGICAL DETERMINISM

My intervention cut against the prevailing techno-optimism on two crucial fronts. First, I explicitly rejected technological determinism. I criticized figures like Alvin Toffler, George Gilder, and Bill Gates for assuming that "third-wave" technologies would automatically produce decentralized harmony, "conflict-free capitalism," or enhanced democracy. Instead, I argued that outcomes would depend on organizational, legal, and political choices, not on the tools themselves.

This resistance to determinism was particularly important in 1996, when much discussion about the internet and digital communication assumed that technology itself had democratic properties. The very architecture of networks, decentralized, peer-to-peer, open, seemed to many observers to guarantee more egalitarian outcomes. I insisted that this was wishful thinking. The same technologies could concentrate power, enable new forms of surveillance and control, or fragment public discourse, depending on how they were deployed within existing structures of economic and political power.

Second, and more provocatively, I questioned the emerging democratic narrative around networked communication. While acknowledging the explosion of online news, email, and internet services, I observed how "bulletin-board politics" and "battling web pages" risked fragmenting the public into isolated communities of the like-minded.

The proliferation of choice reinforced by cable and satellite television might not deepen democratic deliberation but instead erode any shared public sphere, raising the fundamental question: Is there still an "American public" capable of framing common choices or merely segmented markets with diminishing capacity to understand perspectives different from their own?

## FROM CONVERSATION TO ECHO CHAMBERS

Writing before the rise of social media platforms, algorithmic curation, or personalized news feeds, I underscored how increased "choice" in media consumption could paradoxically diminish genuine public conversation. When individuals can curate their information environment to reflect only views they already hold, when they can find communities that reinforce rather than challenge their assumptions, the result is not enhanced freedom but epistemic closure.

Today we call these phenomena "echo chambers" and "filter

bubbles," and we have extensive research documenting how social media platforms algorithmically reinforce division. We understand how recommendation systems optimize for engagement rather than understanding, how outrage travels faster than nuance, and how people increasingly inhabit separate informational universes with incompatible basic facts. But in 1996, when the internet was still predominantly text-based and social media platforms did not yet exist, I argued that the structural logic of the new systems would produce these outcomes.

My warning about bulletin-board politics fragmenting deliberation into niches anticipated not just the technical architecture of contemporary platforms but the broader crisis of shared reality that defines our current political moment. When there is no common space where different perspectives must encounter each other, when individuals can select into communities where everyone thinks alike, the capacity for democratic self-governance, which requires citizens to negotiate differences and forge compromises, deteriorates.

## THE CRISIS OF LISTENING AND EMPATHY

My analysis connects directly to the central argument of this book on empathy, listening, and conversation as leadership capacities. The fragmentation I warned about is fundamentally a breakdown in the practices that make genuine understanding across difference possible. When people inhabit separate informational worlds, when they can avoid encountering perspectives that challenge their assumptions, the disciplines of listening and conversation atrophy.

In my seminar presentation, I described how new communication technologies were reconfiguring not just media consumption but organizational forms, work patterns, and social identities. The shift from bounded national communities to global networks meant that traditional mechanisms for building shared understanding, face-to-face interaction, common media consumption, shared civic rituals, no longer functioned as they once had. The blurring of "inside" and "outside" meant that the assumptions and frameworks people used to make sense of the world were increasingly divergent.

This analysis anticipated the current epidemic of disconnection despite unprecedented connectivity. We are more able to communicate across distances than ever before, yet we are experiencing a profound crisis in our capacity to understand those who think differently. We mistake exposure for engagement, volume for dialogue. We scroll through feeds algorithmically designed to reinforce our existing beliefs, "liking" and "sharing" without truly engaging. We respond to headlines without reading articles, participate in comment threads that generate heat but rarely light.

The result, as I warned in 1996 and elaborate in this book, is a society segregated into tribes of the like-minded, where the ability to understand perspectives different from our own has dangerously diminished. Building the "adaptive organizations" capable of responding to complex challenges, whether in military contexts, corporate environments, or democratic governance, requires reviving practices of empathetic listening and genuine conversation that the information society has systematically undermined.

## THE ENDURING RELEVANCE OF EARLY WARNINGS

Reading my 1996 contribution today is both illuminating and sobering. Nearly thirty years before terms like "filter bubble," "echo chamber," and "post-truth" entered common parlance, he identified the structural dynamics that would produce them. While others celebrated the democratic potential of networked communication, I warned that the same technologies could fragment publics, concentrate power in new ways, and export instability globally.

My insistence on the primacy of institutional and political infrastructure over technical infrastructure remains crucial. The challenges we face are not primarily about network capacity, encryption standards, or copyright provisions, though these matter, but about maintaining the social practices and institutional frameworks that enable people to understand those who think differently, to forge common purpose across divisions, and to sustain legitimate democratic authority in an age of global information flows.

This is why my current work on empathy, listening, and conversation as foundational leadership capacities connects so directly to my

1996 analysis. The fragmentation I warned about can only be addressed by deliberately cultivating the practices that networked communication undermines: genuine listening that seeks to understand rather than to rebut, conversation that builds bridges across difference rather than reinforcing tribal boundaries, and the empathetic engagement necessary to forge shared projects among people with divergent perspectives and priorities.

The "cauldron of change" I described in 1996 is now the world we inhabit. My warning that legal and technical fixes alone would not produce a democratic information society has been validated.

The question now is whether we can heed the deeper lesson of his early intervention: that building adaptive organizations and sustaining democratic community in a networked age requires not better algorithms or platforms but renewed commitment to the fundamentally human capacities for listening, understanding, and genuine conversation across difference.

These are not "soft skills" peripheral to effectiveness but the foundational infrastructure upon which everything else depends.

# UNDERSTANDING EMPATHY IN
# AN AGE OF FRAGMENTATION

Several years ago, I watched a team disintegrate not from lack of talent or resources, but from the erosion of their capacity to hear one another. They had fallen into what I now recognize as the defining pattern of our age: each person inhabited a separate informational universe, convinced of the rightness of their perspective, unable to genuinely engage with viewpoints that challenged their assumptions.

The project manager called endless meetings, but these gatherings generated only heat, never light. People waited to speak rather than seeking to understand. They interrupted, redirected conversations to their priorities, and mistook the volume of their advocacy for the quality of their thinking.

The dysfunction was palpable. Engineers dismissed marketing concerns as superficial. Marketing professionals viewed technical constraints as obstacles to be overcome through better communication with customers rather than genuine limitations to be respected. Finance saw both groups as insufficiently disciplined about resource allocation. Each faction had developed its own vocabulary, its own metrics of success, its own tribal identity. They occupied the same physical space but inhabited fundamentally different cognitive worlds.

Then something shifted. A new leader joined the team, someone whose presence was neither dominating nor deferential, but deeply attentive. In the first meeting, this leader did something radical: she listened. Not the performative listening we often see, where someone waits politely for their turn to speak while mentally rehearsing their response. Real listening. She asked questions that invited reflection rather than defensiveness. She created space for people to articulate thoughts they hadn't fully formed. She heard not just words, but the concerns and possibilities beneath them.

I watched as she worked with the engineering lead, not by dismissing his technical concerns but by helping him articulate them in ways that connected to marketing's customer focus. She engaged the marketing director, not by accepting every customer request as sacrosanct but by exploring what underlying needs those requests revealed. She brought finance into conversations early, not as gatekeepers of resources but as partners in understanding constraints and possibilities. Within weeks, the team's dynamic transformed. People began building on each other's ideas rather than competing with them. Solutions emerged from unexpected combinations of perspectives. The team didn't just complete their project:. They became something they hadn't been before: genuinely adaptive.

This transformation illuminated something I had been observing throughout my career but hadn't fully articulated: the crisis of our age is fundamentally a crisis of communication. We live in an era of unprecedented connectivity yet experience an epidemic of disconnection. The art of listening has atrophied. The practice of genuine conversation has become endangered. And the consequences extend far beyond individual relationships. They threaten our capacity to build the adaptive organizations and resilient communities that our complex, rapidly changing world demands.

## THE COMMUNICATION CRISIS: ECHO CHAMBERS AND ISOLATION

To understand empathy's role today, we must first understand the landscape in which it must operate. We inhabit a communication environment fundamentally different from any previous era. Social media algorithms curate our information feeds to reinforce existing beliefs. We scroll through content designed to confirm rather than challenge our worldview. We "like" and "share" without truly engaging. We participate in comment threads that generate outrage but rarely understanding. We respond to headlines without reading articles, and we mistake exposure for engagement.

This technological shift has profound psychological and social consequences. When we encounter information that challenges our existing beliefs, our brains register it as a threat. We don't evaluate challenging information objectively, we marshal arguments against it, seek flaws in its reasoning, question its sources. Meanwhile, information confirming our beliefs creates feedback loops that reinforce our existing perspectives. Social media platforms exploit these psychological vulnerabilities, optimizing for engagement metrics that correlate with emotional arousal rather than understanding or truth.

The result is a society increasingly segregated into tribes of the like-minded. People cluster in echo chambers where their views are constantly validated and opposing perspectives are either absent or caricatured. When we do encounter opposing views, we often experience them through the most extreme or poorly articulated examples, reinforcing our conviction that "those people" are not just wrong but irrational or ill-intentioned. This dynamic extends across virtually every dimension of contemporary life: political affiliation, professional identity, geographic location, generational cohort, and countless other categorical divisions.

This fragmentation represents perhaps the greatest challenge to effective leadership and organizational adaptation in our time.

- How do you build a cohesive team when members inhabit entirely different informational universes?
- How do you foster innovation when diverse perspectives cannot productively engage?
- How do you create adaptive organizations when the very capacity for dialogue across difference has deteriorated?

These are not theoretical questions. They define the daily reality of contemporary leadership.

This crisis extends beyond the digital realm into our organizations and communities. I have watched leadership teams fragment along lines of specialty or hierarchy, each group developing its own language and priorities, unable to bridge the divides that separate them. I have seen departments within the same organization become as isolated as warring tribes, hoarding information and resources, viewing collaboration as threat rather than opportunity. I have observed how this fragmentation undermines organizational resilience, leaving institutions brittle and unable to respond effectively to complex challenges.

Consider a typical large organization. Engineering speaks the language of technical feasibility and system architecture. Sales focuses on customer relationships and revenue targets. Operations emphasizes efficiency and process optimization. Finance prioritizes resource allocation and return on investment. Each function develops its own worldview, its own success metrics, its own tribal identity. These divisions might seem natural or even necessary for specialization. But they create barriers to the cross-functional collaboration that complex problem-solving requires.

The costs are measurable and substantial. Organizations struggle to innovate because breakthrough ideas emerge at the intersection of different perspectives, and those intersections no longer exist. Teams fail to adapt because they lack the diverse input necessary to recognize changing conditions and respond effectively. Leaders make poor decisions because they surround themselves with people who think exactly as they do, missing crucial information and blind spots. Projects fail not from technical impossibility but from organizational fragmentation that prevents necessary coordination. The quality of organizational conversation directly determines organizational capability, and conversation quality has declined precipitously.

## EMPATHY AS THE PRACTICE OF BRIDGE-BUILDING

In this fragmented landscape, empathy becomes not merely a "soft skill" but a foundational capacity for effective leadership and organizational adaptation. But we must be precise about what empathy means in this context. It is not simply the ability to feel what others feel, though emotional resonance matters. It is not about being "nice" or avoiding difficult conversations. It is not about abandoning standards or accepting every perspective as equally valid. Empathy, properly understood, is the disciplined practice of seeking to understand experiences, perspectives, and reasoning different from your own.

This kind of empathy requires more than good intentions or abstract commitment. It demands the cultivation of specific practices that our current environment actively undermines. Chief among these is the lost art of listening, not just to words but to meanings, concerns, and possibilities. Genuine listening means setting aside your mental rehearsal of responses. It means remaining genuinely curious about perspectives that challenge your assumptions. It means being willing to be surprised, to have your thinking changed, to discover that the person across from you possesses insights you lack.

Consider how rarely this occurs in contemporary discourse. In most conversations, people wait to speak rather than seeking to understand. We formulate responses while others are still talking. We interrupt to redirect conversations to our priorities. We listen for what we expect to hear rather than remaining open to being surprised. We interpret others' words through the filter of our existing beliefs, rarely questioning whether we have truly grasped their meaning. When someone offers a perspective that challenges us, our first impulse is usually defensive: to marshal counterarguments, to identify flaws, to protect our position. This is human nature, but it is also a recipe for organizational and societal stagnation.

This failure of listening is not merely a personal failing. It is a leadership catastrophe. A leader who cannot listen cannot learn. Information flows poorly when people don't feel heard, so crucial insights never reach decision-makers. A leader who cannot learn cannot adapt, and in rapidly changing environments, the inability to adapt is lethal. Organizations led by people who cannot listen become rigid and brittle, unable to recognize emerging challenges or opportunities until it's too late. The capacity to listen deeply, to understand not just what people are saying but why they're saying it, what concerns and possibilities animate their perspective, represents perhaps the most fundamental leadership skill.

Distinguished from sympathy which involves feeling "for" someone from a position of separation, empathy creates shared space. Sympathy maintains distance: the helper and the helped, the one who knows and the one who suffers. There is a place for sympathy in human relations, but it creates hierarchy and separation. Empathy seeks parity, recognizing that understanding flows in multiple directions and that wisdom can emerge from unexpected sources. In organizational contexts, this distinction proves crucial. Sympathetic leaders may feel concern for their teams but still make decisions in isolation, assuming their position grants them superior insight. Empathetic leaders recognize that those closest to problems often possess the deepest understanding of potential solutions, and that their job is to create conditions where that distributed intelligence can be accessed and integrated.

This shift from sympathy to empathy requires a fundamental reorientation of leadership identity. Traditional leadership models emphasized the leader as the person with answers, the expert whose superior knowledge and experience qualified them to direct others. This model made sense in stable environments where accumulated experience translated reliably into future effectiveness.

But in rapidly changing environments characterized by complex interdependencies, no individual possesses sufficient knowledge or perspective to make consistently good decisions alone. Leadership becomes less about having answers and more about creating processes through which collective intelligence can be accessed and applied. This requires empathy or the capacity to understand diverse perspectives and to facilitate their productive engagement. The quest for the relevant questions becomes more important than skillful answers based on past realities.

## THE ENDANGERED ART OF CONVERSATION

Closely connected to listening is the art of conversation, another practice that has atrophied in our age. A true conversation is not a sequential exchange of monologues or a debate to be won. It is collaborative exploration, a shared journey toward understanding. Good conversations have rhythm and flow. They build energy rather than dissipate it. They open possibilities rather than close them down. They create conditions where people think better together than they could alone. This description might sound abstract, but the difference is viscerally obvious to anyone who has experienced both genuine conversation and its pale substitutes.

A skilled conversationalist knows how to ask questions that invite reflection rather than defensiveness. The difference often lies in subtle shifts of framing. "Why did you make that decision?" can feel accusatory, triggering defensive responses. "What were you trying to accomplish with that approach?" invites the person to share their reasoning and constraints, creating conditions for genuine understanding.

Skilled conversationalists offer observations that spark insight rather than judgment. They create space for others to think aloud, to explore half-formed ideas without fear of premature critique. They know how to build on others' contributions, finding value even in perspectives they ultimately disagree with. They weave together diverse contributions into something larger than any individual could create alone.

These capabilities matter enormously in organizational contexts because the quality of conversation within an organization directly determines its capacity for innovation and adaptation. Think about the last meeting you attended.

- Was it genuine conversation, people building on each other's ideas, exploring possibilities, challenging assumptions constructively?
- Or was it a series of presentations and positional statements, where people advocated for predetermined positions and "discussion" consisted mainly of defending turf?

Most organizational meetings fall into the latter category, which explains why they feel so draining and accomplish so little.

When conversations are shallow, defensive, or dominated by hierarchy, organizations become brittle. Information flows poorly, moving up and down formal channels while crucial insights remain trapped in silos. Problems are hidden or ignored because raising them feels risky. People have learned that bringing bad news or challenging assumptions leads to being shot as the messenger. Innovation stagnates because novel ideas require collaborative refinement.

The initial spark might come from an individual, but transforming that spark into something valuable requires input from multiple perspectives, iterative development, and willingness to fail and learn. None of this happens without genuine conversation characterized by psychological safety and collaborative spirit.

People bring compliance rather than commitment when conversations are poor. They do what they are told but withhold their full intelligence and creativity. They follow procedures without questioning whether those procedures still make sense. They implement strategies without bringing their ground-level knowledge to bear on adaptation and improvement. This represents an enormous waste of human potential and organizational capacity.

But when leaders cultivate genuine dialogue or conversation characterized by authentic curiosity, respectful challenge, and collaborative exploration, organizations become resilient and adaptive. People surface problems early because they trust their concerns will be heard thoughtfully and addressed constructively. Novel solutions emerge from unexpected combinations of perspectives because diverse viewpoints can productively engage rather than merely collide. Individuals bring their full intelligence and commitment to their work because they experience themselves as valued contributors to a shared enterprise rather than interchangeable parts in a machine. The quality of work improves dramatically when people feel genuinely engaged rather than merely compliant.

Creating conditions for genuine conversation requires intentional practice. It means establishing ground rules that encourage exploration over advocacy, questions over certainty, building on ideas over shooting them down. It means modeling vulnerability, admitting when you don't know something, acknowledging when you've changed your mind, sharing your reasoning process rather than just your conclusions. It means protecting time and space for genuine dialogue rather than allowing all discussion to be squeezed into the margins of overloaded agendas. It means being willing to slow down initially in order to speed up overall, investing in the quality of collective thinking rather than rushing to premature closure.

## BUILDING ADAPTIVE ORGANIZATIONS THROUGH EMPATHETIC PRACTICE

The central premise of this book is that empathy in communication empowers individuals and paves the way to effective leadership. But achieving this requires moving beyond platitudes about "the importance of empathy" to examine the specific practices through which empathy operates: listening and conversation. These are not innate talents distributed unequally among people but learnable skills that can be deliberately cultivated through disciplined practice.

Building adaptive organizations in our fragmented age means creating cultures where listening and genuine conversation are valued and practiced. This is harder than it sounds because it requires swimming against powerful currents in contemporary organizational life. The pressure for speed militates against taking time to listen well. The premium placed on decisiveness conflicts with the patience genuine conversation requires. The hierarchical structures of most organizations create power dynamics that inhibit authentic dialogue. Overcoming these obstacles requires sustained commitment from leadership and willingness to invest in practices that may initially feel slow or inefficient but ultimately enhance organizational capability.

It means recognizing that the silos and echo chambers fragmenting society also fragment our organizations, and that breaking down these barriers requires patient, empathetic bridge-building. This bridge-building is not about pretending differences don't exist or papering over genuine conflicts. Organizations contain legitimate tensions between competing priorities. Sales wants to promise customers everything possible; operations wants to streamline and standardize. Innovation requires investment and risk; finance requires discipline and return. Long-term sustainability demands different choices than short-term performance. These tensions are inherent and healthy. The question is whether they are managed through empathetic dialogue that seeks creative integration, or through political maneuvering that fragments the organization into warring camps.

It is about creating conditions where people with different perspectives, experiences, and priorities can engage each other productively. This requires psychological safety or the confidence that speaking honestly won't result in punishment or marginalization. It requires conversational skill or the ability to inquire appreciatively into perspectives different from your own. It requires structural support or time and space for genuine dialogue rather than rushed decisions. And it requires leadership that models these behaviors consistently, demonstrating that empathetic engagement is valued not just in rhetoric but in practice.

Throughout my career spanning more than four decades, I have worked across diverse contexts, military organizations, corporations, government agencies, non-profit institutions, and academic settings. I have engaged with leaders at every level, from frontline supervisors to senior executives and military commanders. I have observed organizations in times of growth and crisis, stability and transformation. What distinguishes the most effective leaders is their capacity to listen deeply, to engage others in genuine conversation, and to build bridges across the divides that fragment organizations and communities.

I have seen empathy break down barriers that seemed insurmountable. In military settings, I watched commanders transform unit cohesion by genuinely understanding the concerns of different ranks and specialties. In corporate environments, I observed executives revitalize stagnant organizations by creating space for honest conversation about challenges everyone knew existed but no one felt safe to name. In government agencies, I witnessed leaders navigate political minefields by building coalitions across partisan divides through patient, empathetic engagement that found common ground without sacrificing principle.

I have watched leaders transform hostile groups into collaborative teams through the disciplined practice of ensuring every voice was heard and understood. This doesn't mean giving everyone veto power or achieving unanimous agreement on every decision. It means creating processes where diverse perspectives are genuinely considered before decisions are made, and where people feel their views have been understood even when final choices go against their preferences.

This distinction proves crucial: people can accept decisions they disagree with when they trust the decision-making process included genuine consideration of their concerns. They cannot sustain commitment to decisions that feel imposed without understanding or dialogue.

I have observed organizations revitalize themselves when leaders created space for honest conversation about challenges everyone knew existed but no one felt safe to name. Every organization has elephants in the room or problems or dysfunctions that everyone recognizes but no one discusses openly. These "undiscussable" issues fester and multiply, consuming enormous energy as people navigate around them.

Leaders who create conditions for these issues to be addressed openly unlock tremendous organizational energy and capability. But this requires empathy or the ability to understand why these issues became "undiscussable" in the first place, and the skill to create sufficient safety for honest dialogue.

These experiences convinced me that empathy, manifested through listening and conversation, is not peripheral to leadership effectiveness. It is the foundational capacity upon which all other leadership capabilities rest. You cannot develop people without understanding them. You cannot build effective teams without facilitating productive dialogue across differences. You cannot navigate change without understanding how it affects different stakeholders. You cannot innovate without integrating diverse perspectives. Every dimension of leadership effectiveness ultimately rests on the capacity for empathetic engagement.

# EMOTIONAL INTELLIGENCE: THE FRAMEWORK FOR EMPATHETIC LEADERSHIP

Empathy operates within the broader framework of emotional intelligence or the ability to recognize and manage our own emotions while understanding the emotions of others. Daniel Goleman's influential research identified emotional intelligence as a better predictor of leadership success than traditional measures of cognitive ability. This finding initially surprised many who assumed intellectual capacity mattered most. But reflection reveals why emotional intelligence proves so crucial: leadership is fundamentally about influencing others, and influence requires understanding both yourself and those you seek to influence.[*]

Emotional intelligence encompasses several interconnected capabilities. Self-awareness involves understanding your own emotional landscape and recognizing how feelings influence behavior. Leaders lacking self-awareness remain mysteries to themselves, unaware of how their moods and triggers affect their judgment and impact on others. They make decisions influenced by emotions they don't recognize, alienate people through behaviors they don't perceive, and wonder why their intentions don't match their results.

Self-regulation pertains to managing emotional responses and maintaining composure in challenging situations. This doesn't mean suppressing emotions or presenting a false front of constant equanimity. It means experiencing emotions fully while choosing responses thoughtfully rather than reactively. A leader might feel angry about a team member's repeated mistakes but chooses to address the pattern through coaching conversation rather than venting frustration. This capacity for response flexibility proves essential for navigating complex organizational dynamics.

Together, self-awareness and self-regulation enable the external-facing dimensions of emotional intelligence: understanding others' emotions and managing relationships effectively. When we are attuned

---

[*] Daniel Goleman, *Emotional Intelligence: Why It Can Matter More than IQ* (New York: Bantam Books, 1995).

to our own emotions, we become more adept at recognizing similar states in others. This self-awareness creates the foundation for genuine empathy rather than projection—understanding others as they experience themselves rather than assuming they feel as we would in their situation.

Leaders with high emotional intelligence create environments of psychological safety where people feel comfortable expressing concerns, raising problems, and offering novel ideas. This safety proves essential for building adaptive organizations because adaptation requires learning, and learning requires the freedom to acknowledge what you don't know, to question assumptions, to propose ideas that might fail. None of this happens when people fear judgment, punishment, or marginalization for honest engagement.

Practical strategies for enhancing emotional intelligence begin with developing present-moment awareness. Most people spend most of their time on autopilot, reacting to situations based on habitual patterns rather than conscious choice. Mindfulness practices cultivate the capacity to observe your own mental and emotional states, creating space between stimulus and response. This space allows for choice: instead of reacting automatically to a triggering situation, you can observe your reaction, understand its source, and choose a more constructive response.

Emotional regulation techniques help manage responses to triggering situations. Consider a leader facing a team member's angry outburst about a decision. A leader with low emotional intelligence might respond defensively, escalating the conflict into a power struggle that damages the relationship and undermines psychological safety for everyone watching. A leader with high emotional intelligence might recognize their own defensive impulse, pause to regulate it, then respond with genuine curiosity about the concerns underlying the anger. "I can see you're really upset about this. Help me understand what's driving your reaction." This approach de-escalates tension while surfacing information crucial for better decisions.

Research consistently shows that emotional intelligence correlates with leadership effectiveness across diverse contexts. Leaders with high emotional intelligence build stronger teams characterized by higher trust, better communication, and more effective collaboration.[*] They navigate conflicts more effectively, transforming potentially destructive disputes into productive problem-solving. They create more innovative organizations because they establish conditions where diverse perspectives can engage productively rather than fragmenting into silos.[†]

# EMPATHY AS STRENGTH: OVERCOMING MISCONCEPTIONS

A persistent misconception undermines empathy's adoption in leadership contexts: the belief that empathy represents weakness. This view particularly pervades environments that prize decisiveness and authority, where leaders fear that showing empathy will compromise their ability to make tough decisions or maintain discipline. Yet this misconception fundamentally confuses empathy with indecisiveness, with being "soft," or with avoiding difficult conversations. Nothing could be further from the truth.

Empathetic leaders make better decisions precisely because they understand the human element involved. They don't make decisions in abstract isolation from implementation realities. They anticipate how decisions will land with different stakeholders, recognizing that even the best strategy fails if people cannot or will not implement it. They recognize potential implementation challenges that might escape analysis focused purely on abstract strategy or technical feasibility. They build buy-in by ensuring people feel heard even when final decisions go against their preferences.

This is not weakness: it is strategic sophistication. Consider a leader who must implement an unpopular reorganization necessary for organizational survival. A non-empathetic approach might involve announcing the decision and expecting compliance. This generates resistance, passive-aggressive subversion of the reorganization, loss of key talent, and erosion of trust. An empathetic approach involves

---

[*]  https://ijsra.net/sites/default/files/IJSRA-2024-1875.pdf
[†]  https://pmc.ncbi.nlm.nih.gov/articles/PMC10543214/

genuinely understanding people's concerns about the change, addressing them honestly, explaining the reasoning behind difficult choices, and involving people in shaping implementation details where possible. This builds trust even through adversity and dramatically increases the likelihood that the reorganization will actually achieve its objectives.

Empathy's power also roots in vulnerability, another concept often misunderstood as weakness. Authentic leadership embraces vulnerability, showing that leaders are human and relatable rather than infallible. This doesn't mean oversharing or displaying every emotional fluctuation. It means being willing to admit uncertainty, to acknowledge mistakes, to say "I don't know" when you don't. When leaders admit they don't have all the answers but are open to collaboration, they invite genuine contribution rather than mere compliance.

This openness creates conditions for innovation because breakthrough ideas often emerge when people feel safe to propose unconventional approaches that might fail. In organizations where leaders project infallibility and punish mistakes, people learn to avoid risk and stick to established approaches even when those approaches no longer work. A leader who says, "I don't know the best path forward, but I value your insights and I'm confident we can figure this out together," transforms uncertainty from a threat into an opportunity for collective problem-solving. This is not weakness—it is courage and strategic wisdom.

## THE PATH FORWARD: EMPATHY AS PRACTICE

Understanding empathy's nature and importance represents only the beginning. The crucial question is how to cultivate it deliberately as a leadership capability and organizational practice. This requires moving beyond abstract appreciation to concrete discipline, particularly the disciplines of listening and conversation that will occupy subsequent chapters of this book.

As you reflect on your current communication patterns, consider these questions:

- How often do you find yourself truly listening to others, giving them complete attention without mentally preparing responses?
- When was the last time you had a conversation that genuinely changed your thinking or opened new possibilities?
- How effectively do you bridge divides in your organization or community, connecting people who might otherwise remain isolated in separate spheres?
- Do you create conditions for genuine dialogue even among groups with deep disagreements?
- Are your meetings characterized by genuine conversation or sequential monologues?
- Do people in your organization feel safe raising difficult issues and challenging assumptions?

The potential benefits of enhancing empathy skills through dedicated practice in listening and conversation extend far beyond individual interactions. Imagine organizations where genuine conversation replaces superficial exchange, where listening is valued as highly as speaking, where bridges are built across divides rather than walls erected to reinforce them. Imagine teams that can harness diverse perspectives for innovation rather than fragmenting along lines of difference. Imagine leadership that guides adaptive organizations capable of responding effectively to complex, rapidly changing environments.

This vision is not merely aspirational. It is achievable and urgently necessary. Our organizations face challenges of unprecedented complexity. Climate change, technological disruption, geopolitical instability, demographic shifts, and countless other forces create environments where past approaches no longer suffice. The problems we must solve require bringing together diverse expertise and perspectives in ways that generate genuine innovation rather than political compromise. The pace of change demands organizations capable of learning and adapting quickly, recognizing emerging patterns and responding before they become crises.

None of this is possible without the foundational capacity for empathetic communication. You cannot integrate diverse perspectives if you cannot understand them. You cannot learn quickly if information flows poorly because people don't feel heard. You cannot adapt effectively if your organization fragments into isolated silos. The capacity for empathy, manifested through disciplined practices of listening and conversation, represents perhaps the most crucial organizational capability for navigating our complex, fragmented, rapidly changing world.

In the chapters that follow, we will examine the specific practices through which empathy operates in organizational and leadership contexts. Throughout this journey, remember that empathy is not a fixed trait you either possess or lack. It is a capability you can develop through deliberate practice. The practices of listening and conversation are learnable skills, not mystical talents distributed unequally by fortune. The capacity to bridge divides and build adaptive organizations rests on specific behaviors you can cultivate through sustained attention and effort. This is work that requires patience and persistence.

You will not master these capabilities overnight. But it is work that yields profound returns, in leadership effectiveness, organizational capability, and ultimately in your ability to navigate and shape our complex, fragmented world.

The crisis of our age is a crisis of communication, an epidemic of disconnection despite unprecedented connectivity, an atrophy of listening despite constant noise, an erosion of genuine conversation despite endless exchange.

The remedy is not technological but fundamentally human: the disciplined cultivation of empathy through the practices of listening and genuine conversation.

This is the pathway to effective leadership and adaptive organizations in our fragmented age. This is how we build bridges across divides rather than walls that reinforce them.

This is how we transform organizations from brittle hierarchies into resilient learning systems. Let us begin this essential work together.

# 3

# RECOVERING THE LOST ARTS OF LISTENING AND CONVERSATION

You sit across from a colleague in a coffee shop. She is explaining a problem which the team has to deal with to make a deadline. You nod periodically. You maintain eye contact. But if someone stopped you ten seconds after she finished speaking and asked you to summarize what she just said, you would struggle. Your mind was elsewhere: mentally composing your response, thinking about your next meeting, rehearsing the point you wanted to make. You were present in body but absent in attention. This is not an aberration. This is the default mode of contemporary communication.

The art of listening has become endangered in our time. So too has the practice of conversation as a collaborative exploration rather than a competitive exchange. These are not peripheral skills relegated to interpersonal niceties. They are foundational capacities upon which all effective communication, leadership, and organizational adaptation depend.

Without them, empathy remains an abstraction. With them, empathy becomes the bridge that connects people across the divides that fragment our organizations, communities, and societies.

This chapter examines why these arts have atrophied, what we lose when they disappear, and how we might deliberately cultivate them in an environment that actively undermines both. The goal is not merely skill development but the recovery of practices essential to building the adaptive organizations our complex world demands.

# THE LOST ART OF LISTENING

Listening appears simple. Someone speaks; you hear the words; you understand the message. This mechanical view misses everything important. True listening is an active, demanding practice that requires sustained attention, intellectual humility, and genuine curiosity about perspectives different from your own. It involves not merely processing words but discerning meanings, recognizing unstated concerns, and remaining open to being changed by what you hear.

Consider what genuine listening requires.

- First, it demands that you quiet your own internal monologue. Most people, when another person is speaking, are not listening; they are waiting to speak. They are formulating their response, marshaling their arguments, preparing their rebuttal. This is not listening; it is competitive turn-taking disguised as dialogue. Real listening requires that you temporarily suspend your own agenda and make space for another's thoughts to fully form and be expressed.

- Second, listening demands that you resist the urge to immediately categorize and judge what you hear. We filter incoming information through our existing frameworks, searching for familiar patterns and established categories. When someone begins to express a view, we often prematurely conclude we know what they will say and where they are heading. This prediction impulse short-circuits actual listening. We stop attending to their specific words and reasoning, instead hearing only our projection of what we expect them to think.

- Third, genuine listening requires tolerance for ambiguity and incompleteness. People rarely articulate their thoughts in polished, linear fashion. They circle back, qualify statements, explore tangents that turn out to be relevant. They contradict themselves as they work through complexity. A good listener creates space for this meandering process rather than rushing to pin down a definitive position or pushing for premature clarity.

- Finally, listening at its best involves what might be called generative attention. You are not merely absorbing information but actively helping the speaker discover what they think. Through your quality of presence, your questions, your ability to reflect back what you hear in ways that illuminate rather than flatten meaning, you create conditions for deeper thought. The best listeners function almost as intellectual midwives, helping others birth ideas they did not know they possessed.

Why has this practice become so rare?

Multiple forces conspire against it. Our information environment prioritizes speed over depth, reaction over reflection. We consume content in fragments, scrolling through feeds designed to capture attention for seconds before moving on. This constant partial attention becomes habitual, eroding our capacity for sustained focus on any single thing, including another person speaking.

The incentive structures of contemporary communication actively punish listening. In meetings, visibility comes from speaking, not from the harder work of synthesizing what others have said. Too often, thoughtful questions and genuine curiosity are interpreted as weakness or lack of conviction. We have created systems that reward apparent performance over understanding.

Perhaps most insidiously, we increasingly inhabit informational echo chambers where we are surrounded by people who think as we do. When everyone you interact with shares your basic framework and assumptions, listening becomes less necessary. You can predict what they will say; they will generally affirm what you already believe. The muscle of listening atrophies from disuse. You lose practice in the difficult work of truly understanding perspectives that differ from your own.

The cost of this loss is profound. A leader who cannot listen cannot learn. Organizations where people do not genuinely listen to each other become brittle. Information flows poorly. Problems are hidden rather than surfaced. The diversity that should be a source of resilience and innovation instead becomes a source of fragmentation, as different groups talk past each other from within their separate spheres.

Recovering the art of listening begins with recognizing that it is indeed an art and a discipline requiring conscious practice, not a natural state that occurs automatically. It means creating conditions that support focused attention in an environment designed for distraction. This might involve simple practices: putting away phones during conversations, scheduling meetings with sufficient time for actual dialogue rather than mere information transfer, or instituting norms where questions are valued as highly as assertions.

More fundamentally, it requires cultivating what we might call intellectual humility or the recognition that no matter how expert you are, the person speaking possesses knowledge and perspective you lack. This humility is not weakness. It is the foundation of learning. The leader who assumes he already knows what his team members will say has stopped learning from them. The consultant who cannot genuinely listen to a client because he is already certain of the solution has ceased to provide real value.

Practical techniques can help. The simple practice of pausing before responding and taking three seconds to ensure you have actually processed what was said rather than immediately launching into your prepared remarks can transform the quality of dialogue. The discipline of asking at least one clarifying question before offering your own view ensures you have genuinely understood the other person's position rather than your caricature of it.

Perhaps most powerful is the practice of reflective listening or articulating back what you heard in your own words and checking whether you understood correctly. This serves multiple purposes. It forces you to actually comprehend what was said rather than simply waiting for your turn. It demonstrates to the speaker that they were heard, which itself is a profound gift in an age of pervasive inattention. And it surfaces misunderstandings immediately, when they can be corrected, rather than allowing them to compound.

The barriers to listening are not merely individual habits but structural features of how we organize communication. Meetings that involve too many people or insufficient time make genuine listening nearly impossible. Communication technologies that eliminate silence and allow instant response encourage reaction rather than reflection. Organizational cultures that equate decisiveness with speed create pressure to form judgments before fully understanding situations.

Addressing these structural barriers requires deliberate design. Some organizations have instituted a no devices norm for certain meetings, creating islands of focused attention in a sea of distraction. Others have experimented with different meeting formats, rotating facilitators whose role is not to contribute content but to ensure everyone is heard, or building in structured silence where people write down thoughts before speaking, preventing the loudest voices from dominating.

In high-stakes context negotiations involving conflict resolution or crisis management, the quality of listening often determines outcomes more than the substantive positions involved. A negotiator who can genuinely understand not just what the other party is demanding but why they want it, what concerns drive their position, what would constitute success for them, possesses enormous advantage. This understanding comes only through disciplined listening, not through clever argumentation.

I often discussed the art of negotiation with my friend Harald Malmgren who had many years of experience in conducting trade negotiations for the U.S. government and for private corporations. In my book on his life and his published work with me, I discussed with his daughter Pippa Malmgren her father's approach.

> *My father negotiated on so many different issues with so many different nations at the highest level. He taught me the importance of getting to know those who you are negotiating with, what their interests are and what constitutes a win for them.*

*Negotiation succeeds when each side gets something of value to the other and you cannot succeed if you don't know who you are dealing with. This is not a strong point today in people's training and background. But it certainly was for my father. Today we tend to treat the other negotiator as the opponent rather than as a collaborator. This is a mistake.* [*]

Listening across differences, whether cultural, ideological, generational, or professional, presents particular challenges. The frameworks and assumptions that shape how different groups understand the world may be sufficiently different that surface-level listening misses crucial meanings. What sounds like irrational resistance may reflect legitimate concerns rooted in different experiences. What appears as poor communication may be translation difficulties across distinct conceptual vocabularies.

In these situations, listening well requires more than good intentions. It demands explicit inquiry into how the other party understands key terms, what historical experiences shape their perspective, what they are trying to protect or achieve. It requires checking your understanding repeatedly rather than assuming comprehension. And it often requires third parties who can bridge between different conceptual worlds, translating not just words but meanings.

The payoff for recovering this lost art extends far beyond individual interactions. Organizations characterized by genuine listening become learning organizations. Problems surface early because people feel safe raising them. Innovation accelerates because ideas from unexpected sources get serious consideration rather than premature dismissal. Trust builds because people experience being understood even when they do not get their preferred outcome.

## CONVERSATION AS COLLABORATIVE EXPLORATION

If listening is the foundation, conversation is the architecture built upon it. But conversation, properly understood, has become nearly as

---

[*] Robbin Laird, editor, *Assessing Global Change: Strategic Perspectives of Dr, Harald Malmgren* (Second Line of Defense Publisher: 2025).

rare as genuine listening. What passes for conversation in most contemporary settings is actually something quite different: serial monologue, competitive debate, or ritualized exchange of predetermined positions. True conversation and dialogue, characterized by genuine exploration and collaborative thinking, has atrophied as a practice.

A real conversation is not a debate to be won. It is a shared journey toward understanding where participants build on each other's contributions, moving together toward insights none possessed at the outset. Good conversation has rhythm and flow. It generates energy rather than dissipating it. It opens possibilities rather than foreclosing them. Participants leave different than they entered, not necessarily in their conclusions but in their understanding of the terrain.

Consider the difference between debate and dialogue. In debate, the goal is victory. You marshal arguments to defeat the other side. You identify weaknesses in their position while fortifying your own. You interpret charity as weakness and concession as failure. The underlying assumption is that truth emerges from combat between opposing positions, and the most skillful combatant wins.

Dialogue operates from entirely different premises. The goal is not victory but discovery. Participants bring different pieces of a larger puzzle, and the work is to fit them together into a more complete picture than any individual possessed. This requires a fundamentally different orientation: you listen for insight in what others say rather than for vulnerabilities to exploit. You build on contributions rather than refuting them. You hold your own views lightly enough that they can evolve through encounter with other perspectives.

The skills required for generative conversation differ markedly from those rewarded in competitive discourse. A skilled conversationalist knows how to ask questions that invite reflection rather than defensiveness. Instead of asking: Why did you make that mistake; they ask: What were you seeing that led you in that direction? The first forecloses exploration by making the other person justify themselves; the second opens space for genuine inquiry into their reasoning and what might be learned from it.

Good conversationalists also know how to build bridges between seemingly opposing views by identifying the legitimate concerns each represents. In organizational disputes that present as binary choices, skilled facilitators often discover that both sides are responding to real risks or opportunities, and that creative solutions exist that address multiple concerns simultaneously. But discovering these requires moving past positional bargaining to understand underlying interests.

The architecture of conversation matters enormously. Who speaks in what order, who sets the agenda, what questions frame the discussion, how silence is interpreted, these structural features shape what becomes possible. In many organizational conversations, hierarchy determines speaking order, with senior people establishing the frame to which others react. This structure, while efficient for information transmission, precludes genuine exploration because it establishes the boss's view as the reference point.

Alternative structures can produce dramatically different outcomes. Some organizations have experimented with structures that democratize participation: everyone writes thoughts individually before sharing, ensuring that introverts and those who think best on paper have equal voice with those who dominate verbal exchanges. Or small groups develop ideas before reporting to the whole, preventing groupthink and allowing multiple lines of thinking to develop in parallel.

The quality of questions shapes the quality of conversation. Closed questions that can be answered yes or no shut down exploration. Leading questions that contain embedded assumptions constrain rather than open thinking. By contrast, genuinely open questions that reflect real curiosity and have no predetermined answer invite people to think freshly rather than defensively.

The best questions are often the simplest.

- What are you seeing? Such a question invites people to
  share their perspective without requiring them to defend it.
- What matters most here? Such a question helps groups
  identify core values and priorities rather than getting lost in
  procedural details.

- What are we missing? This is a question which explicitly
  creates space for dissenting views and unconsidered factors.

These questions work not through sophistication but through genuine inquiry.

Why has the art of conversation atrophied? The same forces undermining listening also damage conversation. The acceleration of communication cycles leaves no time for the patient exploration that good conversation requires. The polarization of public discourse creates a model where opposing camps hurl talking points at each other rather than engaging seriously with different views. The fragmentation into echo chambers means many people rarely experience genuine conversation across difference.

Perhaps more fundamentally, we have lost confidence in the possibility that conversation can produce anything valuable. When groups gather to discuss complex challenges, there is often an unstated assumption that the purpose is to ratify decisions already made or to create the appearance of consultation. Few believe that genuine dialogue might actually surface insights not already held by the smartest person in the room. This cynicism becomes self-fulfilling: if we do not create conditions for productive conversation, it does not occur, confirming our belief that it is not possible.

Recovering the art of conversation requires both individual skill development and structural innovation. At the individual level, people need practice in the disciplines that make dialogue possible: suspending judgment, building on others' ideas, asking genuine questions, tolerating ambiguity, thinking aloud without demanding premature certainty. These skills can be taught and practiced, though they run counter to much of what contemporary culture rewards.

Structurally, organizations need to create protected spaces where genuine conversation can occur. This might mean smaller gatherings where everyone can meaningfully participate rather than large meetings where most people are spectators. It might involve longer time horizons that allow ideas to develop through multiple rounds of reflection rather than forcing premature closure. It certainly requires explicit norms about how people engage and what constitutes productive challenge versus destructive attack, how dissent is expressed, what it means to genuinely consider another's view.

The role of leadership in fostering conversational culture cannot be overstated. When leaders model genuine curiosity and openness to being influenced, they create permission for others to do the same. When they ask questions to which they genuinely do not know the answer and take seriously what they hear in response, they demonstrate that conversation is not performance but inquiry. When they acknowledge what they have learned from dialogue rather than presenting themselves as already knowing, they make learning safe.

Conversely, leaders who use questions as rhetorical devices to make points they have already decided, who punish people for raising uncomfortable issues, or who interpret disagreement as disloyalty create cultures where genuine conversation becomes impossible. People learn to tell leaders what they want to hear rather than what they need to know. The organization loses its capacity to learn from experience or adapt to changing circumstances.

## BUILDING BRIDGES ACROSS DIVIDES

The fragmentation of contemporary society into increasingly isolated groups, ideological, demographic, professional, and geographic poses one of the great challenges to organizational effectiveness and social cohesion. People increasingly inhabit separate informational universes, consuming different media, trusting different authorities, operating from different frameworks for understanding events. This fragmentation creates silos within organizations and makes collective action across groups extraordinarily difficult.

Empathetic communication, grounded in listening and genuine conversation, provides the means to bridge these divides. But such bridge-building is not about papering over differences or pretending genuine conflicts do not exist. It is about creating conditions where people with different perspectives, experiences, and priorities can engage each other productively rather than simply talking past each other or retreating into hostile camps.

The first step in building bridges is acknowledging that the divide exists and that it represents something real rather than a mere communication failure. Different groups often have genuinely different interests and experiences that shape their perspectives. The engineer who worries about technical feasibility and the marketer who focuses on customer needs are not simply failing to communicate; they are looking at the same situation from vantage points that highlight different concerns. Both perspectives have validity; the challenge is integrating them rather than having one dominate.

Effective bridge-building requires what might be called multilingual capacity or the ability to understand and operate within multiple conceptual frameworks. Someone who can translate between the technical language of engineers and the customer-focused vocabulary of marketing, understanding the legitimate concerns each represents, can facilitate dialogue that neither group could achieve on its own. This translation work is not about finding a bland middle ground but about helping each party understand what matters to the other and why.

Frankly, much of my career has been precisely doing this. And by so doing, I have learned a great deal from different communities in my role of finding ways for them to connect more effectively.

Genuine projects provide powerful vehicles for bridge-building. When people with different perspectives collaborate on addressing a challenge they all care about, they experience working together effectively. This shared accomplishment builds trust in ways that abstract appeals to unity never achieve. The key is identifying projects that genuinely require diverse capabilities and where success is clearly defined and mutually valued.

Consider a technology company where engineering and sales teams operate in mutual incomprehension and subtle hostility. Engineers see salespeople as making unrealistic promises; sales sees engineering as obstinate and divorced from market reality. No amount of exhortation about teamwork will bridge this divide. But establishing a cross-functional team to develop a new product, where engineers learn directly from customers through sales visits and salespeople understand technical constraints through participating in design decisions, creates conditions for mutual understanding.

Such bridge-building projects must be designed carefully. They require clear objectives that matter to all parties, structures that ensure genuine collaboration rather than parallel work, and sufficient time for relationships to develop. They also need leadership commitment to learning from both successes and failures rather than simply declaring victory or assigning blame.

The practice of perspective-taking becomes crucial in bridging divides. This means more than intellectually acknowledging that others see things differently. It requires the imaginative work of inhabiting another's vantage point, understanding not just what they think but why, given their experiences and responsibilities, their position makes sense to them. This empathetic understanding does not require agreement, but it transforms conflict from tribal warfare into problem-solving.

Practical exercises can develop perspective-taking capacity. Role-playing where people argue for positions they oppose forces engagement with the logic and concerns underlying different views. Shadowing colleagues from other departments reveals the daily pressures and constraints that shape their priorities. Structured dialogues where people from different groups share their experiences and concerns without immediate debate create understanding that subsequent negotiations can build upon.

Perhaps the most challenging bridge-building occurs across ideological or values-based divisions. When people's fundamental commitments differ about what constitutes fairness, how to balance individual liberty and collective responsibility, finding common ground appears impossible. Yet even here, empathetic communication can make progress if the goal is understanding rather than conversion.

The key is distinguishing positions from interests. Positions are what people say they want; interests are why they want it. Two groups may have diametrically opposed positions while having compatible underlying interests. Union and management may take opposing positions on work rules, but both care about the company's long-term viability and fair treatment of employees. Getting past positional bargaining to identify shared interests creates space for creative solutions.

Building bridges also requires attention to power dynamics. When groups have systematically different access to resources, decision-making authority, or platforms to be heard, symmetric dialogue becomes difficult. Those with less power often rightly suspect that conversations are designed to co-opt rather than genuinely incorporate their concerns. Effective bridge-building in these contexts requires more than good facilitation; it requires changes in structure and governance that redistribute voice and influence.

Organizations that successfully build bridges across internal divides do not eliminate differences or conflicts. Rather, they develop the capacity to engage differences productively. They create forums where different perspectives can be aired and taken seriously. They develop processes for integrating diverse inputs into decisions rather than simply allowing the most powerful to prevail. They cultivate leaders who can facilitate dialogue across difference rather than simply advocating for their own group.

The payoff extends beyond conflict reduction. Organizations that bridge internal divides tap into the cognitive diversity that should be their greatest asset. Problems are examined from multiple angles. Solutions are stress-tested against different criteria. Innovation emerges from unexpected combinations of perspectives. What initially appears as the friction of difference becomes the creative tension that drives adaptation and growth.

## PRACTICAL DISCIPLINES FOR DAILY PRACTICE

Understanding the importance of listening and conversation as empathetic practices is one thing; developing the discipline to actually practice them in the rush of daily organizational life is quite another. What distinguishes effective leaders and communicators is not superior understanding of principles but consistent application of practices, day after day, in contexts that often resist them.

Start with the simple practice of the three-second pause. Before responding to anything, a question, a proposal, or a criticism, count silently to three. This micro-intervention creates space between stimulus and response, allowing you to actually process what was said rather than simply reacting. Three seconds feels like an eternity in fast-paced conversation, yet it transforms the quality of engagement. In those three seconds, you can check: Did I actually understand what was just said? Am I responding to their point or to my assumption about their point?

Another foundational practice: the clarifying question before the assertion. Before offering your view on anything, ask at least one question to deepen your understanding. Can you say more about what led you to that conclusion? What would success look like from your perspective?

This discipline serves multiple purposes. It prevents you from arguing against strawmen positions. It often surfaces information that changes your view. And it demonstrates respect in a way that makes others more receptive to your eventual input.

Reflective listening or articulating back what you heard in your own words and checking your understanding should become habitual in any consequential conversation. This practice catches misunderstandings immediately and creates moments where the speaker feels genuinely heard.

In meetings, practice the discipline of building on rather than refuting. When someone makes a contribution, train yourself to first identify what is valuable or insightful in it before pointing out limitations or problems. This orientation fosters collaborative exploration rather than competitive point-scoring.

The practice of acknowledging when you have changed your mind or learned something from dialogue might be the most powerful but least practiced discipline. This public acknowledgment of influence makes it safe for others to do the same, creating a culture where people can evolve their thinking rather than defending initial positions.

Create structural supports for these practices. Designate certain meetings as device free zones, eliminating the constant temptation of email and messaging. Start some gatherings with two minutes of silent individual reflection before discussion begins, allowing introverts and those who think best on paper to formulate thoughts. End meetings by having everyone share one thing they learned rather than just deciding action items.

For leaders specifically, the practice of asking genuine questions to which you truly do not know the answer and where you are genuinely open to being surprised cannot be overstated. Most leaders questions are actually statements in interrogative form, used to make points or test whether people are thinking what the leader wants them to think. Genuine questions signal that the leader values other's insights and is willing to be influenced by them.

Develop the habit of explicitly naming the mode of conversation you are engaging in. I want to think aloud about this problem for a few minutes, and I value your help stress-testing my thinking? Being explicit about whether you are seeking input, making a decision, or exploring a problem creates clarity that improves the quality of dialogue.

Practice perspective-taking not as an occasional exercise but as a daily discipline. When you disagree with a colleague's position, force yourself to articulate the strongest case for their view before explaining your objection. When you encounter a perspective that strikes you as obviously wrong, ask yourself: What would someone have to experience or value for this view to make sense to them? This practice builds the empathetic imagination essential to both leadership and collaboration.

Finally, build in reflection practices that help you learn from experience. After consequential conversations or meetings, take five minutes to consider: What worked? What did not? When did I listen well and when did I slip into reactive mode? What did I learn about the other person or the situation? This reflective discipline prevents you from simply repeating patterns and allows conscious improvement over time.

## CONCLUSION: FROM LOST ARTS TO LIVING PRACTICE

The arts of listening and conversation have not disappeared because people no longer value them. Most people, if asked, would say they want more meaningful dialogue and genuine understanding in their professional and personal lives. These practices have atrophied because the environments we inhabit, informational, technological, and organizational, systematically undermine the conditions they require.

Recovering these lost arts is not about returning to some idealized past. It requires deliberately creating conditions that support focused attention, genuine inquiry, and collaborative exploration in contexts that make them difficult. It means individual discipline in practicing specific techniques and structural innovation in how we organize communication and decision-making.

The stakes could not be higher. Organizations that cannot engage in genuine dialogue across their internal divisions become brittle and blind. Leaders who cannot listen cannot learn from their environment or their people. Communities fragmented into echo chambers lose the capacity for collective action on shared challenges. The bridge-building work that empathetic communication enables is not optional in our complex, interconnected world. It is foundational.

Yet this work is also deeply hopeful. When people experience genuine listening and productive conversation and when they feel truly heard and see dialogue actually produce insight, they remember what is possible. They become advocates for creating more such opportunities. They develop skills that make them more effective in every interaction. They begin to challenge the forces that fragment and isolate, creating alternatives that reconnect and integrate.

The practices outlined in this chapter, the three-second pause, clarifying questions, reflective listening, perspective-taking, building rather than refuting, may appear modest. Yet their consistent application transforms the quality of communication and the nature of relationships. They move empathy from abstraction to practice, from sentiment to skill, from individual virtue to organizational capability.

I close this chapter with an invitation to begin practicing. Pick one discipline from this chapter. Apply it consistently for a week in your daily interactions. Notice what changes. Then add another. The journey from lost art to living practice begins with a single conversation, approached with renewed attention and genuine curiosity about the person across from you.

4

# EMPATHETIC CONFLICT RESOLUTION

The most profound conflicts I have witnessed in four decades of working with leaders and organizations rarely begin as conflicts at all.

They begin as failures of listening. They begin when people stop engaging in genuine conversation and retreat into defensive positions. They begin when the capacity for empathetic understanding atrophies, replaced by the rigid certainty that comes from inhabiting echo chambers where everyone thinks exactly as we do.

In our fragmented age, where social media algorithms reinforce existing beliefs and people increasingly live in isolated informational universes, the art of resolving conflicts empathetically has become both more difficult and more essential than ever before.

Consider a situation I encountered several years ago at a defense manufacturing company undergoing a major technological transformation. Management and the engineering team had reached an impasse over the implementation of new automation systems. From the executive suite, the resistance seemed irrational, the engineers were blocking obvious improvements that would enhance efficiency and competitiveness. From the engineering floor, management appeared reckless and dismissive, pushing marketing changes without understanding their technical implications or operational risks. Both sides marshaled arguments. Both sides held meetings. Yet the conflict deepened with each exchange.

What finally broke the deadlock was not a brilliant compromise or a decisive executive mandate. It was the patient work of listening. When I facilitated a series of conversations, genuine conversations, not presentations or debates, a different picture emerged. The engineers were not resistant to change; they were concerned about specific technical vulnerabilities in the proposed systems that management had not understood. Management was not reckless; they were responding to competitive pressures and market realities that the engineers had not fully grasped.

Neither side had been listening to the other. Each had been waiting to speak, formulating rebuttals, defending positions. Once genuine listening began, collaborative problem-solving became possible.

This experience encapsulates the central insight of this chapter: empathetic conflict resolution is not primarily about techniques for managing disagreements. It is about cultivating the capacity to listen deeply and engage in genuine conversation even, especially when tensions run high and stakes are significant. It is about building bridges across divides rather than fortifying defensive positions. And in our current environment, where communication fragmentation poses perhaps the greatest challenge to organizational adaptation, these capacities have become leadership essentials.

The outsider position I occupy as a consultant proves invaluable in such situations, but only when properly understood and accepted by the organization. I must be recognized as someone who possesses sufficient knowledge of the organization's history, culture, and technical realities to engage credibly with various stake holders, yet remains fundamentally uncommitted to any particular faction's predetermined outcome. This balanced positioning creates the necessary space for genuine dialogue to emerge where internal actors, constrained by organizational politics and career considerations, often cannot.

My role is not that of an arbiter who renders judgments, nor an advocate who champions one side's position over another. Instead, I function as an intellectual facilitator whose primary contribution lies in creating and protecting the conditions under which authentic conversation becomes possible. This means asking the questions that internal stakeholders may fear to raise, surfacing assumptions that have calcified into unexamined orthodoxies, and persistently redirecting energy from positional defense toward collaborative problem-solving. The facilitator's power comes not from authority or expertise in the traditional sense, but from the legitimacy granted by detachment from internal power struggles.

This facilitation requires more than neutrality, it demands active engagement informed by deep contextual understanding. I must know enough about the technical details to recognize when engineering concerns reflect genuine risk rather than resistance to change, and enough about market dynamics to appreciate when management pressures stem from competitive necessity rather than executive ego. Yet this knowledge must be wielded in service of mutual understanding rather than personal judgment. The consultant who succeeds in this role becomes a trusted translator between organizational subcultures, enabling the various stake holders to hear not just the words but the legitimate concerns embedded in the other's perspective.

## THE CRISIS OF CONFLICT IN ORGANIZATIONS

Conflicts in contemporary organizations increasingly reflect the broader fragmentation of our communication landscape. Just as society has splintered into tribes of the like-minded, organizations often fragment into silos where different groups develop their own languages, priorities, and worldviews. Marketing speaks past operations. Technology teams and business teams inhabit different universes. Senior leadership and frontline workers might as well be speaking different languages. These divides are not merely inconvenient; they are catastrophic for organizational adaptation.

An adaptive organization, one capable of responding effectively to rapid change and complex challenges, requires the ability to forge understanding across such divides. It needs people from different functional areas, with different expertise and different perspectives, to engage each other productively.

But this is precisely what has become so difficult in our age of fragmented communication. People no longer possess shared frameworks for understanding problems or common grounds for discussion. They inhabit separate informational ecosystems, exposed to different sources, different framings, different "facts."

The conflicts that emerge from this fragmentation are particularly intractable because they are not merely disagreements about solutions. They are collisions between different ways of understanding reality itself. When an engineering team and a marketing team clash, they are often not just disagreeing about the best course of action. They are operating from fundamentally different assumptions about what the problems are, what matters, and how to evaluate potential solutions. Traditional conflict resolution techniques, focused on negotiation, compromise, and finding middle ground, prove inadequate for such fundamental disconnects.

This is where empathetic listening and genuine conversation become essential. They provide the means to bridge divides that cannot be bridged through argumentation or negotiation alone. They create possibilities for understanding across differences so profound that the parties might not even recognize they are speaking about the same thing. But cultivating these capacities in our current communication environment requires deliberate practice and organizational commitment.

## LISTENING AS THE FOUNDATION OF CONFLICT RESOLUTION

The most common failure in organizational conflicts is the failure to listen. Not the failure to hear: people hear each other perfectly well. The failure is to listen with genuine openness to being changed by what one hears. In conflicts, we typically listen defensively, filtering everything through our existing frameworks, listening for what confirms our views or what we can rebut. We formulate responses while others are still speaking. We interrupt when we hear something we disagree with. We hijack conversations to return to our own points. This is not listening; it is waiting to speak.

Genuine listening requires something different. It requires the disciplined practice of seeking to understand before seeking to be understood. It requires suspending judgment long enough to truly grasp another person's perspective, even when or rather especially when that perspective conflicts with your own. It requires attending not just to words but to meanings, concerns, and the reasoning behind positions. Most fundamentally, it requires the humility to recognize that the person you are in conflict with possesses insights you lack.

I learned this lesson forcefully early in my career during an intense debate about strategic direction within a defense organization I was working with. A senior analyst and I had deeply conflicting views about how to interpret emerging data about adversary capabilities. The debate was technical, detailed, and grew increasingly heated. I was convinced he was missing obvious implications. He was equally convinced I was drawing unwarranted conclusions. We were at an impasse, and the stakes were significant for recommendations would flow from our analysis.

What broke through was a simple intervention by a colleague: "Robbin, can you articulate his argument in a way he would recognize as his own?" The question stopped me. I realized I could not. I could articulate my critique of his argument, but I could not represent his actual reasoning in a way he would accept as accurate. My colleague then turned to him with the same question. He, too, struggled. We had been so busy defending our positions and formulating rebuttals that neither of us had truly listened to the other.

The next hour changed everything. We each took turns articulating the other's perspective, with the other person providing corrections until we got it right. This process was difficult. It required setting aside our need to be right, at least temporarily. But once we could each genuinely articulate the other's reasoning, the conversation shifted.

We were no longer adversaries defending positions. We were colleagues exploring a complex question from different analytical angles. Within that shift, synthesis became possible. We identified the specific points of genuine disagreement and the assumptions underlying them. More importantly, we recognized that both perspectives contributed essential insights to a more complete understanding.

This experience taught me that genuine listening in conflict situations requires specific practices:

- First, the practice of articulation: Before responding to someone you disagree with, practice articulating their position until they confirm you understand it correctly. This is harder than it sounds. It requires setting aside your rebuttals and critiques long enough to genuinely grasp their reasoning. But it is transformative. Once you can articulate another person's position to their satisfaction, the tenor of the conflict changes. They feel heard. You gain genuine understanding. Common ground becomes visible.

- Second, the practice of inquiry: Replace assertion with questioning. Instead of declaring your disagreement, ask questions that help you understand the reasoning behind the position you find problematic. "What led you to that conclusion?" "What evidence are you weighing most heavily?" "What concerns are you trying to address?" These questions should not be rhetorical or disguised critiques. They should be genuine attempts to understand. Often, this inquiry reveals that what appeared to be an irrational position is actually quite reasonable given different information or different priorities.

- Third, the practice of attention: Give your complete attention to the other person when they speak. This means not just refraining from interrupting, but truly focusing on understanding rather than on formulating your response. In our multitasking culture, complete attention has become rare. But it is essential for genuine listening. When someone feels your complete attention, they often articulate thoughts and concerns they did not know they possessed. The quality of conversation deepens dramatically.

- Fourth, the practice of patience: Resist the urge to jump in with solutions or rebuttals. Let conversations breathe. Allow silence. Some of the most important insights emerge not in the initial statements but in the reflections that follow when people feel they have space to think aloud. In our fast-paced environment, where efficiency is prized, this patience feels counterintuitive. But it is often the most efficient path to genuine understanding and resolution.

These practices sound simple. They are not. They require disciplined effort, particularly in high-stakes conflicts where emotions run strong and pressures for quick resolution are intense.

But they are learnable. And organizations that cultivate these practices in their leaders and teams dramatically enhance their capacity for adaptive conflict resolution.

In my work with a major aerospace company, I witnessed how systematic cultivation of these listening practices transformed conflict dynamics throughout the organization. The company was facing severe tensions between engineering teams and program management over schedule pressures and technical risk assessments. Engineers felt their concerns about technical readiness were being dismissed in favor of schedule targets. Program managers felt engineers were using technical concerns as excuses for delays and perfectionism.

The transformation began when senior leadership committed to a simple but profound change: before any major program decision involving technical risk, there would be a structured listening session where program managers had to articulate engineering concerns to the satisfaction of the engineering team, and engineers had to articulate program constraints to the satisfaction of program management. This was not negotiation or debate. It was pure listening practice with each side demonstrating they genuinely understood the other's perspective before any decision discussion began.

The initial sessions were awkward and frustrating. Program managers struggled to articulate technical concerns without dismissing them. Engineers struggled to articulate schedule pressures without being condescending. But over months of practice, something shifted. The quality of mutual understanding improved dramatically.

More importantly, the nature of conflicts changed. Instead of adversarial disputes about whether concerns were legitimate, conversations became collaborative problem-solving about how to address genuine technical issues within genuine schedule constraints. Neither side had compromised their core priorities. But both sides had developed the capacity to understand and work with the other's constraints and concerns.

This example illustrates a crucial point about listening in conflict resolution: it is not merely a preliminary step before real problem-solving begins. Genuine listening often is the problem-solving. When people truly understand each other's perspectives, constraints, and concerns, solutions often emerge that were invisible from positions of mutual incomprehension. The adversarial frame dissolves not through compromise but through expanded understanding that reveals possibilities neither side could see from their initial perspectives.

## THE ART OF CONVERSATION IN CONFLICT

Listening is necessary but not sufficient for resolving conflicts empathetically. Genuine listening must be paired with the art of conversation or the capacity to facilitate dialogue that moves beyond defensive exchanges toward collaborative exploration. In my experience working with organizations facing significant internal conflicts, the quality of conversation within the organization determines whether conflicts become destructive or generative.

Destructive conflicts are characterized by positional exchanges. Each side states their position, defends it against critique, and attempts to persuade or overpower the other. Energy dissipates. Frustration builds. Even when temporary resolutions are reached, they often feel like imposed settlements rather than genuine agreements. Worse, they leave underlying issues unaddressed, setting the stage for future conflicts.

Generative conflicts, conflicts that actually strengthen organizations and relationships, are characterized by different conversational dynamics. They involve genuine exploration of different perspectives. They build energy rather than dissipate it. They surface underlying issues rather than papering over them. Most importantly, they create new understanding and possibilities that transcend the original positions. Facilitating generative conversation in the midst of conflict is perhaps the most important leadership skill for building adaptive organizations.

What makes a conversation generative rather than destructive?

Based on my observations across diverse contexts, several elements consistently appear.

The first is shared focus on real problems rather than positions: Generative conversations redirect attention from "my position versus your position" to "the problem we both want to solve." This shift requires deliberate facilitation. When a facilities manager and a finance director are locked in conflict about budget allocations, the conversation can remain stuck in positional bargaining, more money versus fiscal responsibility.

But when a skilled facilitator helps them focus on the underlying challenge, how to maintain necessary infrastructure while managing costs, new possibilities emerge. The facilities manager might acknowledge areas where efficiencies are possible. The finance director might recognize where investment is essential. Together, they can explore creative solutions neither would have considered from their defensive positions.

Second is the openness to being surprised. Generative conversations require participants to remain open to hearing something unexpected, something that might change their thinking. This openness is rare in conflicts, where people typically know exactly what they think and are focused on defending it. But the most productive conflicts I have witnessed involved moments where someone genuinely surprised themselves and where they heard something that shifted their perspective or forced them to question their assumptions.

Creating conditions for surprise requires specific conversational practices. It requires asking questions that invite reflection rather than defensive response. Instead of "Why did you do that?" try "What were you hoping to accomplish?" Instead of "Don't you see the problem with your approach?" try "What concerns do you have about alternative approaches?" These subtle shifts in questioning create space for genuine exploration rather than defensive justification.

Third is building understanding incrementally. Complex conflicts cannot be resolved in single conversations. They require patient accumulation of understanding over time. Each conversation should aim not to resolve everything but to deepen understanding of some aspect of the situation. This incremental approach runs counter to our desire for quick resolution, but it is essential for addressing truly difficult conflicts.

I learned this working with a multinational team facing severe internal conflicts rooted in different cultural expectations about communication and decision-making. American team members expected direct communication and quick decisions. Asian team members valued indirection and consensus-building. Each side viewed the other as dysfunctional. The American members thought their Asian colleagues were impossibly slow and indirect. The Asian members thought their American colleagues were impossibly blunt, reckless and slick.

Resolution required a series of conversations that gradually built mutual understanding. We did not attempt to resolve everything at once. Instead, each session focused on understanding one dimension of the differences, communication styles in one session, decision-making processes in another, concepts of hierarchy in a third. Over time, as understanding accumulated, the team developed hybrid practices that honored both sets of cultural values. This was only possible because we resisted the pressure for immediate resolution and allowed understanding to build slowly.

Fourth is creating genuine dialogue rather than debate. The most fundamental distinction between generative and destructive conflict conversations is the difference between dialogue and debate. Debate assumes opposed positions and aims for one side to prevail. Dialogue assumes shared concern and aims for collaborative understanding. In organizational conflicts, the instinct is almost always toward debate with each side marshaling arguments and evidence to support their position.

Shifting from debate to dialogue requires active facilitation. It means interrupting argumentation and redirecting energy toward exploration. When someone makes an assertive claim, the facilitator might respond: "That's an interesting perspective. Help us understand the reasoning behind it." When someone attacks another's position, the facilitator might intervene: "Before we critique that idea, let's make sure we understand it fully. Can you articulate what concerns led to that proposal?"

These interventions feel simple, but they fundamentally alter conversational dynamics. They signal that the goal is understanding, not victory. They create permission for people to think aloud, to acknowledge uncertainty, to modify their positions based on new information. In debate, changing your position is weakness. In dialogue, it is intellectual honesty and growth.

## BRIDGING DIVIDES THROUGH GENUINE PROJECTS

Even with skilled listening and facilitated conversation, some organizational conflicts prove intractable because the divides are simply too wide. When different groups have genuinely different priorities, values, and frameworks for understanding problems, conversation alone may not be sufficient. This is where genuine projects, collaborative endeavors that unite people across their differences, become essential.

Genuine projects share certain characteristics that make them powerful tools for conflict resolution. They address real challenges that multiple stakeholders care about. They require diverse perspectives and capabilities to succeed. They create opportunities for people to experience working together effectively, building trust through shared accomplishment rather than through abstract appeals to unity. Most importantly, they shift the focus from abstract disagreements to concrete collaboration.

I encountered the power of genuine projects dramatically in a government agency where policy analysts and field operations staff had developed deep mutual contempt. Analysts viewed operations staff as unsophisticated and resistant to evidence-based approaches. Operations staff viewed analysts as disconnected ivory-tower types who did not understand ground realities. The conflict was not merely interpersonal; it reflected fundamental tensions between different kinds of expertise and different relationships to problems.

The breakthrough came when both groups were brought together to address a specific operational challenge that recent policy changes had created. Neither group could solve it alone. The analysts had essential understanding of policy constraints and regulatory requirements. The operations staff had essential understanding of implementation realities and practical constraints. Working on this concrete problem and designing practical implementation protocols for new regulations required genuine collaboration.

The transformation was not immediate. Initial meetings recreated the adversarial dynamics. But as the groups worked together on the genuine challenge, relationships began to shift. Analysts gained respect for operations staff's practical intelligence and problem-solving capabilities. Operations staff gained respect for analysts' ability to navigate complex regulatory environments. More fundamentally, both groups began to see how their different forms of expertise complemented each other. The project created an experience of productive collaboration that abstract discussions about "working together better" could never have achieved.

Identifying and catalyzing such projects is crucial leadership skill for resolving organizational conflicts. It requires understanding what different groups genuinely care about, their authentic concerns and priorities, not their stated positions. It requires identifying challenges where collaboration is necessary, not optional. And it requires structuring the work so that mutual dependence is clear and success requires genuine integration of different perspectives.

This approach does not eliminate disagreements. The policy analysts and operations staff in my example did not suddenly agree about everything.

But the shared project created a different context for their disagreements. Instead of abstract conflicts about whose approach was superior, disagreements became concrete questions about how to balance different considerations in specific situations. This shift from abstraction to concreteness makes conflicts dramatically more tractable.

# THE PAPER CHASE EXAMPLE

The TV series "The Paper Chase" offers one of the most enduring portraits of legal education as a crucible where raw ambition is both sharpened and challenged. The series follows first-year law student James T. Hart and his classmates as they struggle under the relentless pressure of Professor Charles Kingsfield, a contracts scholar at an elite law school modeled on Harvard.

Kingsfield's classroom, dominated by the Socratic method and a constant threat of humiliation, is engineered to test not only intellect but character, forcing students to confront what it means to be a lawyer in a profession that prizes both individual excellence and collective responsibility.

One of the most revealing episodes centers on an elaborate contracts assignment that functions as a kind of academic scavenger hunt across the university. Kingsfield issues a sprawling problem set composed of numerous, obscure questions, announcing that every student must reach a minimum number of correct answers or risk failing the exercise.

The class immediately fragments into small teams, each convinced that their best chance lies in internal cohesion and external secrecy. Study groups that already operate as semi-competitive cells now double down, hoarding sources, hiding research leads, and treating information as a private asset rather than a shared resource.

At first glance, this reaction seems entirely rational. Law school, particularly as depicted in "The Paper Chase," is built around ranking: class standings, exam scores, and the relentless sorting of students into future winners and losers. The social contract among students is informal but clear: mutual support is acceptable so long as it does not interfere with one's competitive edge. Kingsfield's reputation for destroying the complacent and rewarding the prepared only intensifies this ethos, encouraging students to think of success as a strictly individual achievement secured against peers, not alongside them.

However, the structure of Kingsfield's assignment quietly undermines that logic from the start. No single team can realistically find and correctly answer enough questions within the time allowed. The task is too broad, the sources too scattered, and the interpretive work too demanding for any isolated group, no matter how talented or disciplined. In effect, the problem is engineered as a collective-action puzzle disguised as a competitive test.

The students initially misread the assignment as a zero-sum contest, but the underlying design assumes a very different model: that genuine success will require the class to behave like a coordinated legal enterprise rather than a set of warring solo practitioners.

As the deadline approaches, the limits of competitive individualism become impossible to ignore. Each team discovers gaps: missing citations, unresolved ambiguities, and entire clusters of questions for which they have neither the time nor the expertise to assemble a competent answer. The more they push within their siloed groups, the more they run into structural constraints that no amount of individual effort can overcome.

This is precisely where the assignment becomes a lesson in contracts beyond doctrine. The students have, in effect, entered into an implicit contract with one another, shaped by the culture of the law school: they will compete fiercely, share selectively, and accept that some will fail so others can rise. Kingsfield's design exposes that informal contract as irrational under conditions of genuine complexity.

The eventual breakthrough occurs when the students begin to share their work across team boundaries. What starts as tentative information trading evolves into an implicit class-wide consortium as they realize that pooling outlines, research threads, and partial answers is the only viable path to meeting Kingsfield's minimum threshold. In contract terms, the students are renegotiating the terms of their relationship: they move from a fragmented network of competing micro-alliances to something closer to a joint venture.

The benefits are immediate. Different teams have strengths in different areas, some excel at doctrinal analysis, others at tracking down obscure sources in the library, others at synthesizing interpretations into clear, defensible conclusions. Once combined, these disparate assets produce a composite performance no single group could achieve.

Kingsfield's reaction underscores the deeper pedagogical point. He does not punish the students for "cheating" by collaborating; instead, he uses the episode to illustrate how the practice of law actually works in complex institutional settings. Large transactions, intricate litigation, regulatory investigations—none of these can be managed by a lone, heroic lawyer operating in isolation.

They demand teams, often multi-disciplinary and multi-institutional, coordinated under formal contracts and informal norms. The lawyer's task is not only to be personally brilliant but also to design structures, partnership agreements, service contracts, governance frameworks, that enable distributed competence to function effectively.

Seen this way, the episode stages a collision between two different ideals of professionalism.

On one side stands the myth of the purely competitive individual: the top-of-the-class student or rainmaking partner who dominates by superior talent and relentless self-assertion.

On the other side stands a more collaborative professional identity, in which excellence is measured by the capacity to contribute to and orchestrate joint performance.

"The Paper Chase" does not fully abandon the first ideal, Hart and his peers still care deeply about rankings and recognition, but it complicates it, suggesting that an overreliance on competitive individualism can become maladaptive when the work itself is collaborative by nature.

The contracts assignment thus functions as a kind of microcosm of modern professional life beyond law. Many fields are still organized around individual metrics, grades, bonuses, promotion tracks, even as the real work becomes more interdependent, technologically mediated, and organizationally complex.

Kingsfield's genius, in this episode, lies in forcing his students to experience the failure of a purely competitive model from the inside rather than merely lecturing about teamwork. The resulting lesson is not sentimental; it does not ask them to abandon ambition or standards. Instead, it invites them to reconceive ambition itself: not as a solitary climb up a ranking table, but as the pursuit of roles and structures where individual capability and professional collaboration rein-force each other.

In the end, "The Paper Chase" uses the drama of law school to explore a larger question: what kind of professionals do institutions actually need?

Kingsfield's contracts assignment suggests an answer. Institutions need individuals who are sharp enough to stand on their own, yet wise enough to recognize when the only rational move is to reshape the "contract" with one's peers and work together. Competitive individu-alism may get students into the classroom, but it is professional collab-oration that allows them and the systems they will one day serve to solve the hardest problems.

# POWER DYNAMICS AND EMPATHETIC CONFLICT RESOLUTION

One dimension of organizational conflict that demands particular attention is power asymmetry. Many organizational conflicts involve parties with dramatically different levels of formal authority, resource control, or institutional standing. These power differences fundamen-tally shape conflict dynamics in ways that empathetic approaches must recognize and address.

The naive approach to empathetic conflict resolution assumes symmetrical conditions where two parties meeting as equals, each able to speak freely, each with equivalent capacity to influence outcomes.

But organizational reality is rarely symmetrical. A junior employee disagreeing with their manager faces very different stakes and constraints than the manager faces. A small department competing for resources with a large, politically powerful department enters the conflict from a position of structural disadvantage. Cross-functional conflicts often involve groups with very different proximity to execu-tive power and decision-making authority.

These power asymmetries create several challenges for empathetic conflict resolution. Those with less power may not feel safe expressing their genuine concerns. They may self-censor, or they may express concerns in indirect or coded ways that those with more power fail to recognize or take seriously. Those with more power may not recognize how their structural advantages shape the conflict. They may interpret others' caution or indirection as lack of serious concern rather than as reasonable responses to power differences.

My experience in dealing with both public and private organizations has taught me several crucial lessons about power and empathetic conflict resolution:

- First, empathetic listening across power differences requires explicit attention to how power shapes communication: You cannot simply facilitate conversation and assume power will not matter. Those with less power need explicit assurance that honest communication is safe. Those with more power need explicit awareness of how their structural position affects what others feel safe to say.
- Second, inquiry is especially important when power is asymmetrical: When someone with power asserts their position, those with less power may not feel safe challenging it. But when someone with power genuinely inquires seeking to understand concerns and perspectives rather than defending decisions space opens for authentic expression from those with less power.
- Third, facilitation becomes essential in asymmetrical conflicts: Without skilled facilitation, power differences typically dominate conversational dynamics. Those with more power speak more, interrupt more, and have their views taken more seriously. Facilitation can create more symmetrical conversational conditions even within asymmetrical organizational relationships.
- Fourth, separating understanding from decision-making helps: When conversations mix understanding and decision-making, power differences contaminate the understanding phase. Those with less power may not express genuine concerns because they are already thinking about what decisions will be acceptable to those with more power. Separating these phases, establishing that a conversation is

purely about understanding, with decisions to come later, creates more space for authentic expression.

- Fifth, those with power bear special responsibility: In asymmetrical conflicts, empathetic resolution depends crucially on those with more power using that power to create conditions for genuine dialogue. They must recognize that their structural advantages create responsibilities, not just privileges. They must actively work to hear perspectives that their power might otherwise silence.

Organizations that understand these dynamics develop practices that systematically address power asymmetries in conflict engagement. They create forums where hierarchical power is temporarily suspended to allow genuine dialogue. They train leaders to recognize how their positional power shapes communication and to use that power to create conditions for others to speak freely. They build accountability systems that reward leaders not just for making decisions but for seeking and incorporating diverse perspectives in their decision-making.

None of this eliminates the reality of organizational hierarchy or the necessity of authoritative decision-making. But it does mean that conflicts can be engaged more empathetically even within hierarchical structures. Those in positions of power can resolve conflicts more effectively not by imposing solutions but by genuinely understanding the full range of perspectives and concerns that their structural position might otherwise keep hidden from them.

## BUILDING ORGANIZATIONAL CAPACITY FOR EMPATHETIC CONFLICT RESOLUTION

Individual skills in empathetic listening and conversation are necessary but not sufficient for building adaptive organizations. Organizations themselves must develop cultures and structures that support empathetic conflict engagement. This requires deliberate effort because our default organizational patterns, hierarchical decision-making, siloed structures, metrics-driven management, often undermine the conditions necessary for genuine dialogue and empathetic conflict resolution.

The organizations I have seen successfully build this capacity share several characteristics:

- They normalize conflict as natural and potentially generative: Rather than treating conflict as failure or aberration, these organizations frame conflict as inevitable wherever people care deeply about their work and have different perspectives. Leaders model this by engaging conflicts openly rather than suppressing them. They distinguish between generative conflicts that strengthen understanding and capability and destructive conflicts that poison relationships and paralyze decision-making. The goal is not to eliminate conflict but to channel it productively.
- They invest in conversational infrastructure: These organizations create regular opportunities for genuine conversation across organizational boundaries. This might include cross-functional working groups, leader dialogues with frontline staff, collaborative problem-solving sessions, or simply structured time for conversations not focused on immediate operational demands. These forums provide protected space for the kind of listening and dialogue that empathetic conflict resolution requires.
- They develop facilitation capacity throughout the organization: Rather than relying on outside mediators or limiting facilitation skills to senior leaders, these organizations systematically develop conversational facilitation skills at multiple levels. Middle managers learn to facilitate difficult conversations within and across their teams. Team leaders learn to create conditions for genuine dialogue. Even individual contributors learn questioning and listening techniques that shift conversational dynamics. This distributed capacity means that conflicts can be engaged empathetically at the point where they emerge rather than escalating up hierarchies.

- They reward bridge-building rather than just problem-solving: Traditional performance management rewards individual achievement and clear accountability. But building adaptive organizations requires rewarding people who build bridges across divides, who facilitate difficult conversations, who help disparate groups understand each other. These bridge-building activities are often invisible in traditional metrics. Organizations serious about empathetic conflict resolution make them visible and valued.

- They create genuine projects that span boundaries: As discussed earlier, genuine collaborative projects are powerful tools for resolving conflicts. Organizations that understand this deliberately structure work to require cross-functional, cross-level, and cross-cultural collaboration. They avoid letting different groups become so separated that they can function independently and thus never need to develop mutual understanding.

Building this organizational capacity is not quick work. It requires sustained leadership commitment over years, not months. It requires willingness to invest in capabilities, listening, dialogue, facilitation, that may seem soft or peripheral compared to technical skills and operational expertise. But the organizations that make this investment develop profound competitive advantage.

They can adapt more rapidly because information flows more freely. They can innovate more effectively because diverse perspectives can be integrated. They can weather crises more successfully because they have practiced working through conflicts under less extreme conditions.

## THE PRACTICE OF EMPATHETIC CONFLICT RESOLUTION

Throughout this chapter, I have emphasized practices rather than techniques because empathetic conflict resolution is fundamentally about cultivated capacity rather than applied methods. You cannot resolve conflicts empathetically by following a protocol or applying a framework. You can only do so through disciplined practice of listening, through patient development of conversational skill, through sustained commitment to understanding across differences.

This practice begins with the conflicts you encounter daily. Each difficult conversation is an opportunity to practice genuine listening. Each disagreement is a chance to practice inquiry rather than assertion. Each moment of tension is an opportunity to practice patience rather than reaction. The cumulative effect of this practice sustained over months and years is the development of genuine capacity for empathetic conflict engagement.

But practice alone is insufficient. You also need reflection on that practice. After difficult conversations or conflicts, take time to consider: What went well? What made genuine understanding possible? Where did conversation become defensive or positional? What might you have done differently? This reflective practice accelerates learning and prevents the mere repetition that does not constitute genuine development.

Equally important is learning from others. Observe leaders who are skilled at facilitating difficult conversations. Notice what they do that shifts conversational dynamics. Pay attention to how they ask questions, how they redirect energy when conversations become defensive, how they help groups move from positions to shared problems. Seek feedback on your own conflict engagement from people who can observe it. Their perspective often reveals patterns you cannot see from inside the interaction.

Finally, remember that empathetic conflict resolution is not about being nice or avoiding hard truths. Some of the most empathetic conversations I have witnessed involved people saying difficult things to each other. The difference was that they said those difficult things in ways that invited engagement rather than triggered defensiveness. They combined honesty with respect, clarity with curiosity, firm commitment to their concerns with genuine openness to understanding others' concerns.

In our fragmented age, where organizations and communities struggle with conflicts rooted in profound disconnection, the capacity for empathetic conflict resolution has become essential leadership capability. It is the foundation upon which adaptive organizations are built. It is the means by which diverse teams become capable of genuine collaboration. It is the bridge across divides that otherwise fragment organizations and paralyze adaptation.

The path forward requires sustained commitment to cultivating empathy through the patient practice of listening and genuine conversation. It requires building organizational cultures and structures that support rather than undermine these capacities.

Most fundamentally, it requires recognizing that in our complex, rapidly changing world, the ability to resolve conflicts empathetically is not a peripheral "soft skill" but a strategic imperative upon which organizational survival increasingly depends.

# EMPATHY AS KEY ELEMENT FOR LEADERSHIP

In a military command center I visited several years ago, I witnessed something remarkable. A senior officer was briefing his staff on a complex operational challenge when a junior analyst raised a concern about intelligence gaps. Rather than dismissing the question or offering a quick reassurance, the commander stopped. He asked the analyst to walk him through the specific data points that troubled her. For fifteen minutes, the room focused on understanding not just what the analyst was saying, but what what the analyst was seeing that others had missed. That conversation changed the operation's entire approach and potentially saved lives.

What struck me most was not the commander's decision to listen though that mattered immensely but how he listened. He didn't wait for the analyst to finish so he could respond. He didn't formulate his answer while the analyst spoke. He gave the analyst his complete attention, asked clarifying questions that showed he was genuinely trying to understand the analyst's perspective, and created space for others in the room to engage with the analyst's concerns. The quality of that conversation transformed what could have been a hierarchical exchange into collaborative problem-solving.

This incident crystallizes what empathy as leadership skill actually means. It is not about being nice or making people feel good, though those may be byproducts. Empathetic leadership is the disciplined practice of seeking to understand the experiences, perspectives, and reasoning of those you lead, not because it feels good, but because it is essential for effective decision-making in complex environments. In an age where organizations face unprecedented challenges requiring rapid adaptation, leaders who cannot listen cannot learn. Leaders who cannot learn cannot adapt. And organizations that cannot adapt do not survive.

Yet the practice of genuine listening has become extraordinarily rare in leadership. Walk into most organizational meetings and you will observe leaders who interrupt frequently, redirect conversations to their own priorities, listen primarily to confirm what they already believe, and mistake hearing words for understanding meaning.

This failure is not merely unfortunate: it is catastrophic. When leaders cannot truly hear what their people are telling them, critical information never reaches decision-makers, problems metastasize in silence, and the organization's collective intelligence remains untapped.

## THE LISTENING IMPERATIVE

Empathy in leadership begins with a recognition that listening is not a passive act of courtesy but an active discipline requiring sustained effort and practice. Consider what genuine listening demands. It requires setting aside your own agenda temporarily, not abandoning it, but consciously suspending it to create space for understanding another person's perspective fully. It means attending not just to words but to the meanings beneath them, the concerns driving them, the context shaping them.

Effective leaders listen for several distinct layers simultaneously. They listen to the explicit content, what is actually being said. They listen to the emotional undertones and how the speaker feels about what they're saying. They listen to what is not being said, the gaps, hesitations, and topics carefully avoided. And they listen for the deeper concerns or priorities that animate the conversation, what really matters to this person and why.

This kind of listening is exhausting. It demands cognitive resources. You cannot do it while multitasking, while checking your phone, while mentally rehearsing your response. It requires you to be fully present in a way that has become increasingly difficult in our fragmented attention economy. Yet this is precisely why it has become so powerful. In a world where superficial engagement is ubiquitous, deep attention stands out dramatically.

The mechanics of genuine listening are worth examining in detail. When a leader truly listens, several things happen simultaneously.

- First, they maintain consistent eye contact and open body language that signals full attention.
- Second, they resist the nearly universal urge to interrupt or redirect the conversation to familiar territory.
- Third, they ask questions that deepen rather than deflect, questions that show they are following the speaker's logic and want to understand it more fully.

Consider a specific example from my work with a corporate leadership team. The chief operating officer had a reputation for brilliant strategic thinking but poor implementation. Projects he championed frequently stalled. In conversations with his direct reports, a pattern emerged. He would ask them about project challenges, but the moment they began explaining obstacles, he would interrupt with solutions. His mind moved so quickly that he believed he was being helpful by immediately solving problems. But his team members felt unheard. They stopped bringing him real problems because they knew he would not listen long enough to understand the full context.

When we discussed this pattern, the COO was genuinely surprised. He thought he was listening, after all, he asked about problems. But asking is not listening. Listening requires creating space for complete expression before moving to solutions. When he consciously practiced holding his response until others had fully articulated their thinking, something remarkable happened. He discovered that many problems his teams faced were not the ones he had assumed. His brilliant solutions were often addressing the wrong challenges. When he actually understood the real problems, better solutions emerged—often from the teams themselves, who had been trying unsuccessfully to tell him what they needed.

This is the paradox of listening in leadership. Leaders believe they must have answers, so they focus on formulating responses rather than understanding problems. But the best answers come from genuine understanding of problems. Time spent truly listening is not time taken away from solving problems—it is the essential investment that makes problem-solving effective.

I have observed across military, corporate, government, and nonprofit contexts that leaders who cultivate genuine listening capacity develop several advantages.

- First, they receive better information. People share more honestly with leaders who they believe actually hear them.
- Second, they make better decisions because they draw on a fuller range of perspectives and insights.
- Third, they build loyalty not through charisma but through the profound experience of being truly heard, something many people experience rarely in their professional lives.

The practice of listening also changes what leaders notice. When you commit to really hearing people, you begin to detect patterns that would otherwise remain invisible.

In one government agency I worked with, the director committed to holding monthly listening sessions with employees at all levels. No agenda, no formal presentations, just open conversation about what was working and what wasn't. Over several months, she began hearing similar concerns from different parts of the organization about how information flowed between departments.

No single conversation revealed this pattern clearly. But by listening consistently and attentively across multiple conversations, she recognized a systemic issue that was impeding the agency's effectiveness. Had she been listening casually or sporadically, this crucial insight would have been lost in the noise of daily operations.

But listening alone is not sufficient. The information gathered through listening must be engaged through conversation, and it is here that many leaders fail even when they succeed at listening. They hear what people tell them, but they do not know how to transform that understanding into productive dialogue.

## THE EMPOWERING IMPERATIVE OF LEADERSHIP

A crucial leadership element is empowering people within the organization so that their conversations directly shape how policy is framed and executed.

That what was done on a regular basis by one of the most effective leaders I have ever had the opportunity to work with, Michael W. Wynne who served as both Secretary of Acquisition and as Secretary of the U.S. Air Force.

In this recounting by Dr. Mark Lewis, Chief Scientist of the USAF and a leading architect of hypersonics research, Lewis recounted an event which shows how empowerment works to generate effective organizational evolution through dialogue.

*Here is one quick anecdote to illustrate his style. In order to kick start the Air Force's alternate fuel activities, an industry day was announced at the USAF's Arnold Engineering Development Center in Tullahoma, TN.*

*Arnold is the Air Force's premiere ground test and evaluation center and was then doing early work to certify manufactured "Fischer-Tropsch" fuels in existing jet engines. The Fischer-Tropsch process was well-established, having been used by the Germans during World War II, and more recently by the South African aviation industry in place of petroleum-based fuels; as such, it was a logical starting point for our alternate fuels work.*

*The event at Tullahoma turned into one of the most poignant days I experienced on the Air Staff. A group of us flew down together with Mike on his military flight – always a good experience, as we got uninterrupted quality time with the Boss.*

*Part of the day was spent dedicating a memorial to Mike Wynne's brother,* who was lost in combat over the skies of Vietnam. To have been included in such a meaningful event with the entire Wynne family was one of those special moments that are hard to describe. Suffice it to say, it was an incredible honor to be there by the Secretary's side, and to join a family that was mourning a loss of four decades previous.

Later in the day we witnessed a fuel test in an engine cell, and Mike Wynne impressed each of the engineers and technicians with his interest, knowledge, and engagement. What a thrill it was to tour lab facilities and test cells with him!

Then we went to the industrial round table. The meeting began with Mike Wynne at the head of the table, and me at his right hand, with the leaders of industry on either side. Secretary Wynne suggested that we go around the room and introduce ourselves, and so we began.

When it was Mike Wynne's turn, he explained of course that he was the Secretary of the Air Force and spoke a little about why we were all in the room. Then, before I could speak, he jumped in and said: "I don't want this gentleman to introduce himself; instead, I'd like to introduce him to you all. This is Mark Lewis, my Chief Scientist. He is my 'rod' and my 'staff,' my right hand. When you are speaking with him, it's the same as if you are speaking with me."

I'm not usually at a loss for words, but at that particular instance I was completely dumbstruck. That the Secretary of the Air Force had so empowered his Chief Scientist was amazing; it was also quintessential Mike Wynne. His words of course had the desired effect, as our industrial partners treated me accordingly. After the meeting, I was the most popular man in the room.

One other event of that day is worth noting, for it says something else about Secretary Wynne. A few weeks before this trip, I had offered some technical advice on an issue, but Secretary Wynne disagreed and decided to go in a different direction.

On the flight home, in the middle of a conversation, he suddenly turned to me and asked: "By the way, are you still mad with me?"

I insisted I was not, that I was mostly disappointed in myself for not making the convincing argument, but he was having none of it.

We talked about his reasons for disagreeing, he explained his reasoning, and at the end of the conversation I realized there were some political dimensions to the technical issues that I had not considered.

That was also very special for me. The Secretary of the Air Force is under no obligation to explain himself to his subordinate Chief Scientist. At that

*moment it became clear that though he disagreed with me, he respected me
enough to explain why, and he wanted me to respect and understand his decision.
I don't think I could have ever appreciated him more than at that moment.* *

# THE ART OF LEADERSHIP CONVERSATION

A conversation is not an exchange of monologues. It is not a leader broadcasting decisions and employees acknowledging them. Real conversation is collaborative exploration, a shared journey toward understanding and, ideally, toward solutions that no individual could have reached alone.

I learned this most powerfully in a series of workshops I facilitated for a European defense ministry facing major reorganization. The various services, army, navy, air force, each had deeply entrenched positions about resource allocation. Initial meetings were predictable position statements followed by defensive counterarguments. Nothing moved.

The breakthrough came when we changed the nature of the conversation. Instead of asking each service to defend its budget request, we asked them to help us understand the operational challenges they faced and why current approaches weren't working. Instead of debating whose programs deserved priority, we explored what capabilities the integrated force actually needed and what combinations of service contributions might deliver those capabilities effectively.

This shift from positional bargaining to collaborative problem-solving required changing how people engaged in conversation. Leaders had to ask different questions, not "Why do you need this?" but "Help me understand what problem you're trying to solve and what constraints you're operating under." They had to create space for people to think aloud without immediately judging or countering. They had to weave together diverse contributions into emerging shared understanding.

The quality of conversation in an organization directly determines

---

* Robbin Laird, editor, *America, Global Military Competition, and Opportunities Lost: Reflections on the Work of Michael W. Wynne* (Second Line of Defense Publications, 2025.)

its adaptive capacity. Organizations with shallow, defensive, or hierar-chy-dominated conversations become brittle. Information flows poorly. Problems are hidden. Innovation stagnates. But organizations where leaders cultivate genuine dialogue, characterized by authentic curiosity, respectful challenge, and collaborative exploration, become resilient and creative.

What does this look like in practice?

An effective leadership conversation has certain recognizable characteristics:

- It begins with real questions, not rhetorical ones. The leader genuinely wants to understand something and asks questions that invite substantive engagement rather than simple confirmation.
- It creates space for thinking. The leader tolerates silence while people formulate thoughts. They don't rush to fill every pause. They recognize that good thinking often requires time.
- It builds on contributions. When someone offers an idea or perspective, the leader acknowledges it specifically before moving forward, not with empty praise but by showing how it connects to or extends the discussion.
- It surfaces disagreements productively. Rather than papering over conflicts or forcing false consensus, the leader helps the group articulate precisely where and why they disagree, often revealing that apparent contradictions stem from different but compatible perspectives on different aspects of a problem.
- It moves toward action. While comfortable with exploration and ambiguity, the conversation ultimately orients toward decisions and commitments. The leader helps the group identify what has been learned and what follows from that learning.

These practices may sound straightforward, but they run counter to how most organizational conversations actually function. They require leaders to relinquish certain forms of control, the ability to dominate discourse, to have the final word on everything, to be the smartest person in the room. In exchange, leaders gain access to their organization's collective intelligence and the commitment that comes when people genuinely participate in shaping decisions that affect them.

## BUILDING TRUST THROUGH UNDERSTANDING

Trust in leadership does not primarily come from competence or charisma, though these matter. Deep trust comes from the experience of being understood. When people believe their leader genuinely comprehends their situation, concerns, and constraints, they extend trust even when they disagree with specific decisions.

I saw this principle tested severely in a corporate context during a painful restructuring. The organization faced market pressures requiring significant workforce reduction. Leaders could not avoid difficult decisions that would harm people's lives and livelihoods. What they could control was how they engaged with those affected.

One executive team decided to hold extensive listening sessions before finalizing restructuring plans. They met with employees at all levels, asking them to explain their work, what obstacles they faced, what they believed the organization should prioritize. They made clear that the economic pressures were real and that reductions would occur, but they wanted to understand as fully as possible what capabilities and functions mattered most before making decisions.

These conversations were difficult. People were angry, scared, and skeptical. But something important happened through the process. Employees began to believe that leaders were genuinely trying to understand the organization's actual work, not just managing spreadsheets. When final decisions came, many people disagreed with specific choices. But the organization retained most of its key talent through the transition because people trusted that decisions had been made with real understanding of their implications, not in ignorance or indifference.

This is what empathetic leadership delivers in practice. Not avoidance of hard decisions. Not making everyone happy. But making difficult decisions with genuine understanding of their human impact, and communicating those decisions in ways that respect people's intelligence and dignity.

The foundation of this trust is the patient, sustained practice of listening and conversation. There are no shortcuts. You cannot fake genuine understanding. People know the difference between a leader who has truly listened and one who is performing empathy while fundamentally uninterested in perspectives that don't confirm their own views.

## FROM UNDERSTANDING TO ACTION: EMPATHETIC DECISION-MAKING

Leadership ultimately requires making decisions, often with incomplete information and competing priorities. Empathy does not remove these challenges, but it changes how leaders approach them. Empathetic decision-making integrates diverse perspectives not as a box-checking exercise but as essential intelligence.

Consider how most strategic decisions get made in organizations. Senior leaders gather data, consult experts, perhaps hold focus groups, then retire to make decisions. This model treats decision-making as separate from the organization, something leaders do to or for the organization rather than with it.

Empathetic decision-making looks different. It begins with the recognition that the people doing the work often understand crucial aspects of challenges and potential solutions that leaders removed from daily operations cannot see. The question becomes how to surface and integrate this distributed knowledge.

One approach I have seen work effectively is what might be called "empathy mapping" in strategic planning. Before making major decisions, leaders systematically work to understand how different stakeholder groups experience the current situation and would experience proposed changes. This is not market research. It is structured effort to see the challenge from multiple vantage points.

In one defense acquisition program I studied, leaders mapped how a proposed system change would affect not just end users but maintainers, trainers, logisticians, and others in the support ecosystem. This exercise revealed that a technically elegant solution would create impossible maintenance burdens. The design was modified based on this understanding, producing a more successful program.

The key is treating empathy not as a feeling but as a method, a disciplined way of gathering and integrating knowledge that would otherwise remain siloed. This requires specific techniques:

- Structured listening sessions with diverse stakeholders, using consistent questions to enable comparison across groups
- Collaborative analysis where people from different organizational areas work together to interpret what they're hearing and identify patterns
- Scenario planning that explicitly considers how different groups would experience various futures
- Decision criteria that include implementation feasibility and human factors alongside technical and economic considerations

These techniques formalize empathy, making it a systematic input to decision-making rather than a vague aspiration.

## THE EMPATHY-AUTHORITY BALANCE

Leaders face a persistent tension between empathy and authority. Too much empathy without clear direction can create drift. Too much authority without understanding can create brittle organizations that break under pressure. The balance point is not fixed but must be continually negotiated.

I have learned through observation that effective leaders maintain this balance through transparency about both empathy's role and authority's necessity. They make clear that understanding perspectives does not mean all perspectives determine decisions. They listen genuinely to concerns while being honest that some concerns cannot be accommodated within real constraints.

A military commander I worked with explained his approach this way: "I tell my people I need to understand their view completely, and they need to understand mine completely. Then I'll make the best decision I can with what I know. Sometimes they'll disagree. But they'll know their perspective was genuinely considered, not dismissed."

This clarity prevents empathy from being mistaken for weakness or indecision. The leader listens deeply, engages in genuine dialogue, then decides and acts. The empathy makes the authority more effective because decisions are better informed. The authority makes the empathy productive because understanding leads to action.

The balance requires leaders to develop comfort with difficult conversations. Empathy does not mean avoiding conflict or discomfort. Sometimes the most empathetic thing a leader can do is name a difficult reality clearly rather than soft-pedaling it.

I observed this in a nonprofit organization facing fundamental questions about its mission. Staff had passionate but contradictory views about strategic direction. The executive director held a series of conversations where she pushed people to articulate not just what they wanted but why, what problem they were trying to solve, what they believed was at stake, what they feared might happen if the organization went a different direction.

These conversations were uncomfortable. People had to explain their reasoning, defend their assumptions, engage with criticism. But through this process, the organization identified some genuine shared commitments beneath apparent disagreements and some irreducible differences that required executive decision. The director decided, some people disagreed, but the organization moved forward more coherently because the decision emerged from real understanding rather than political maneuvering.

# ADAPTIVE ORGANIZATIONS AND THE QUALITY OF CONVERSATION

The ultimate test of empathetic leadership is whether it produces organizations capable of adapting to complex, rapidly changing environments. My four decades working across diverse organizations have convinced me that adaptive capacity correlates directly with the quality of internal conversation.

Organizations that can learn and evolve are characterized by rich dialogue across boundaries, vertical conversations between hierarchical levels, horizontal conversations across functional areas, and temporal conversations that connect past experience to present challenges to future possibilities. These conversations share certain qualities:

- They surface problems early rather than hiding them. In organizations with good conversational culture, people raise concerns when they first emerge rather than waiting for them to become crises. This happens when leaders consistently demonstrate they want to hear about problems and respond to them constructively rather than punishing messengers.
- They integrate diverse expertise effectively. Complex challenges require combining insights from multiple specialties. Organizations with strong conversational cultures develop protocols for bringing different perspectives into productive dialogue rather than siloing expertise.
- They enable rapid course correction. When conversations are honest and informed, organizations can recognize quickly when approaches aren't working and adjust. Organizations with poor conversational cultures commit to failing strategies because acknowledging problems feels too threatening.
- They build institutional memory while remaining open to new approaches. Good conversations connect people who remember past lessons with people bringing fresh

perspectives, enabling organizations to learn from history without being trapped by it.

These characteristics don't emerge accidentally. They result from leaders who consistently model and reinforce the practices of genuine listening and productive conversation.

I saw this powerfully demonstrated in a European air force's approach to operational lessons learned. Rather than formal after-action reports that sanitized problems, they created conversational forums where crews could discuss challenges candidly. Leaders participated not as judges but as engaged learners. Over time, this created an organization with extraordinary capacity to identify and address emerging issues.

The quality of conversation determines how effectively organizations bridge internal divides. Most organizations are fragmented, by function, by geography, by generation, by expertise, by a hundred other factors. These divisions can be sources of strength, providing diverse perspectives and capabilities. But they become weaknesses when they prevent integration and learning.

Empathetic leadership addresses this fragmentation not through organizational restructuring but through conversational bridging. Leaders create forums and occasions for people from different areas to engage each other in substantive dialogue about shared challenges. They facilitate conversations that help people understand not just what their colleagues do but why it matters and how it connects to broader organizational purpose.

## LEADING THROUGH CHANGE WITH EMPATHY

Organizational change tests empathy most severely. Change creates uncertainty, anxiety, and resistance. Leaders must move organizations forward while respecting that people's concerns about change are often legitimate, not merely obstacles to overcome.

I have observed countless organizational transformations, successful and failed. The successful ones share a characteristic approach to empathy during change. Leaders distinguish between empathy for people's experience of change and agreement with resistance to change. They validate that change is difficult while maintaining clarity that change is necessary.

This plays out in how leaders communicate about change. Ineffective leaders either sugarcoat reality, pretending change will be painless, or dismiss concerns as resistance to overcome. Effective leaders acknowledge difficult truths while explaining why change is essential and how the organization will support people through transition.

Empathy during change does not mean avoiding difficult decisions or indefinitely delaying necessary changes. It means making those decisions and managing those changes with understanding of their human impact and with support systems that address real concerns.

## THE GENUINE PROJECT AS EMPATHY IN PRACTICE

Perhaps empathy's most powerful expression in leadership comes through what might be called "the genuine project" or a shared endeavor that brings diverse people together around real challenges that matter to them all. These projects create conditions where empathy becomes operational rather than abstract.

I have seen this principle work across contexts. A military unit preparing for deployment, where diverse specialties must integrate their capabilities toward mission success. A corporate product development team, where engineering, design, marketing, and operations must collaborate to create something valuable.

Genuine projects share certain characteristics. They address real challenges that multiple stakeholders care about. They require diverse perspectives and capabilities to succeed. They create opportunities for people to experience working together effectively, building trust through shared accomplishment rather than abstract appeals to unity.

Leaders who understand empathy's role in adaptation actively identify and catalyze such projects. They look for challenges that naturally require bridging organizational divides. They create teams that bring together people who might not otherwise engage. They structure work to require genuine collaboration rather than parallel effort.

A technology company I studied faced persistent conflicts between product development and operations teams. Rather than mediating their disputes, leadership identified a critical customer problem that required both teams' expertise to solve. Working together on this genuine project, team members developed understanding of each other's constraints and capabilities. This understanding transferred to other work, reducing friction throughout the organization.

The genuine project works because it makes empathy practical and consequential. People develop understanding not through training exercises but through actual collaboration on work that matters. They learn to listen because they need information. They learn to have productive conversations because they need to solve problems together.

Let me describe in more detail how this works. In the technology company example, the customer problem centered on system performance degradation that users experienced during peak usage periods. Product development saw this as an infrastructure scaling issue, they needed more resources. Operations saw it as a code efficiency issue, the application wasn't optimized. Each side had data supporting their view. Neither was entirely wrong, but neither had the complete picture.

The breakthrough came when leadership created a joint task force with explicit mandate to solve the problem completely, not to advocate for either team's preferred solution. This changed the conversation. Instead of defending positions, team members had to understand each other's analysis. Product developers had to learn operations' perspective on system behavior under load. Operations staff had to understand product design constraints and customer feature priorities.

Through working together on actual problem-solving, not abstract team-building but real work with real stakes, they discovered the issue was more complex than either side had recognized. It involved interaction effects between application design and infrastructure configuration that neither team could see from their separate vantage points. The solution required changes on both sides, coordinated carefully.

More importantly, the collaboration created relationships and understanding that persisted beyond this single project. Product developers gained appreciation for operational complexity they had previously dismissed. Operations staff developed respect for product development constraints they had not fully grasped. Future disagreements didn't disappear, but they became more productive because each side better understood the other's legitimate concerns.

This is what genuine projects accomplish. They create contexts where empathy develops naturally through shared purpose rather than being imposed artificially through training or exhortation. The project provides reason to listen, framework for conversation, and stakes that make understanding matter.

## CULTIVATING EMPATHETIC LEADERSHIP CAPABILITIES

Empathetic leadership is not an innate trait but a set of capabilities that can be developed through practice. Based on extensive observation, I believe several specific practices enhance leaders' empathetic effectiveness:

Scheduled listening time: Effective empathetic leaders build regular, protected time for conversations with diverse people across their organization. This is not casual management by walking around but disciplined effort to understand different perspectives systematically. One executive I worked with blocked out every Thursday afternoon for what he called "listening rounds" or scheduled conversations with employees at different levels and in different functions, rotating to ensure he heard from across the organization over time. These weren't problem-solving meetings or status updates. They were conversations focused on understanding people's work, challenges, and perspectives. Over months, this practice gave him an understanding of organizational dynamics that no amount of reading reports could provide.

The discipline here is treating listening as important work deserving protected time, not something to squeeze in when convenient. Leaders must fight the persistent pressure to fill calendars with "productive" meetings and recognize that genuine listening is perhaps the most productive use of leadership time.

Reflection practice: After significant interactions, empathetic leaders pause to consider what they learned, what they might have missed, and how their own assumptions might have shaped their understanding. This reflection prevents listening from becoming superficial. One military officer I knew kept a brief leadership journal where he noted key conversations each day and reflected on what he learned and what questions the conversation raised. This practice helped him identify patterns over time and recognize his own blind spots. He noticed, for instance, that he was more patient with technical explanations than with interpersonal issues, a bias that had been making him miss important signals about team dynamics.

Reflection also involves considering what was not said. After a staff meeting where everyone nodded agreement with a new policy, an effective leader might reflect: who didn't speak? whose concerns weren't voiced? what might people be thinking that they didn't feel safe saying? This kind of reflection often reveals important information that surface-level listening would miss.

Structured dialogue protocols: Leaders who facilitate good conversations often use light frameworks, questions to ensure multiple perspectives are heard, ground rules for respectful engagement, techniques for surfacing and working through disagreements constructively. These protocols need not be elaborate. In one organization I worked with, the leadership team adopted a simple practice for important decisions: before discussing solutions, they required everyone to articulate their understanding of the problem. This ensured they were addressing the same challenge before debating approaches. The practice revealed numerous instances where apparent disagreements about solutions stemmed from different understandings of problems.

Another effective protocol involves structuring brainstorming sessions to separate idea generation from evaluation. Leaders ask people to offer possibilities without immediate judgment, creating space for diverse thinking. Only after multiple ideas are visible does the group begin evaluating them. This simple separation prevents premature closure and allows perspectives that might initially seem tangential to get considered.

Seeking disconfirming evidence: Empathetic leaders actively look for information that challenges their current understanding rather than seeking only confirmation. They ask questions like "Who might disagree with this assessment and why?" or "What aren't we seeing?"

This practice guards against the confirmation bias that plagues most decision-making.

I watched one CEO implement this through a deliberate practice he called "designated skeptic." For major decisions, he would ask someone to take on the role of challenging the emerging consensus, not contrarian for its own sake, but genuinely trying to identify what might be wrong with the favored approach. This role rotated among senior leaders. What made it work was his genuine receptiveness to the challenges raised. He didn't want perfunctory criticism: he wanted real engagement with weak points in their thinking. This practice surfaced concerns that might otherwise have remained unvoiced, leading to better decisions and sometimes revealing that what seemed like consensus was actually thin agreement masking significant doubts.

Developing other leaders' conversational capacity: Empathy scales when leaders develop these capabilities throughout their organization. Effective leaders explicitly teach and model listening and dialogue skills rather than treating them as personal attributes. This might involve bringing teams together to discuss how they have conversations, not just what they talk about. What makes our discussions productive? Where do we get stuck? How do we handle disagreements?

In one government agency, senior leaders implemented a practice of debriefing important meetings to examine the quality of conversation itself. After particularly difficult or particularly productive discussions, they would spend fifteen minutes reflecting: What enabled us to work through that challenge? Where did we struggle to hear each other? What could we do differently next time? This meta-conversation about conversation gradually improved the team's collaborative capacity.

Another approach involves leaders narrating their own listening and thinking process. Rather than simply announcing conclusions, they sometimes walk their team through how they arrived at understanding, what they heard, how they weighed different perspectives, where they remain uncertain. This transparency helps others develop similar analytical habits.

These practices are simple to describe but difficult to maintain amid daily pressures. They require treating empathetic engagement as important work, not something to squeeze in when you have time. The challenge is that listening and reflection do not feel urgent in the way that immediate problems do. A leader can always justify postponing listening time to handle a crisis. Over time, this pattern creates a deficit in understanding that makes crises more frequent and harder to resolve.

The most effective leaders I have observed treat empathetic practices with the same discipline they apply to financial management or strategic planning. They build them into their routines, measure themselves against them, and hold themselves accountable for maintaining them even under pressure. They recognize that organizational adaptive capacity, the ability to sense and respond to challenges effectively, depends fundamentally on the quality of understanding that flows through leadership practices.

## THE LEADER AS BRIDGE-BUILDER

Ultimately, empathetic leadership is about building bridges, across organizational divides, across different perspectives, across past and future. In our fragmented age, where echo chambers and silos threaten organizational coherence, this bridging capacity becomes essential.

The bridges are built through listening and conversation. By genuinely understanding diverse perspectives, leaders can identify both genuine conflicts requiring resolution and false conflicts arising from miscommunication. By facilitating quality dialogue, they help people discover common ground and creative solutions.

This bridging is not about forcing unity or pretending differences don't exist. It is about creating conditions where people with different views can engage each other productively. It requires leaders who can facilitate difficult conversations, who can help groups move beyond positional bargaining to collaborative problem-solving.

I have watched this bridging capacity transform organizations in crisis. A government agency riven by internal conflict, where empathetic leadership created space for honest conversation about underlying concerns and rebuilt working relationships. A corporation where generational divides threatened knowledge transfer, where leaders facilitated dialogue that connected experienced employees' institutional knowledge with younger employees' fresh perspectives.

The bridge-building metaphor captures something essential about empathetic leadership. Bridges don't eliminate the distance between places, they enable movement across it. Similarly, empathetic leaders don't eliminate differences between people or groups—they enable productive engagement across those differences.

## CONCLUSION: THE EMPATHY IMPERATIVE

Empathy in leadership is not optional in today's complex, rapidly changing environment. Leaders who cannot listen, who cannot engage in genuine conversation, who cannot understand and bridge across differences will find themselves increasingly ineffective. Their organizations will become brittle, unable to adapt to challenges that demand integration of diverse knowledge and perspectives.

The path forward requires commitment to specific practices: genuine listening as a discipline, conversation as collaborative exploration, decision-making that integrates diverse perspectives, balancing empathy with authority, creating genuine projects that unite people across divisions.

These practices demand effort. They require treating human understanding as essential intelligence, not a soft skill peripheral to real work. But the return on this investment is organizational capacity for adaptation, innovation, and resilience, precisely the capabilities most critical in our uncertain age.

As you continue your leadership journey, I encourage you to examine your own practices.

- How often do you truly listen, giving complete attention without formulating responses?
- When did you last have a conversation that genuinely changed your thinking?
- How effectively do you bridge divides in your organization?

The transformation begins with recognizing that empathy is not about being nice. It is about being effective. It is about accessing and integrating the intelligence distributed throughout your organization. It is about building organizations capable of learning and adapting in our complex, turbulent world.

The leader who cultivates empathy through listening and conversation does not have all the answers. But they have something more valuable: the capability to discover answers through genuine engagement with the people doing the work, facing the challenges, and living with the consequences of decisions. This is the foundation of adaptive leadership for our time, and facing the challenge of chaos management and shaping adaptive organizations.

**6**

# LEADERSHIP FOR CHAOS MANAGEMENT

We inhabit an era characterized by cascading, interconnected disruptions that defy traditional categorization. This pervasive disruption stems from three interlocking forces: the compression of time, the ubiquity of crisis, and the paradox of connectivity that provides unprecedented information while overwhelming our capacity to process it meaningfully.

Traditional leadership frameworks built for stability and predictability prove dangerously inadequate.

The uncomfortable truth is that our conventional approaches assumed equilibrium was the natural state and chaos temporary exception. But when disruption becomes permanent, these assumptions collapse. Successfully navigating this reality demands transformation in how we conceive of leadership itself.

This transformation must be built on the foundation established in the previous chapter. Empathy or that disciplined practice of genuinely understanding diverse perspectives through listening and conversation is not merely helpful in chaotic environments. It is the essential capability without which organizations cannot develop the adaptive capacity chaos demands.

# FROM CRISIS MANAGEMENT TO CHAOS MASTERY THROUGH EMPATHETIC UNDERSTANDING

Traditional crisis management treats disorder as temporary aberration to be eliminated so normal operations can resume. The methodology is linear: identify the problem, analyze its causes, develop a solution, implement it, and return to stability.

But this framework fails in environments of permanent chaos because it rests on a critical misconception. It assumes problems can be objectively defined, analyzed by experts, and solved through technical solutions. This assumption breaks down when you recognize that in genuinely chaotic environments, the very definition of "the problem" is contested among diverse stakeholders who see different aspects of complex challenges through the lens of their distinct positions, experiences, and concerns.

This is where empathy becomes operationally essential. Chaos management or the ability to operate effectively within ongoing disruption requires leaders who can genuinely understand and integrate multiple, often conflicting perspectives to construct working understanding of challenges that exceed any individual's comprehension.

To understand why empathy is foundational to chaos management, consider what operating effectively in permanent disruption actually requires. You cannot predict all challenges. You cannot rely on established procedures because conditions change faster than procedures can be updated. You cannot depend on complete information.

What you can do is build organizational capacity to sense changes quickly, integrate diverse perspectives to understand what those changes mean, and adapt responses faster than conditions deteriorate. This is adaptive capacity or the ability to respond effectively to whatever actually emerges.

Building this capacity requires solving several interconnected challenges. Organizations must surface problems early. They must integrate specialized knowledge across silos. They must enable rapid course correction. They must maintain institutional memory while remaining open to new approaches. They must bridge internal divisions that fragment understanding.

Every single one of these is fundamentally an empathy challenge. Early problem detection requires people to share concerns when they first emerge rather than hiding them. This happens only when leaders have demonstrated they genuinely want to hear about problems and will respond constructively. This requires the listening culture we explored in Chapter 4.

Integrating diverse expertise requires leaders who can facilitate productive dialogue across functional boundaries, helping specialists understand each other's perspectives well enough to collaborate effectively. This demands the conversational facilitation skills discussed in the previous chapter: asking questions that deepen understanding, creating space for thinking, building on contributions, surfacing disagreements productively.

Rapid course correction depends on honest assessment of what is and is not working. Organizations that punish failure create conditions where people hide problems and resist acknowledging when situations have changed. Only where leaders have built trust through demonstrated understanding can organizations maintain the radical honesty chaos demands.

Bridging internal divisions requires leaders who can help people from different organizational tribes genuinely understand each other's legitimate concerns and constraints. This bridge-building cannot be accomplished through reorganization or policy. It requires patient, sustained empathetic engagement that creates human connections across differences.

In short, every capability essential for chaos management rests on a foundation of empathetic leadership. You build adaptive organizations through leaders who practice disciplined empathy at scale.

## EMPATHY AND WICKED PROBLEMS

The challenges leaders face in chaotic environments are not conventional problems solvable through technical analysis. They are "wicked problems" or challenges where the problem definition itself is

contested, where there is no clear stopping point, where every intervention creates new complications.

Empathy becomes operationally essential because wicked problems
are wicked precisely because different stakeholders perceive fundamentally different problems requiring fundamentally different
responses. You cannot solve this through better analysis because there
is no objectively correct definition. The challenge is inherently
perspectival.

Managing wicked problems effectively requires "empathetic
problem construction" or the disciplined practice of understanding
how different stakeholders experience and frame the challenge, identifying both genuine conflicts requiring negotiation and false conflicts
arising from miscommunication, and constructing working problem
definitions that integrate enough diverse perspectives to enable coordinated action.

## THE EMPATHETIC LEADER'S ADAPTIVE TOOLKIT

Earlier we explored specific practices that develop empathetic leadership capacity: scheduled listening time, reflection after significant
interactions, structured dialogue protocols, actively seeking disconfirming evidence, and developing conversational capacity throughout
the organization. In chaotic environments, these practices must be
extended and integrated with additional capabilities.

Cognitive flexibility or the capacity to shift mental frameworks
rapidly depends fundamentally on empathetic engagement. Leaders
who listen only to confirm existing understanding become trapped in
rigid frameworks. But leaders who practice genuine listening continuously encounter perspectives that challenge and extend their understanding.

The discipline of empathy forces cognitive flexibility. When you
genuinely try to understand how someone with completely different
background perceives a situation, you must temporarily suspend your
own framework to enter theirs. Practicing this regularly builds mental
muscle to hold multiple frameworks simultaneously and shift between
them fluidly.

Pattern recognition, detecting meaningful signals amid overwhelming noise, is enhanced dramatically by empathetic engagement. Complex patterns in organizational dynamics, emerging threats, and systemic changes often become visible only through integrating diverse perspectives. The signals that matter are rarely obvious from any single vantage point.

Consider intelligence analysis in national security contexts. The best analysts combine technical skills with capacity to understand how diverse actors with different motivations and cultural contexts perceive situations. This empathetic understanding enables recognition of patterns that would remain invisible to purely technical analysis.

Emotional regulation, maintaining effective cognitive function under pressure, is both enabled by and necessary for empathetic leadership. Leaders who practice consistent empathetic engagement build psychological resources that support emotional regulation. Leaders who create empathetic environments help everyone regulate emotions more effectively, enabling better collective performance under stress.

Simultaneously, emotional regulation makes empathetic engagement possible when stakes are highest. During genuine crises, leaders face powerful impulses to shut down empathetic engagement, to stop listening and just decide. These impulses are understandable but often counterproductive. The discipline of emotional regulation enables leaders to maintain empathetic practices precisely when they matter most.

Collaborative sensemaking, harnessing collective intelligence to construct shared understanding, is essentially applied empathy at scale. It requires all the conversational skills we explored earlier. But in chaotic environments, collaborative sensemaking becomes the primary mode of leadership work rather than occasional practice.

The leader's role shifts from being the person with answers to being the person who facilitates collective construction of working hypotheses that the group can test and refine through action. This shift requires profound comfort with empathetic practice because it means consistently prioritizing understanding over certainty, dialogue over direction.

# BUILDING ORGANIZATIONAL EMPATHY AT SCALE

Individual leaders practicing empathy matters, but it is not sufficient. Chaos management requires empathetic capacity distributed throughout the organization, what we might call organizational empathy. Building this requires leaders to architect organizational structures, processes, and cultures that enable and reward empathetic engagement at all levels.

This means creating forums for regular cross-boundary conversation that builds understanding across organizational divides. Many organizations inadvertently prevent empathy by siloing different functions, creating separate communication channels, minimizing interaction across levels and specialties. People cannot understand perspectives they are never exposed to.

Effective leaders deliberately design opportunities for diverse organizational groups to engage in substantive dialogue about shared challenges. These might include regular forums where people from different functions explain their work and constraints to each other, rotation programs that move people across boundaries, or project teams deliberately composed to include diverse perspectives.

The goal is not generic teambuilding but genuine understanding. People need to comprehend not just what their colleagues do, but why it matters, what makes it difficult, how it connects to broader purpose. This understanding builds over time through sustained interaction.

Building organizational empathy also requires leaders to model and reinforce the conversational norms explored earlier. When leaders consistently demonstrate genuine listening, when they visibly incorporate diverse perspectives into decisions, when they acknowledge how different viewpoints shaped their thinking, they establish standards others follow.

Perhaps most importantly, building organizational empathy requires creating "genuine projects" or shared challenges that naturally require diverse groups to collaborate in ways that build understanding through actual work rather than abstract discussion. These projects make empathy practical and consequential.

I have observed this principle work across remarkably diverse contexts. A military joint task force integrating capabilities from different services discovers through operational collaboration what classroom instruction could never teach. A corporate product development team learns to genuinely understand each other's constraints through shared challenge of creating something valuable. A government interagency working group builds empathetic understanding by wrestling together with genuinely difficult tradeoffs.

The genius of genuine projects is that they make empathy instrumental rather than idealistic. People do not engage empathetically because they are told it is important. They engage empathetically because they cannot succeed at work they care about without genuinely understanding their collaborators' perspectives, constraints, and concerns.

Leaders who understand this principle actively identify challenges that naturally require cross-boundary collaboration and structure work to necessitate genuine engagement across differences. Over time, this builds organizational empathy as cultural norm rather than depending on individual leaders' personal commitment.

## EMPATHY AND AUTHORITY IN CHAOS

Leaders face persistent tension between empathy and authority. In chaotic environments facing wicked problems, this tension intensifies. The temptation to abandon empathetic engagement and simply decide becomes powerful when uncertainty feels overwhelming.

But this temptation must be resisted. In genuinely chaotic environments, authority without understanding produces worse outcomes than empathetically informed action even when that action rests on provisional understanding. Leaders who decide without genuinely understanding diverse perspectives make predictable errors: they solve wrong problems, overlook critical constraints, generate resistance that undermines implementation, and miss opportunities that different perspectives would have revealed.

The balance in chaotic environments requires what we might call "empathetically informed decisiveness." Leaders maintain the discipline of genuine listening and dialogue. They invest real effort to understand diverse perspectives and construct the most comprehensive understanding circumstances permit. But they do not mistake this empathetic engagement for consensus-seeking or endless deliberation.

After genuine engagement, leaders decide. They act. They provide direction. Sometimes this means making choices that disappoint people whose perspectives were genuinely understood but whose preferences cannot be accommodated within real constraints. The empathy does not eliminate difficult decisions. It makes those decisions better informed and helps people accept them even in disagreement because they know their perspectives were genuinely considered.

This balance requires transparency about both empathy's role and authority's necessity. Effective leaders explain that they are seeking to understand as completely as possible, that diverse perspectives will genuinely inform decisions, but that ultimately decisions will be made and may not satisfy everyone. This honesty prevents empathetic engagement from being mistaken for weakness while maintaining the trust that makes empathy operationally effective.

I have watched leaders navigate this balance successfully in high-stakes situations. A military commander making deployment decisions held extensive conversations with his command to understand their assessment of readiness and concerns, then decided and explained his reasoning transparently even when others disagreed. A corporate executive leading restructuring invested genuine effort to understand human impact while maintaining clarity that difficult changes were necessary.

In every case, the empathetic engagement made decisions better, more informed, more implementable, more accepted even by those who disagreed. And the leader's willingness to ultimately decide and take responsibility maintained the authority necessary for effective action. The empathy did not replace authority. It made authority more effective.

# CONCLUSION

We began recognizing that we inhabit an era of permanent disruption, where traditional leadership frameworks prove dangerously inadequate. Empathy through disciplined listening and conversation builds trust and understanding essential for effective leadership. Now we can see how this foundation becomes absolutely critical for chaos management.

Empathy is not peripheral soft skill. It is the hard skill that makes adaptive capacity possible. In chaotic environments filled with wicked problems that exceed individual comprehension, empathetic leadership provides the only viable path to organizational learning, collective intelligence, and coordinated adaptation.

The path forward requires commitment to specific practices: genuine listening as discipline, conversation as collaborative exploration, decision-making that integrates diverse perspectives, balancing empathy with authority, creating genuine projects that build understanding through shared work. These practices demand sustained effort. They require treating human understanding as essential intelligence.

But the return on this investment is organizational capacity for precisely what chaos demands: the ability to sense changes quickly through distributed awareness, to integrate diverse perspectives into comprehensive understanding, to adapt faster than conditions deteriorate, to maintain coordination across differences while responding to local variation, to learn continuously from experience while taking action with incomplete information.

Organizations that cultivate empathetic leadership at scale develop resilience not through rigid structures that resist change but through flexible cultures that embrace it. They build adaptive capacity not by trying to predict all challenges but by developing collective capability to respond effectively to whatever actually emerges. They manage wicked problems not by solving them in any final sense but by engaging with them productively over time.

As you continue your leadership journey, examine not just your own empathetic practices but whether you are building organizational empathy at scale.

- Are you creating forums for genuine cross-boundary dialogue?

- Are you facilitating collaborative sensemaking around your most complex challenges?
- Are you modeling the balance between empathetic understanding and decisive authority? Are you identifying genuine projects that build understanding through shared work?

The transformation our age demands cannot be accomplished by individual leaders alone, no matter how empathetic their personal practice. It requires building organizations where empathetic engagement becomes the cultural norm, where understanding across differences is recognized as essential intelligence, where listening and conversation are treated as important work deserving serious investment.

This is the foundation for chaos management: not the fantasy of controlling disruption or returning to stability, but the reality of building human organizations capable of learning, adapting, and thriving within permanent complexity.

The leader who cultivates empathy in themselves, in their teams, and in their organizational cultures does not have all the answers. But they have something more valuable: the capability to discover answers through genuine engagement with the people facing the challenges and living with the consequences.

This is adaptive leadership for our time. This is the empathy imperative for chaos. The question is not whether you will face permanent disruption: that much is certain. The question is whether you have built, through patient empathetic practice at scale, the organizational capacity to thrive within it.

## 7

# CULTURAL EMPATHY AS LEADERSHIP PRACTICE

D r. Harald Malmgren and I met in 1980 and since then and until his death in early 2025, we talked frequently about our work. He was a political economist and trade expert with decades of negotiating experience. I worked on defense issues on three continents and dealt with many organizations and we shared insights into the art of negotiating and cultural learning.

In one conversation, he told me about one of his experiences, He was in a conference room in Singapore watching a carefully planned negotiation unravel. On one side of the table sat executives from a German manufacturing firm, armed with detailed specifications and implementation timelines. On the other sat representatives from a family-owned business in Indonesia, who had traveled for two days to attend the meeting. The Germans presented their proposal with characteristic precision and directness. The Indonesians nodded politely, asked few questions, and offered gracious but noncommittal responses. The Germans interpreted this as agreement and moved forward with confidence. Three months later, the partnership collapsed, leaving both sides frustrated and confused.

What went wrong? The easy answer would point to cultural differences and such differences certainly played a role. But the deeper failure was one of empathetic practice. Neither side engaged in the patient work of listening beneath the surface of words. Neither invested in the kind of sustained conversation that builds genuine understanding across difference. Both groups possessed goodwill and economic interest in success. What they lacked was not cultural knowledge in the abstract, but the practiced capacity to bridge cultural divides through disciplined listening and genuine dialogue.

This pattern repeats itself daily across the interconnected world. Organizations speak of embracing diversity and cultural intelligence. Leaders attend workshops on cultural awareness.

Yet the fundamental capacity to connect empathetically across cultural boundaries continues to atrophy. We collect facts about other cultures, their holidays, their etiquette, their communication preferences, as if cultural understanding were merely information to be downloaded. We mistake awareness for empathy, and knowledge about cultures for the capacity to engage meaningfully across them.

The challenge facing leaders today is not primarily one of cultural literacy, though such knowledge matters. It is the challenge of cultivating empathy as practice in contexts where cultural differences complicate the already difficult work of genuine listening and conversation.

In an age where teams span continents, where markets are global, and where problems require coordination across diverse perspectives, the capacity for cultural empathy is not a nice-to-have competency.

It is a leadership imperative. Yet this capacity cannot be developed through reading alone, or through abstract commitment to diversity. It requires the patient cultivation of specific practices that our current environment actively undermines.

## BEYOND CULTURAL AWARENESS: EMPATHY AS DISCIPLINED PRACTICE

When leaders speak of cultural empathy, they often mean something like cultural sensitivity or an awareness of differences, an avoidance of obvious offenses, a surface respect for alternative ways. This is necessary but insufficient. Cultural sensitivity without empathetic practice remains thin and brittle, collapsing under the pressure of genuine engagement. True cultural empathy demands something more rigorous: the disciplined practice of listening and conversation across profound difference.

Consider what genuine listening requires in cross-cultural contexts. When you listen to someone from your own cultural background, you share tacit assumptions about communication norms, social hierarchies, emotional expression, and countless other factors that shape how meaning is made. These shared assumptions operate invisibly, allowing you to focus on explicit content.

But when cultural backgrounds differ significantly, these invisible assumptions diverge. What one person intends as respect, another experiences as coldness. What one views as directness, another perceives as aggression. The words remain the same, but their meanings shift beneath them.

Genuine listening across cultures means attending not just to words but to the entire context of communication. It means noticing not only what is said but what remains unspoken, what is emphasized and what is minimized, what sparks energy and what creates discomfort.

This requires more than cultural knowledge. It demands sustained attention, patient observation, and the willingness to question your own interpretations continually. It means resisting the impulse to fill silence with your own voice or to resolve ambiguity prematurely with your own assumptions.

In that Singapore conference room, the German executives heard agreement in the Indonesians' responses because they interpreted politeness and non-contradiction as consent. They had read about high-context versus low-context cultures. They knew in the abstract that many Asian cultures prioritize harmony and indirect communication. But this knowledge did not translate into practice. They failed to listen for what the Indonesians were not saying, for the absence of concrete commitments beneath the gracious words, for the cultural dance of relationship-building that needed to occur before business decisions could be made. Their listening remained within their own cultural frame, hearing only what their expectations prepared them to hear.

The art of conversation across cultures demands similar discipline. A genuine conversation, as I have argued throughout this book, is not a sequential exchange of monologues or a negotiation to be won. It is a collaborative exploration toward understanding. But cultural differences profoundly complicate this collaborative work.

The rhythms of conversation vary across cultures, who speaks when, how long silences last, whether interruption signals engagement or disrespect, whether questions express curiosity or challenge.

The purposes of conversation differ, whether dialogue aims primarily at task completion or relationship building, whether it should surface disagreement or maintain harmony, whether it exists to reach decisions or to create shared understanding that enables later action.

Skilled cross-cultural conversation requires conscious attention to these variations. It means learning to read the conversational patterns of others while remaining aware of your own patterns and their effects. It means developing flexibility in your conversational approach, sometimes leading, sometimes following, sometimes simply creating space for others to find their voice. It means recognizing when to push for clarity and when such pushing violates cultural norms around directness. Most fundamentally, it means approaching conversations not with a script to execute but with genuine curiosity about how meaning is being made collaboratively across difference.

The German executives in Singapore approached the negotiation as a transaction to be completed efficiently through clear communication. The Indonesian representatives approached it as the beginning of a relationship that might eventually support business collaboration. These different purposes shaped how each side engaged in conversation. The Germans focused on specifications and timelines. The Indonesians wanted to understand the people they might work with, their values and intentions, their reliability as partners. Each side conversed according to their cultural script, but neither adjusted their approach to bridge the gap. The result was parallel monologues, not genuine dialogue.

# THE FRAGMENTATION PROBLEM IN GLOBAL CONTEXT

The communication crisis I described in this book's introduction takes on particular urgency in cross-cultural contexts. When people already inhabit different linguistic and cultural worlds, the tendency to cluster in echo chambers of the like-minded intensifies dramatically. Expatriate communities often form bubbles insulated from the surrounding culture. International businesses create headquarters-centric communication patterns that marginalize local perspectives. Global teams fragment along national lines, with inadequate bridges connecting them.

This fragmentation is not merely unfortunate: it is organizationally catastrophic. In a globalized economy where competitive advantage often depends on the capacity to integrate diverse perspectives and adapt to varied markets, organizations cannot afford the luxury of cultural silos.

Yet without deliberate cultivation of cross-cultural empathy, such silos are inevitable. People naturally gravitate toward those with whom communication feels easiest. The transaction costs of bridging cultural differences, the extra time, the higher risk of misunderstanding, the discomfort of operating outside familiar patterns, create powerful incentives to avoid such bridges.

Leaders must therefore work deliberately against these natural tendencies. Building organizations capable of genuine cross-cultural collaboration requires creating structures, practices, and cultures that make empathetic engagement across difference not merely possible but routine. This is not accomplished through diversity statements or cultural awareness campaigns. It requires embedding cross-cultural listening and conversation into the daily work of the organization.

Consider language, the most obvious cultural barrier. Many global organizations adopt English as their working language, treating this as a solution to the language problem.

But this apparent solution often masks deeper issues. When non-native speakers conduct business in English, they operate with a double burden, managing not only the substance of conversations but also the linguistic challenges of expressing complex thoughts in a second language. Meanwhile, native English speakers often fail to recognize this asymmetry, expecting the same conversational fluency from everyone regardless of linguistic background.

Empathetic practice in such contexts means native speakers learning to listen differently, attending more carefully to meaning beneath imperfect language, creating space for non-native speakers to find words, resisting the impatience that cuts off those who speak more slowly or search for vocabulary. It means non-native speakers feeling empowered to ask for clarification, to request slower speech, to acknowledge when understanding breaks down rather than pretending comprehension to avoid embarrassment. These practices do not emerge spontaneously. They must be cultivated deliberately through leadership modeling, explicit norms, and patient practice.

Beyond language, the hierarchical assumptions embedded in different cultures create persistent challenges for global teams. Cultures vary dramatically in their acceptance of power distance, the degree to which less powerful members expect and accept unequal power distribution. In high power distance cultures, subordinates rarely question authority, and leaders expect deference. In low power distance cultures, hierarchy is more fluid, and questioning authority is viewed as appropriate or even expected.

These differences create predictable pathologies in global teams. A leader from a low power distance culture may solicit input from team members, expecting open dialogue and debate. Team members from high power distance cultures may interpret such solicitation as a test, offering only responses they believe the leader wants to hear. The leader mistakes their silence or agreement for genuine consent, missing the concerns that remain unvoiced. Alternatively, team members from low power distance cultures may challenge ideas or offer contrary perspectives that members from high power distance cultures view as insubordinate or disrespectful.

Empathetic leadership in such contexts requires explicit conversation about these dynamics. It means making visible the invisible assumptions about hierarchy and authority that different team members bring to interactions. It means creating structures that enable genuine input across hierarchical divides, perhaps soliciting written feedback before meetings, or organizing smaller conversations where junior members feel more comfortable speaking. It means learning to read silence not as agreement but as a signal requiring investigation. None of this is natural or automatic. It requires conscious attention and sustained practice.

## THE PRACTICE OF CULTURAL LISTENING

If empathy across cultures begins with listening, what does such listening entail practically?

Cultural listening is not passive reception but active construction of understanding across difference. It requires multiple complementary practices, each demanding conscious development.

- First, cultural listening requires managing your own anxiety and discomfort. Cross-cultural interactions often generate anxiety, fear of giving offense, concern about being misunderstood, discomfort with unfamiliar patterns, awareness of incompetence in navigating new cultural terrain. This anxiety creates a powerful temptation to retreat to familiar ground, to speak rather than listen, to control the interaction rather than remain open to what emerges. Skilled cultural listeners recognize this anxiety as normal and develop strategies to manage it without letting it dominate the interaction.
- Second, cultural listening demands suspending judgment and interpretation. Your first interpretation of someone's words or actions in a cross-cultural context is almost always colored by your own cultural lens. The raised voice that seems aggressive to you may be passionate enthusiasm in another cultural context. The indirect response that frustrates you with its ambiguity may be a culturally appropriate way of expressing disagreement without direct

confrontation. Cultural listening means holding your initial interpretations lightly, treating them as hypotheses to be tested rather than conclusions to be acted upon.

- Third, cultural listening involves attending to multiple channels of communication simultaneously. In high-context cultures especially, enormous information flows through non-verbal channels, tone of voice, facial expressions, body language, the relationship dynamics in the room, the way people position themselves relative to each other. A skilled cultural listener learns to notice these channels, even while recognizing that interpreting them across cultures is risky. The key is not to become an expert decoder of all cultural signals, an impossible task, but to recognize that explicit verbal content represents only part of the communication occurring.

- Fourth, cultural listening requires checking your understanding through careful questioning. But the form such questioning takes matters enormously. In some cultural contexts, direct questions work well and signal engagement. In others, such questions may be experienced as confrontational or as putting someone on the spot uncomfortably. Skilled cultural listeners develop sensitivity to when and how to check understanding, sometimes through direct questions, sometimes through indirect approaches that invite rather than demand clarification, sometimes through simple restatement that allows the other person to correct misunderstandings without losing face.

- Fifth, cultural listening means attending to patterns over time rather than interpreting isolated interactions. A single conversation provides limited data for understanding across cultures. Patterns that emerge over multiple interactions provide more reliable guidance. The person who seems reticent in full group meetings but speaks more freely in smaller settings may be managing cultural norms around hierarchy rather than lacking opinions. The colleague who

never disagrees directly but later raises concerns through
indirect channels may be working within cultural norms
about conflict. Cultural listening involves patient
observation across contexts, building understanding
gradually rather than rushing to conclusions.

Return to the Singapore conference room. What would cultural
listening have looked like in that context? The German executives
might have noticed that while the Indonesians expressed no direct
disagreement, they also offered no specific commitments, no names of
people who would implement the plan, no concrete timelines, no questions about details that implementation would require. This absence
might have prompted exploration: "We have outlined our proposal.
We want to understand your perspective on whether this approach fits
with your organization's way of working. What concerns or questions
should we address?"

Such a question creates space for indirect expression of concerns
without forcing direct confrontation. It signals that the German executives are attending to more than just the absence of explicit disagreement. It invites deeper conversation while respecting cultural norms
around directness. But this requires the Germans to resist their own
cultural pattern of interpreting polite reception as agreement, to listen
for what is not being said as carefully as for what is explicit.

## THE ART OF CROSS-CULTURAL CONVERSATION

If listening provides the foundation for cultural empathy, conversation
is where understanding gets built collaboratively. Cross-cultural
conversation demands particular attention to process, not just what
gets discussed but how the discussion unfolds.

Effective cross-cultural conversation begins with explicit attention
to conversational norms themselves. In monocultural settings, such
norms usually operate invisibly, people simply know how conversations
work in their context.

But in cross-cultural settings, making norms explicit becomes
essential. This might involve opening a conversation with discussion of

how the group will work together: How will decisions be made? How will disagreements be handled? How will quieter voices be heard? What role will the formal leader play?

While such meta-conversation may feel awkward initially, it prevents far greater awkwardness later when implicit norm violations generate conflict or misunderstanding.

Cross-cultural conversation also requires conscious management of speaking time and conversational space. In some cultures, conversations are competitive, people interrupt, speak over each other, fight for airtime. In others, people wait for clear openings, speak in turn, avoid interruption. When members of both types of cultures participate in the same conversation, predictable patterns emerge: those from competitive conversational cultures dominate the discussion while others remain quiet. The result is not representative of the full group's thinking but rather reflects cultural differences in conversational style.

Skilled facilitators of cross-cultural conversation address this directly. They might use structured techniques that ensure all voices are heard, round-robin speaking, written contributions before verbal discussion, small group conversations before large group reporting. They might explicitly name the dynamic: "I notice that some people have contributed a lot while others have said little. I want to make sure we hear from everyone. Let me ask those who haven't spoken yet to share your thoughts." Such interventions feel artificial initially, but they prevent the natural outcome where cultural conversational patterns determine whose perspectives shape collective understanding.

The emotional dynamics of cross-cultural conversation demand particular attention. Cultures vary enormously in their norms around emotional expression, what emotions are appropriate to display in professional settings, how intensely they can be expressed, what emotional displays signal about the speaker. When someone from a culture that values emotional restraint in professional contexts encounters someone from a culture where passionate expression signals engagement and commitment, misunderstanding easily occurs. The restrained person seems cold or disengaged; the passionate person seems unstable or unprofessional.

Empathetic leadership in such contexts involves helping people understand these different emotional languages without judgment. It means creating norms that allow for different styles of engagement while maintaining productivity. It might mean explicitly discussing how conflict will be handled, since cultures vary dramatically in whether direct confrontation is viewed as healthy honesty or unacceptable disrespect. The key is making room for multiple cultural approaches rather than privileging one as the "right" way.

The ultimate goal of cross-cultural conversation is not merely information exchange but the construction of shared understanding that enables effective collaboration. This requires conversations that go beyond surface coordination to deeper alignment about purposes, priorities, and approaches. Such conversations take time, more time than monocultural conversations because the work of bridging cultural difference is genuinely harder. Organizations that fail to invest this time front-end of collaborations pay for it later through misunderstandings, conflicts, and failed implementations.

In the Indonesia-Germany case, genuine conversation might have involved multiple exchanges over time, not a single meeting. Initial conversations might have focused less on business specifications and more on understanding each organization's values, ways of working, and expectations for partnership. These conversations would have created relationship foundations that enabled later business discussions. They would have surfaced the different cultural approaches to decision-making, whether decisions get made in meetings or after meetings, whether consensus is required or hierarchical approval suffices, what role written agreements play versus relationship trust.

This patient conversation-building feels inefficient to cultures that prize rapid decision-making. But it proves far more efficient than investing heavily in implementations that fail because foundational cultural differences were never addressed. The time invested in genuine cross-cultural conversation is not time wasted but time spent building the collaborative capacity that everything else depends upon.

# FROM AWARENESS TO PRACTICE: DEVELOPING CULTURAL EMPATHY

Cultural empathy as I have described it, grounded in disciplined listening and genuine conversation, does not develop through training programs alone, though good training can help. It develops through sustained practice in contexts where stakes are real and feedback is available. Leaders seeking to build organizational capacity for cultural empathy must therefore think about creating practice fields where people can develop these skills.

One powerful approach involves deliberately structuring cross-cultural working relationships around projects that matter. When people work together toward shared goals that require genuine collaboration, they must develop cross-cultural empathy or fail. The pressure of real work forces attention to cultural dynamics that abstract training can only describe.

The key is ensuring such projects include reflection on the cross-cultural collaboration process itself, not just the task outcomes. This might involve regular check-ins where team members discuss what is working well and what is proving difficult in their cross-cultural collaboration, making challenges explicit rather than allowing them to fester.

Another approach involves creating cultural mentoring relationships where someone with deep experience in a particular cultural context helps others develop their understanding and skills. Unlike training that delivers general cultural knowledge, mentoring provides contextualized guidance tailored to specific situations. The mentor can help interpret confusing interactions, suggest appropriate responses to challenging situations, and provide feedback on cultural missteps before they become serious problems. Effective cultural mentors do not simply tell mentees what to do but help them develop their own capacity for cultural listening and conversation.

Leaders themselves must model the practices they seek to cultivate. When leaders visibly invest time in cross-cultural listening, when they acknowledge their own cultural learning edges, when they adjust their communication approaches to bridge cultural differences, they signal that such practices are valued and expected. Conversely, when leaders demonstrate impatience with cultural differences, when they expect others to adapt to their cultural preferences without reciprocal adaptation, when they make decisions without genuine cross-cultural input, they undermine any stated commitment to cultural empathy.

The organizations most successful at building cross-cultural empathy make it an explicit aspect of performance expectations and evaluation. They recognize and reward employees who bridge cultural divides effectively. They make cross-cultural collaboration skills a factor in promotion decisions. They invest in ongoing development of these capabilities rather than treating cultural training as a one-time event. Most importantly, they create organizational cultures where admitting cultural ignorance or confusion is acceptable and where asking for help in navigating cultural differences is viewed as strength rather than weakness.

This requires acknowledging that cultural empathy is difficult and that mistakes are inevitable. The goal is not cultural perfection but cultural humility, the recognition that your cultural perspective is partial, that others' perspectives are valid, and that genuine understanding requires ongoing work. Organizations that punish cultural missteps harshly create cultures where people avoid cross-cultural risk-taking, defeating the goal of building cross-cultural capacity. Organizations that normalize cultural learning create environments where people develop the skills to bridge differences effectively.

## THE LEADERSHIP IMPERATIVE

The fragmentation and isolation I described in this book's introduction take on particular urgency in global contexts. In an interconnected world, the inability to bridge cultural differences is not merely unfortunate: it is organizationally catastrophic. Organizations compete globally, problems require coordination across borders, teams span continents. The capacity for cultural empathy, grounded in disciplined listening and genuine conversation, is not optional for leaders. It is foundational.

Yet this capacity continues to atrophy. We collect cultural facts without developing cultural practice. We celebrate diversity without doing the hard work of bridging difference. We speak of inclusion while maintaining organizational structures and practices that privilege particular cultural approaches. The result is organizations that struggle to leverage their diversity, teams that fragment along cultural lines, and leaders who wonder why their global strategies falter in implementation.

The alternative requires commitment to empathy as practice rather than sentiment. It demands investing time in genuine cross-cultural conversation even when efficiency pressures make such investment seem costly. It requires creating structures and norms that enable cross-cultural listening despite the natural gravitational pull toward comfortable similarity. It means accepting that global leadership is harder than monocultural leadership precisely because the practices of listening and conversation become more complex and demanding across cultural divides.

But the payoff for this investment is organizational capacity that represents genuine competitive advantage. Organizations that develop deep cross-cultural empathy can integrate diverse perspectives in ways that generate innovation. They can adapt to local markets while maintaining global coherence. They can build teams that are genuinely collaborative rather than merely co-located. They attract and retain talent from around the world who seek workplaces where their cultural identities are not obstacles to be overcome but assets to be valued.

Most fundamentally, organizations that cultivate cultural empathy through the practices of listening and conversation contribute to building the kind of global community our interconnected world desperately needs. In an age of rising nationalism and cultural conflict, where technological connection paradoxically coexists with deepening fragmentation, leadership that bridges cultural divides is not merely organizationally valuable. It is ethically essential.

The practices I have outlined in this chapter are not just tools for organizational effectiveness. They are practices of global citizenship, ways of being in the world that honor human dignity across difference and build connection across the divides that threaten to fragment us.

The work is difficult, unglamorous, and never complete. There is no point at which you achieve cultural empathy and can move on to other concerns. It requires sustained attention, patient practice, and continual learning.

But it is work that matters, for your organizations, your teams, and the broader global community of which we are all part. The question is not whether cultural empathy is important but whether you will commit to developing it through the disciplines of listening and conversation that this chapter has outlined.

# DIGITAL COMMUNICATION AND THE CRISIS OF CONNECTION

Years into my work with organizations navigating digital transformation, I sat in on a video conference that perfectly captured our contemporary communication crisis. Twenty people occupied separate squares on a screen, each isolated in their home office or conference room. The meeting's ostensible purpose was to resolve a conflict over project priorities, but what I witnessed instead was twenty simultaneous monologues. People unmuted themselves to deliver prepared statements, then muted again, visibly checking email or other windows while colleagues spoke. No one built on anyone else's ideas. No one asked clarifying questions. The meeting concluded with the same divisions that began it, only now hardened by the performance of having "communicated."

This wasn't a failure of technology. It was a failure of understanding what communication requires. The digital tools that promise to connect us across distances can paradoxically deepen our isolation when we mistake their presence for genuine connection. The challenge we face isn't learning to use new platforms. It's learning to listen and converse authentically through them.

# THE ILLUSION OF DIGITAL CONNECTION

Consider the trajectory of how we communicate today. We participate in dozens of Slack channels, respond to hundreds of emails, attend countless video meetings, and maintain presence across multiple social media platforms. We have never been more reachable, never more responsive, never more "connected." Yet leaders consistently tell me their organizations feel fragmented, their teams disconnected, their people isolated despite constant digital interaction.

This paradox reveals something fundamental about the nature of communication. Connection isn't created by the transmission of information. It emerges from the quality of attention we give and receive, from the willingness to be genuinely present to another person, from the practice of seeking to understand rather than simply waiting our turn to transmit. These capacities, attention, presence, understanding, are precisely what our contemporary digital environment systematically undermines.

The problem isn't that digital communication lacks non-verbal cues, though that matters. It's that our digital communication practices have atrophied our capacity for the disciplines that make genuine communication possible. We have trained ourselves to scan rather than read, to formulate responses while others speak, to participate in conversations while simultaneously engaging three other platforms. We have optimized for speed and reach while sacrificing depth and understanding.

This deterioration of communication capacity poses particular challenges for organizations. Building adaptive organizations, those capable of learning, evolving, and responding effectively to complex challenges, requires something digital tools alone cannot provide. It requires the patient cultivation of genuine conversation, the practice of listening not just to respond but to understand, and the building of bridges across the differences that fragment our organizations into isolated silos.

# LISTENING ACROSS DIGITAL DISTANCE

In traditional face-to-face settings, certain social pressures encourage at least minimal listening. The person speaking can see if you're paying attention. The social cost of obviously ignoring someone sits across from you creates some constraint on our tendency toward self-absorption. Digital communication removes even these weak safeguards. Mute buttons let us tune out completely while maintaining the appearance of engagement. Multiple windows allow us to multitask through every interaction. The delayed nature of email and messaging removes any immediate accountability for whether we actually absorbed what someone said.

Yet listening, genuine, disciplined listening, is even more critical in digital contexts than face-to-face ones. Without visual cues and physical presence, the only way to bridge distance and build understanding is through the quality of attention we bring to others' words. This demands intentional practice.

Start by recognizing that listening through digital channels requires different disciplines than face-to-face listening. You cannot rely on your unconscious absorption of body language and tone. You must read more carefully, attend to word choice and phrasing more closely, and actively work to understand not just what is said but what concerns, questions, and assumptions lie beneath the surface of the words.

When someone sends you a message, whether email, chat, or document comment, resist the impulse to respond immediately. Instead, read twice. The first time, simply absorb what they've said. Notice your own reactions, but don't act on them yet. The second time, read specifically to understand their perspective. What are they concerned about? What are they trying to accomplish? What assumptions are they working from? What questions are they actually asking, whether explicitly stated or implied?

In video meetings, practice complete presence despite the temptations of multiple windows and notifications. Close everything except what's needed for the meeting. Take notes by hand if possible, it forces you to process and synthesize rather than transcribe. When others speak, watch them. Notice patterns in how they engage, what energizes them, what makes them hesitate. This attention builds understanding that goes far beyond the content of their words.

Perhaps most importantly, develop the discipline of asking clarifying questions before forming your response. In digital communication, where we often lose the immediate back-and-forth of conversation, this practice is essential. "Help me understand what you mean by..." "When you say X, are you thinking about..." "What would success look like from your perspective?" These questions slow down the rush to response and create space for genuine understanding to develop.

One leader I worked with transformed her team's dynamic by implementing what she called "the second question rule" in all digital interactions. Before responding to any message or speaking in any meeting, team members had to demonstrate understanding by asking at least one clarifying question. Initially, people found this frustrating. It seemed to slow everything down. But within weeks, they noticed something remarkable: far fewer misunderstandings, far less need for repeated explanations, and far more productive conversations because people actually understood each other's positions before trying to persuade, negotiate, or decide.

The challenge of listening digitally becomes even more acute when dealing with written communication that arrives at us constantly throughout the day. Email inboxes become battlegrounds where we fight for inbox zero rather than spaces where we genuinely engage with others' thinking. Slack channels become streams of notifications we scan rather than conversations we participate in meaningfully. The sheer volume of digital communication creates pressure to process quickly rather than understand deeply.

I've observed organizations where leaders receive hundreds of messages daily. The inevitable result is triage rather than engagement, quick scans to determine urgency, rapid-fire responses that address surface issues while missing deeper concerns, and a growing backlog of "lower priority" messages that represent real people seeking genuine connection or collaboration. This isn't sustainable, and it certainly doesn't build the understanding necessary for adaptive organizations.

The solution isn't better time management or faster reading. It's making strategic choices about how we allocate our limited attention. This means being honest about what we can genuinely engage with versus what we can only acknowledge. It means creating structures that reduce unnecessary digital communication rather than trying to process ever-increasing volumes. Most importantly, it means recognizing that a single message genuinely understood and thoughtfully responded to builds more organizational capacity than ten messages quickly processed.

Consider implementing designated times for deep engagement with digital communication, periods where you close all other windows, silence all notifications, and genuinely attend to what others are communicating. During these periods, read with the same attention you would bring to an in-person conversation. Take the time to understand not just the explicit content but the underlying concerns and questions. Craft responses that demonstrate this understanding rather than simply disposing of items in your inbox.

Between these periods of deep engagement, acknowledge receipt of messages but resist the pressure to respond substantively. A brief "I've received this and will respond thoughtfully by [specific time]" respects both the sender and your own capacity for genuine attention. This practice runs counter to the expectation of constant availability that characterizes much contemporary digital work culture. But it's precisely this expectation that makes genuine listening impossible.

## CULTIVATING GENUINE CONVERSATION DIGITALLY

If listening is difficult in digital contexts, genuine conversation is even more so. Real conversation, the collaborative exploration that creates new understanding, requires a rhythm and responsiveness that our digital tools often impede. Email's asynchronicity fragments conversation into disconnected exchanges. Chat's brevity and speed can reduce dialogue to rapid-fire exchanges lacking depth. Even video meetings, despite allowing real-time interaction, often devolve into presentations rather than conversations.

Yet adaptive organizations depend on genuine conversation. Innovation emerges from the collision and synthesis of diverse perspectives. Problems get solved through collaborative exploration rather than individual brilliance. Trust builds through the experience of thinking together, not just information exchange. Creating conditions for such conversation through digital channels requires deliberate practice and careful design.

Consider how different digital platforms enable or constrain different aspects of conversation. Email allows thoughtful composition but lacks spontaneity and makes it difficult to build on others' ideas. Video meetings allow real-time dialogue but can feel performative and make it hard for quieter voices to find space. Chat enables quick exchanges but discourages the patient development of complex ideas. None of these platforms is inherently superior for each serves conversation differently.

The key is matching the medium to the conversational purpose and then using it well. For exploratory conversations where you're trying to understand a situation or develop new ideas, use video meetings with small groups. Design these carefully: set clear questions or problems to explore, ensure everyone understands they're there to think together rather than present positions, and actively facilitate to create space for all voices while allowing ideas to build on each other.

For conversations requiring careful consideration of complex issues, use documents rather than email chains. Create a shared document where people can add thoughts, questions, and perspectives, then use video conversation to synthesize and build on what emerges. This separates the gathering of diverse perspectives from the work of integrating them, allowing both to happen more effectively than in real-time discussion alone.

For ongoing dialogue that builds relationships and maintains shared understanding within teams, use chat platforms well. This means resisting the temptation to use chat for everything. Reserve it for quick coordination and for building social connection through informal exchange. Recognize that chat is terrible for making decisions or resolving conflicts but excellent for maintaining the informal conversations that build trust and shared context.

One organization I observed transformed their team dynamics by implementing "thinking hours" or designated times when substantive issues were deliberately explored through structured conversation rather than rapid-fire messaging. During these video sessions, participants came prepared with questions rather than positions. The facilitator's role wasn't to drive toward decisions but to ensure all perspectives were heard and understood, to identify areas of agreement and genuine disagreement, and to help the group see patterns and possibilities that emerged from their collective thinking.

The results were striking. Issues that had generated dozens of fractured email exchanges and chat threads were often resolved in a single well-facilitated conversation. More importantly, the quality of understanding improved dramatically. People left these sessions with genuine clarity about both what was decided and why, about both the perspectives they agreed with and those they didn't.

This organization also discovered something unexpected: these structured conversations built conversational capacity that transferred to their everyday digital interactions. Team members who had experienced well-facilitated dialogue began bringing those practices to their informal exchanges. They asked better questions. They built on each other's ideas more effectively. They became more comfortable with disagreement because they had learned to distinguish between genuine conflicts requiring resolution and differences in perspective that could coexist productively.

The practice of genuine conversation also requires recognizing when digital channels are inadequate for the conversation you need to have. Sometimes the complexity of an issue, the sensitivity of relationships involved, or the number of stakeholders requiring alignment means that no amount of skilled digital communication will suffice. In these cases, the question isn't how to conduct the conversation digitally but whether to attempt it digitally at all.

I've seen organizations waste weeks in email exchanges trying to resolve issues that were settled in a single in-person conversation when that became possible. While geography often makes physical gathering impractical, the cost of digital-only conversation for truly complex or sensitive matters can exceed the cost of bringing people together. Leaders of adaptive organizations make strategic choices about when to insist on richer forms of interaction rather than defaulting to whatever channel is most convenient.

This doesn't mean abandoning digital communication. Rather, it means using it strategically. Use asynchronous digital channels to gather perspectives, share information, and prepare for synchronous conversation. Use video meetings for genuine dialogue and collaborative thinking. Use in-person gatherings for the most complex negotiations, sensitive discussions, or relationship-building that underpins all other collaboration. Each channel serves conversation differently; the art lies in orchestrating them effectively.

This practice transforms digital conflicts from battles to be won into problems to be solved collaboratively. When people feel genuinely understood, even in disagreement, they become far more willing to seek creative solutions rather than dig into positions. The quality of understanding becomes the foundation for productive resolution.

The development of this deeper empathy through digital channels also requires attention to power dynamics and positional authority. In face-to-face settings, social cues often provide information about hierarchies and power relationships that influence how people communicate. Digital communication can flatten these hierarchies in productive ways, a junior team member may feel more comfortable raising concerns via email than in a physical meeting with senior leaders. But it can also obscure power dynamics in ways that undermine genuine understanding.

Leaders must work deliberately to ensure that digital communication doesn't simply recreate or reinforce existing hierarchies and silences. This means actively soliciting input from those who might not volunteer it. It means creating structures that ensure all voices are heard, not just those belonging to people most comfortable with particular digital platforms or communication styles. It means recognizing that some forms of digital communication favor certain personalities and communication styles while disadvantaging others.

I've observed organizations where the shift to primarily digital communication inadvertently silenced important voices. People who thrive in spontaneous verbal exchange but struggle with written communication. Those who need time to process before responding. Individuals whose communication styles don't translate well to brief text-based exchanges. Leaders building adaptive organizations recognize these dynamics and deliberately create diverse channels and formats to ensure all valuable perspectives can be contributed and heard.

This might mean supplementing real-time video discussions with asynchronous opportunities to contribute in writing. It might mean explicitly inviting quiet participants to share their thinking. It might mean using anonymous input gathering for sensitive issues where social dynamics might prevent honest contribution. The specific practices matter less than the underlying commitment to ensuring that the quality of conversation isn't determined by who speaks fastest or most assertively in any particular medium.

## BUILDING BRIDGES ACROSS DIGITAL DIVIDES

Perhaps the most serious challenge digital communication poses is how it reinforces the echo chambers and silos that already fragment our organizations and communities. Without the informal hallway conversations and spontaneous interactions of physical proximity, digital workers increasingly interact only with their immediate teams. Different departments, locations, and functions develop separate vocabularies, assumptions, and priorities. The organization becomes a collection of tribes rather than a coherent whole.

This fragmentation is precisely what adaptive organizations cannot afford. Complex challenges require diverse perspectives working together. Innovation emerges at the boundaries between different domains of expertise. But digital communication, if not deliberately managed, turns boundaries into barriers.

Building bridges across these digital divides requires more than good technology. It requires identifying and pursuing what I call genuine projects, initiatives that matter to multiple groups and require their collaboration to succeed. These projects create contexts where people with different perspectives and priorities must genuinely engage each other. They provide concrete reasons to listen across differences and to find common ground despite disagreement.

The key is to identify projects where the success criteria themselves demand cross-group collaboration. Not top-down initiatives imposed on reluctant participants, but challenges that people from different parts of the organization genuinely care about and recognize they cannot solve alone. Finding these projects requires listening to understand what different groups care about, what frustrates them, what they see as opportunities.

One company I worked with had deep divisions between their engineering and customer support teams. Engineers saw support as simply not understanding the product's sophistication. Support saw engineers as indifferent to user experience. Digital communication had hardened these divisions because the groups rarely interacted directly, and when they did, it was usually in the context of finger-pointing over problems.

The breakthrough came when a mid-level manager identified a genuine project: reducing the support burden of a particularly problematic feature. Both teams cared about this, but for different reasons. Support wanted fewer frustrated customers. Engineering wanted fewer interruptions to focus on new development. By framing this as a shared challenge rather than either team's problem, she created space for genuine collaboration.

The key was how she facilitated their initial digital conversations. Rather than starting with solutions, she had each team articulate what they understood about the problem. This required real listening where support had to understand the technical constraints engineers faced, engineers had to grasp the actual user experience support dealt with daily. Only after this foundation of mutual understanding did they discuss approaches.

The project succeeded in reducing support volume, but its more important impact was transforming the relationship between these teams. They developed shared vocabulary and understanding. They saw each other as resources rather than obstacles. They built trust through the experience of working together effectively. And all of this happened primarily through digital channels, because the quality of conversation improved dramatically once they had a genuine shared purpose.

## CREATING CONDITIONS FOR GENUINE DIGITAL DIALOGUE

For leaders seeking to build adaptive organizations in digital environments, the challenge is creating conditions where listening and genuine conversation can flourish despite the constraints of digital media. This requires moving beyond the instrumental view of communication as information transmission and recognizing it as the practice through which we build understanding, forge relationships, and create shared meaning.

Begin by examining your organization's digital communication norms. What behaviors do they reward? Speed? Volume? The appearance of engagement? Or genuine understanding, thoughtful response, and collaborative exploration? Most organizations inadvertently optimize for the former while claiming to value the latter.

Create space for reflection and genuine response. One leader I worked with implemented a simple rule: any substantive email or message should prompt not immediate response but considered reply after at least one hour. This single change transformed the quality of their team's communication. People stopped firing off quick reactions and started crafting thoughtful responses. Misunderstandings decreased dramatically. The time "lost" to delayed response was more than recovered through reduced back-and-forth clarification.

Design your video meetings to facilitate conversation rather than presentation. This means smaller groups, longer time per topic, and explicit facilitation to ensure all voices are heard. It means starting many meetings not with updates but with questions to explore together. It means ending by reflecting not just on what was decided but on what was learned.

Use documents to think together asynchronously. Rather than discussing complex issues only in real-time meetings, create shared documents where team members can add their perspectives, questions, and insights. Then use video meetings to synthesize, explore tensions, and build shared understanding. This separates the generation of diverse input from the work of integration, allowing both to happen more effectively.

Perhaps most importantly, explicitly value listening and genuine conversation as leadership competencies. Recognize and reward leaders who demonstrate these capacities. Share examples of effective listening and conversation. Create opportunities for people to develop and practice these skills in contexts where the stakes aren't too high.

One organization developed a regular practice they called "difficult conversations." Once a month, they brought together people with genuinely different perspectives on some challenging issue facing the organization. The explicit goal wasn't to resolve the issue but to ensure all perspectives were deeply understood. A skilled facilitator helped participants articulate their views, listen to others', and identify both areas of genuine disagreement and potential common ground. These sessions built tremendous capacity for productive dialogue across difference throughout the organization.

## EMPATHY AS UNDERSTANDING IN DIGITAL CONTEXTS

Much discussion of digital communication focuses on "showing empathy" through word choice, emojis, and response timing. These matter, but they address symptoms rather than causes. The fundamental challenge isn't making our messages seem empathetic. It's actually developing the understanding that genuine empathy requires.

Empathy, in this deeper sense, is not primarily an emotional response but an intellectual and imaginative practice. It's the disciplined effort to understand how situations look from perspectives different than your own, to grasp what others value and fear, to recognize the logic in positions that seem wrong to you. This understanding cannot be signaled through clever phrasing. It must be built through patient listening and genuine conversation.

In digital environments, this is simultaneously harder and more necessary. Harder because the cues that help us understand others in person are absent. More necessary because without this understanding, the distance and asynchronicity of digital communication allow misunderstanding to fester and grow unchecked.

Building this understanding requires systematic practice. When conflicts arise through digital channels, resist the temptation to respond immediately. Instead, work to understand the other person's perspective until you can articulate it in a way they would recognize as accurate. This doesn't mean agreeing with them. It means genuinely grasping how the situation looks from where they sit.

When someone's message frustrates or confuses you, don't respond with your reaction. Instead, ask questions to understand their position more fully. "Help me understand what concerns you about this approach." "What would need to be true for this to work from your perspective?" "What am I missing about the situation you're facing?" These questions aren't rhetorical devices. They're genuine inquiries to build understanding.

This practice transforms digital conflicts from battles to be won into problems to be solved collaboratively. When people feel genuinely understood, even in disagreement, they become far more willing to seek creative solutions rather than dig into positions. The quality of understanding becomes the foundation for productive resolution.

## THE PATH FORWARD

Digital communication will not revert to face-to-face interaction. If anything, geographic distribution of teams and work will continue to increase. The question isn't whether to communicate digitally but how to communicate effectively despite and sometimes because of digital channels' constraints.

The answer lies in deliberately cultivating the practices of listening and genuine conversation that our digital environment undermines. This requires recognizing that technology itself is neutral. It's our practices in using it that determine whether it connects or divides, enlightens or obscures, builds understanding or deepens confusion.

Leaders in adaptive organizations recognize this. They don't simply adopt new platforms and hope for the best. They design their digital communication practices to create conditions for genuine listening and conversation. They identify and pursue genuine projects that give diverse groups reasons to collaborate authentically. They build bridges across the digital divides that fragment their organizations.

This work isn't easy. It requires swimming against powerful currents in our contemporary communication culture. The pressure for speed over understanding, the bias toward broadcasting over dialogue, the preference for agreement over genuine engagement with difference.

But the organizations and leaders willing to do this work build something increasingly rare and valuable: the capacity for genuine connection and collective intelligence despite geographic distance and digital mediation.

As we move forward in an increasingly digital world, the competitive advantage belongs not to organizations with the best technology but to those with the best communication practices. It belongs to leaders who understand that empathy isn't performed through careful word choice but built through disciplined listening and genuine conversation. It belongs to teams that bridge differences not through superficial agreement but through patient understanding and authentic collaboration.

The tools we use to communicate will continue to evolve. The platforms will change. The technologies will improve. But the fundamental requirements for genuine connection remain constant: the willingness to listen deeply, the commitment to understand perspectives different from our own, the patience to engage in real conversation rather than sequential monologue, and the courage to build bridges across the divides that fragment us.

These capacities, more than any technology, determine whether our digital communication connects or divides, builds understanding or deepens confusion, creates adaptive organizations or rigid ones.

The choice before us is clear. We can continue treating digital communication as primarily information transmission, optimizing for speed and reach while accepting shallow engagement and persistent misunderstanding.

Or we can recognize that genuine communication, the kind that builds adaptive organizations and connected communities, requires disciplined practice in listening and conversation, practices that must be deliberately cultivated in digital contexts precisely because our tools and norms systematically undermine them.

The organizations and leaders who choose the latter path will build something increasingly rare and valuable in our digitally mediated age: the capacity for genuine connection, mutual understanding, and collaborative intelligence despite distance and difference.

9

# THE COMING OF ARTIFICIAL INTELLIGENCE AND ITS IMPACT ON LEAD TO LISTEN

In the second decade of the 21st century into which we have just entered, artificial intelligence will become more ubiquitous as a tool in various domains and will clearly have an impact on the challenge of listening to lead.

The arrival of artificial intelligence as a transformative force in human organizations marks not merely a technological shift but a fundamental challenge to the communicative architectures that determine whether institutions can adapt or ossify.

For the framework developed in Listen to Lead, which positions disciplined listening, authentic conversation, and operational empathy as the core capabilities for navigating complexity and chaos, AI represents both an unprecedented threat and an unexpected opportunity.

The question is not whether AI will change leadership communication, but whether leaders will use these tools to deepen human understanding or to accelerate the very disconnection and fragmentation the book identifies as the central crisis of contemporary organizational life.

This chapter examines how AI intersects with the three pillars of Listen to Lead — disciplined listening, authentic conversation, and operational empathy — and argues that AI will sharply raise the premium on leaders who practice these arts while exposing those who have reduced communication to performance, messaging, and metrics. Drawing on insights from military transformation, particularly the shift from platform-centric to network-centric warfare, we can see that AI's impact on leadership mirrors broader patterns: technologies that promise efficiency simultaneously create new vulnerabilities that only human judgment and relational capacity can address.

## THE PARALLEL WITH MILITARY TRANSFORMATION

The defense sector's experience with technological disruption offers a useful lens for understanding AI's impact on leadership communication. Over the past two decades, military organizations have confronted a fundamental shift from platform-centric operations to network-centric operations, where effectiveness depends on sensor-to-shooter integration and distributed decision-making. This transformation has revealed a paradox: the more sophisticated the technology, the more critical becomes the human capacity for sense-making and adaptive collaboration.

The F-35 Lightning II exemplifies this shift. Its value lies not simply in its kinetic capabilities but in its role as an information node within a larger network. Pilots have evolved from individual aviators to cognitive managers who must synthesize data from multiple sources and communicate effectively with both manned and unmanned assets. The technical capability is meaningless without pilots who can listen to what the network tells them and exercise empathetic judgment about second-order effects.

Similarly, the Marine Corps' Force Design 2030 represents a pivot from hierarchical command structures to distributed decision-making. This transformation requires not just new equipment but fundamental cultural shift: from information hoarding to radical transparency. The Marines discovered that technological modernization without cultural transformation produces only expensive failures, platforms that cannot integrate, data that cannot be shared, units that cannot collaborate when traditional communication channels are disrupted.

These examples reveal a critical insight: advanced technology amplifies rather than eliminates the need for the human practices *Listen to Lead* describes. When operations become too complex for any single node to comprehend, the organizations that prevail are those whose members have internalized the disciplines of listening across difference, conversing under pressure, and exercising empathetic judgment amid radical uncertainty.

# AI AS AMPLIFIER OF EXISTING PATHOLOGIES

*Listen to Lead* diagnoses contemporary organizations as suffering from an epidemic of pseudo-communication: leaders who confuse broadcasting with dialogue, meetings structured around performance rather than learning, and cultures where people wait to speak rather than working to understand. AI threatens to supercharge these pathologies by providing leaders with sophisticated tools for avoiding genuine engagement.

AI-generated summaries promise to distill hours of meetings into bullet points. Sentiment analysis claims to reveal team morale without actual conversation. Predictive models offer to anticipate stakeholder reactions. For executives already inclined toward "managing from the dashboard," these tools create the illusion that they can understand their organizations without the slow work of listening.

This dynamic mirrors what military strategists call the "headquarters fallacy" or the belief that comprehensive data feeds can provide situational awareness equivalent to what frontline operators possess through direct experience. In Iraq and Afghanistan, commanders learned that satellite imagery and algorithmic pattern analysis could not substitute for the tacit knowledge embedded in units that had built relationships with local populations. The data looked comprehensive; the understanding was superficial.

The speed bias AI introduces compounds this problem. *Listen to Lead* emphasizes that authentic listening requires patience, the discipline to suspend one's own agenda and allow others space to discover what they think. AI systems are optimized for velocity: instant responses, real-time recommendations. When decisiveness is confused with speed, the leader who pauses to ask an open question can appear inefficient. Yet organizations that cannot slow down enough to actually listen cannot learn, and those that cannot learn cannot adapt.

The echo chamber effect represents perhaps the most insidious risk. AI recommendation systems excel at delivering content that confirms existing assumptions. For leaders, this means AI-curated feeds that systematically filter out dissenting views and perspectives from the organizational periphery. The tribalization *Listen to Lead* identifies becomes algorithmically reinforced, with each executive inhabiting a personalized reality that diverges from both colleagues and frontline teams.

## AI AS ENABLER OF DEEPER LISTENING

Yet AI need not function only as amplifier of dysfunction. Used with intentionality, AI can create conditions that make genuine listening more possible and more systematic.

Consider transcription and documentation. One hidden cost of listening is the cognitive load of simultaneously attending to others while tracking the conversation's evolution. AI transcription captures what was said, freeing leaders to focus on how things are said, the hesitations and emotional undertones that reveal what people really mean. Post-meeting, AI can identify patterns across multiple conversations, surfacing themes no single participant could track.

Translation and accessibility tools offer similar potential. *Listen to Lead* emphasizes the challenge of listening across differences, across functions and cultures that use different vocabularies. AI can help finance professionals understand engineering constraints and vice versa. The risk is treating machine-mediated paraphrases as sufficient. The opportunity is using AI to accelerate the mechanics of understanding so leaders can spend more time on the probing questions that reveal underlying values and assumptions.

More ambitiously, AI can function as a diagnostic tool revealing where listening is breaking down. Network analysis can show which voices are systematically excluded, which teams have stopped exchanging information, and which issues are discussed everywhere except officially. These are not substitutes for human attention but triggers for it, early warnings telling leaders where to direct their capacity for deep listening.

The Marine Corps' adoption of Live-Virtual-Constructive training environments illustrates this principle. By integrating live exercises with simulations, the Marines create training scenarios more complex than traditional exercises allow. These environments generate vast data about how units communicate under pressure. AI analytics help instructors identify communication breakdowns and cognitive overload points, enabling targeted interventions. The technology doesn't replace instructor judgment; it extends perceptual range and allows human mentorship where it matters most.

## CONVERSATION IN THE AGE OF SYNTHETIC SPEECH

*Listen to Lead* distinguishes sharply between debate, which seeks victory, and genuine conversation, which is collaborative exploration where participants think better together than alone. AI complicates this art by flooding the conversational space with plausible but disembodied language.

The proliferation of AI-generated text creates what might be called "conversational pollution": messages optimized for effect but untethered from authentic struggle with difficult questions. When every statement is algorithmically polished, the room for hesitation and genuine co-discovery shrinks. The awkward phrase revealing someone working through confusion, the unfinished sentence inviting collective completion, the productive silence where people are actually thinking, these markers of authentic conversation become increasingly rare.

This echoes challenges in military command as autonomous systems become more prevalent. When AI can generate tactically sound recommendations faster than humans can articulate them, there is pressure to simply execute rather than engage in collaborative planning. Yet combat experience shows that missions succeed not when everyone follows the optimal plan but when everyone understands the intent deeply enough to adapt when plans inevitably fail.

Similarly, organizational breakthroughs often emerge at the intersection of perspectives that initially appear incompatible. This requires leaders who protect space for dissent and unresolved tension who resist premature closure even when AI could synthesize a "consensus" position. The leader's role becomes less about having the answer and more about hosting the conversation: asking the question that reframes the problem, noticing whose voice hasn't been heard, holding the group in discomfort long enough for unexpected insights to emerge.

Structured conversation protocols become more important in an AI-rich environment. Techniques like written reflection before speaking and explicit norms valuing bridge-building questions can counterbalance AI's tendency toward frictionless efficiency. These practices create deliberate inefficiencies, productive slowness, that prevent conversations from collapsing into either algorithmic determinism or performative debate.

# EMPATHY AS COMPETITIVE ADVANTAGE

*Listen to Lead* defines empathy not as sentimentality but as the disciplined effort to understand others' experiences well enough to state their view in a way they would recognize. This operational empathy allows leaders to uncover hidden constraints, foresee implementation challenges, and design decisions people can accept even when they disagree.

AI emotional analytics, sentiment analysis, facial recognition, predictive engagement models, promise to make empathy scalable. Leaders can monitor thousands of employees' morale in real time and tailor communications to anticipated reactions. This is empathy as management technique, extracted from relationship and operationalized as control.

The risk is profound. When leaders treat feelings as data points to be managed rather than realities to be encountered, they practice what *Listen to Lead* calls "performative listening" or simulating attention while remaining unchanged by what they hear. AI makes it possible to simulate empathy at industrial scale: personalized messages generated from sentiment patterns, interventions triggered by algorithmic flags. People sense when concern is scripted. Trust erodes.

Yet the deeper danger is what reliance on algorithmic inference does to leaders themselves. If emotional intelligence requires self-awareness and self-regulation or the capacity to recognize one's own triggers and choose constructive responses under pressure, then outsourcing emotional diagnosis to machines atrophies exactly the capabilities leaders most need. The disciplined pause between stimulus and response gets squeezed out by systems that urge immediate, optimized reactions.

The alternative is treating AI as prosthetic rather than replacement: a tool that expands the leader's field of attention but does not short-circuit empathic encounter. If analytics suggest a team is anxious, the next step is not deploying a pre-written intervention but convening a conversation, listening deeply, and allowing those affected to articulate their own meaning. AI surfaces the question; humans pursue the understanding.

This approach finds support in military lessons about human-machine teaming. The most effective applications of autonomous systems are not those where machines replace human judgment but where they handle routine cognitive tasks, monitoring, pattern recognition, freeing operators to focus on relationship-building and contextual interpretation. Similarly, AI that handles routine emotional monitoring can give leaders more capacity for the face-to-face encounters where genuine empathy actually operates.

## CHAOS MANAGEMENT AND THE EMPATHETIC AI-AUGMENTED LEADER

*Listen to Lead* portrays contemporary organizational life as an era of permanent disruption characterized by compressed time, ubiquitous crises, and overwhelming information flows. It introduces "wicked problems" that cannot be definitively solved, only engaged through continuous learning and collaborative sense-making. Empathy, operationalized through listening and conversation, is the foundational capability for navigating this chaos.

AI amplifies both the chaos and the adaptive possibility. On one hand, AI-driven automation, disinformation, and economic disruption accelerate the rate at which old certainties collapse. On the other, AI can detect emerging patterns, integrate diverse data streams, and support scenario exploration beyond unaided human capacity.

The decisive variable is whether leaders use AI to substitute for or to extend human empathy. Substitution produces exactly the brittle hierarchies and communicative breakdowns the book documents: decisions made far from lived reality, teams reduced to implementers of opaque models, cultures of cynicism. Extension means using AI to widen the circle of voices in sense-making, reveal mismatches between official narratives and ground truth, and create more time for conversations that matter.

In the augmented model, listening, conversation, and empathy become the distinguishing human capacities determining which organizations harness AI for good. Leaders who can listen across disciplines and cultures, host conversations where people think together better than any algorithm alone, and hold authority and vulnerability in tension will integrate AI into genuine projects that unite people around real challenges. Those who cannot will possess sophisticated tools and declining trust.

The potential impact of artificial intelligence on *Listen to Lead*'s framework, then, is not to automate empathy out of existence but to make its presence or absence more visible and consequential. In a world where AI generates flawless talking points and instant answers, what distinguishes credible leaders is their willingness to be fully present, ask questions with no pre-computed response, and let others' perspectives genuinely alter their thinking.

Machines process language; only humans decide to listen. The coming of AI does not change this fundamental truth. It only raises the stakes of ignoring it.

# THE GENERATIONAL FRACTURE: HOW AGE-CODED REALITIES TEST THE LIMITS OF LISTENING

The most disorienting aspect of leading across generations is not simply that younger and older cohorts disagree, It is that they increasingly inhabit mutually unintelligible worlds.

A senior executive who came of age when organizations were information gatekeepers now leads teams socialized in environments where information is commodified to the point of worthlessness, where authority must justify itself constantly, and where peer networks carry more epistemic weight than institutional hierarchies.

These are not superficial differences in style. They represent fundamentally different experiences of how organizations function, how knowledge moves, and what constitutes legitimate grounds for followership.

Generational divergence poses a specific challenge to the "listen to lead" framework: it multiplies the simultaneous realities a leader must track, fragments the shared language necessary for dialogue, and exposes how much of what passes for listening is pattern-matching against one's own generational assumptions.

Leaders who fail to reckon with this systematically misread the people they aim to lead, interpreting resistance as obstinacy, skepticism as disrespect, and silence as consent when each may mean something radically different to cohorts shaped by distinct technological, economic, and social ecosystems.

## THE COLLAPSE OF SHARED REFERENCE POINTS

Previous generations moved through broadly similar informational landscapes. Disagreements existed, but they played out against shared references and mutually comprehensible authority structures.

That common ground has disintegrated. Each generation now develops its professional identity in a distinct media ecology. Older leaders spent formative years where information scarcity made knowledge power, face-to-face interaction was primary, and career progression followed predictable timelines. Younger professionals were socialized where information is hyper-abundant but curation scarce, digital networks allow instant community assembly around shared grievances, and traditional career ladders have been visibly dismantled by successive restructuring, automation, and precariousness.

Identical organizational experiences are processed through incompatible frames. When a senior leader announces restructuring, they may believe they are communicating strategic clarity. A younger employee hears yet another iteration of churn that has characterized their entire working life, interprets it through frameworks learned in online communities, and responds with wariness the leader reads as cynicism rather than reasonable pattern recognition across multiple employers.

This is not communication failure in any conventional sense. It is collision of interpretive frameworks so divergent that identical sentences carry radically different semantic and emotional freight depending on age-coded lens. Leaders operating under the illusion that because they have spoken, they have been understood or that because younger employees nod in meetings, genuine alignment exists are dangerously mistaken.

# DIGITAL PLATFORMS AS
# GENERATIONAL SORTING MECHANISMS

Social media platforms actively deepen generational differences by feeding each age cohort content optimized to confirm existing worldviews. Older leaders consume news reinforcing narratives of meritocracy and institutional stability. Younger professionals encounter streams highlighting systemic inequity and institutional failures.

Within organizations, this manifests as mutual invisibility. Senior leadership discusses strategy and resource allocation. Younger staff circulate analyses of workplace culture and value gaps in age-segregated digital communities. These parallel conversations rarely intersect meaningfully because each generation validates understanding within platforms the other neither sees nor comprehends.

Leaders often have no idea what younger employees are actually thinking or discussing. They mistake silence in formal settings for acquiescence, unaware that robust critique happens continuously in channels they don't access. This invisible discourse shapes how younger employees interpret every leadership action, repeatedly blindsiding leaders with reactions they never anticipated.

This information fragmentation undermines listening at its foundation. When leaders and younger employees consume different informational diets shaped by platforms designed to maximize engagement through confirmation, cognitive distance widens until mutual comprehension requires extraordinary deliberate effort.


# AGE-CODED EMOTIONAL ECOLOGIES

Each cohort brings distinct affective patterns from formative experiences. Older leaders carry emotional substrates from eras when job security was attainable and career progression legible. Even when intellectually aware these conditions no longer hold, their emotional reflexes produce instinctive responses, frustration at "lack of loyalty," bewilderment at "unrealistic expectations", that reference a vanished world.

Younger professionals were emotionally formed in permanent

instability. They watched parents laid off despite decades of service, witnessed industries evaporate, and absorbed messaging that they must be perpetually entrepreneurial and individually responsible for navigating structural risks previous generations addressed collectively. The resulting ecology is strategic detachment, vigilant self-protection, and expectation that organizations will betray commitments when economically convenient.

These patterns collide constantly. An older leader extends what they believe is generous stretch responsibility; a younger employee hears invitation to unpaid overwork yielding no security. A younger professional requests remote flexibility; a senior manager perceives lack of commitment and interprets it through their experience of "paying dues" through presence. Both operate from entirely reasonable emotional logics grounded in incompatible lived realities.

For listening, leaders must recognize and regulate their own age-coded emotional reactions while developing enough generational empathy to understand that younger cohorts express not moral failing but adaptive response to fundamentally different circumstances.

## THE ATROPHY OF CONVERSATIONAL INFRASTRUCTURE

One damaging consequence of generational divergence is erosion of organizational conversational competence. Where age cohorts talk past one another, organizations retreat into bureaucratic process: standardized meetings, templated communications, one-way announcements disguised as dialogue. These forms paper over gaps while allowing misunderstanding to compound beneath procedural compliance.

Genuine conversation, collaborative construction of shared understanding through iterative exchange, becomes vanishingly rare. Town halls become performative rituals with pre-screened questions. "Listening sessions" collect grievances that are acknowledged but not acted upon, teaching participants their input is decorative. Meetings cycle through presentations where speakers wait their turn without genuinely engaging others.

This conversational atrophy hits younger generations particularly hard because they are asked to speak up while experiencing that their perspectives have no material impact. The result is learned cynicism that senior leaders misread as apathy, when it is rational adaptation to pseudo-dialogue. Younger employees perform participation while reserving real thinking for peer conversations where shared generational frameworks make mutual comprehension achievable.

Leaders wanting to listen across generations face a bootstrapping problem: creating conditions for authentic dialogue requires first acknowledging existing conversational infrastructure is failing. This demands fundamental redesign of how conversations are structured, who speaks when, how dissent is invited and protected, and whether leadership will genuinely have its assumptions challenged by people decades younger seeing the organization through incompatible lenses.

## THE PROBLEM OF DUAL-USE LANGUAGE

A particularly insidious dimension of generational fracture is dual-use language, words carrying entirely different meanings depending on age. Terms like "accountability," "flexibility," "teamwork," and "commitment" function as semantic traps, appearing to establish common ground while masking profound disagreement.

When a senior leader speaks of "accountability," they often mean answerability within established hierarchies: you are accountable to your manager, who is accountable upward. When a younger employee hears "accountability," they increasingly mean horizontal transparency: everyone accountable to everyone through mechanisms that make power visible and subject to challenge. These are fundamentally opposed visions of organizational authority.

Similarly, "flexibility" to an older manager might mean generous accommodation of occasional personal needs within a framework where physical presence remains default. To a younger professional, "flexibility" means self-direction over when, where, and how work gets done, a claim to autonomy challenging the entire architecture of supervision many senior leaders take for granted.

This linguistic ambiguity makes listening exceptionally difficult because superficial agreement masks fundamental misalignment until conflict erupts over implementation. To listen effectively across this divide, leaders must develop "semantic suspicion", pausing when apparent agreement comes too easily and explicitly testing whether both parties use terms the same way. This is laborious work, but without it, organizational communication is simply two monologues in different languages sharing superficial vocabulary.

## PROJECTS AS GENERATIONAL TRANSLATION DEVICES

One effective strategy for bridging generational divides is deployment of "genuine projects" or concrete endeavors with clear stakes that cannot succeed without integrating age-diverse perspectives. Abstract appeals to "understand each other" typically fail because they ask for empathy without material incentives for difficult mutual comprehension work. Projects make cross-generational listening instrumental: people learn to translate across age-coded worldviews because failure to do so produces visible, consequential failures.

When an older technical expert and younger professional with digital fluency must jointly solve an operational problem, generational differences become resources rather than obstacles. The older professional's institutional memory prevents reinventing failed solutions; the younger professional's facility with new tools unblocks pathways the senior person would never discover. Shared accomplishment builds trust no amount of training can manufacture.

Leaders who recognize this don't just "manage diversity"; they actively engineer conditions where age-diverse collaboration becomes necessary for success. This requires deliberate team design, explicit articulation of what each generation brings, and protection of junior voices against default hierarchies.

The payoff extends beyond immediate projects. These collaborations create informal bridges, individuals who develop fluency translating concerns and communication styles across generations because they have worked through real problems together. They embody in practice what formal training attempts to teach: that generational differences are conditions to be worked with through disciplined attention and mutual investment.

# FROM AUTHORITY TO FACILITATION: THE GENERATIONAL LEADERSHIP TRANSITION

Underlying these challenges is a deeper shift in leadership itself, one that generational fracture both reflects and accelerates. In stable organizational environments, leadership rested on authority: accumulated expertise, positional power, and information control gave senior leaders legitimate claim to make decisions others would implement. Generational deference reinforced this; younger employees expected direction and gained status demonstrating competence within frameworks elders defined.

This model is collapsing under accelerating change, information abundance, and legitimacy crisis affecting traditional institutions. No single generation possesses sufficient knowledge to make consistently good decisions in isolation. Complexity and velocity of contemporary challenges exceed any individual's cognitive capacity, regardless of experience. Meanwhile, younger cohorts have been taught by repeated institutional failures to be deeply skeptical of leaders claiming special insight simply by virtue of position.

The result is fundamental reorientation of the leadership role: from authority figure providing answers to facilitator creating conditions for collective intelligence to emerge. This does not mean leaders abdicate decision-making or pretend all perspectives carry equal weight. It means acknowledging that knowledge required for adaptive decision-making is distributed across age cohorts, functions, and levels and that extracting and integrating that knowledge requires conversational infrastructure most organizations have not built.

This transition is profoundly difficult for leaders whose professional identity was built on being the person with answers. It requires reframing what leadership means or a shift from "I lead by deciding" to "I lead by creating conditions for better decisions than any of us could make alone." For many senior leaders, this feels like loss of authority, when it is actually recognition that effective leadership in high-complexity environments requires distributing sense-making across diverse cognitive and generational resources.

# CONCLUSION: LISTENING AS CONTINUOUS GENERATIONAL INQUIRY

The generational challenge to "listen to lead" is not a puzzle to be solved but a permanent condition to be managed through disciplined practice. Divergence in formative experiences, informational ecologies, emotional patterns, and adaptive orientations across age cohorts will not diminish; accelerating change suggests it will intensify. Leaders waiting for generational tensions to resolve are waiting for a future that will not arrive.

What is required is institutionalization of generational inquiry as leadership practice. This means building into organizational routines explicit moments where age-diverse groups articulate how they experience the same situation differently. It means treating generational interpretation gaps as intelligence rather than nuisance, as signals about divergent realities leaders need to understand if decisions are to land effectively. It means accepting that genuine listening across generations is slow and awkward but that organizations forgoing this work make decisions in ignorance that compounds over time.

Most fundamentally, it requires leaders to surrender the fiction that because they speak a shared language in a shared organization, they operate in shared reality. They do not. The 25-year-old and 55-year-old in the same meeting process that meeting through frameworks so divergent that mutual comprehension requires deliberate, sustained effort.

Leaders who recognize this and design conversational practices accordingly do not eliminate generational friction, but they prevent it from metastasizing into organizational dysfunction that occurs when people who think they understand each other discover far too late that they have been talking past one another all along.

# CONCLUSION

Empathetic communication is not a decorative extra for leaders; it is the operating system that allows organizations and communities to stay coherent, adaptive, and human in an era of permanent disruption.

Leaders now work inside a cauldron of compressed time, constant crisis, and fragmented information where no one vantage point can see the whole. In this environment, old assumptions that stability is normal and chaos is the exception have collapsed, and attempts to "return to normal" only deepen brittleness.

Digital networks and AI have amplified these pressures by accelerating communication while undermining shared reality, creating echo chambers, generational fractures, and institutions that struggle to hold a common conversation. The result is organizations and polities that are technically connected but communicatively fragmented, with growing gaps between where decisions are made and where consequences are lived.

Across the domains explored in this book, from ministries of defense and joint forces to corporations, public agencies, and families, the same pattern recurs when things go right.

Leaders treat listening as a disciplined practice rather than a courtesy, making room to hear what they have not yet understood instead of rehearsing their next argument.

Conversation is reframed from a contest to be won into a shared exploration where people think better together than they could alone, especially when they begin far apart.

Empathy is exercised as operational intelligence: the effort to understand others' realities well enough that their concerns, constraints, and purposes can be stated in a way they recognize, even when their preferred outcome cannot be delivered.

When these practices are present, wicked problems become more workable, generational divides become sources of insight rather than paralysis, and new organizational forms, like distributed, networked forces or cross-functional teams, gain the human connective tissue they require to function.

The coming wave of AI, digital mediation, and generational realignment does not make empathy obsolete; it raises the premium on it. Tools that summarize, predict, and simulate can easily be used to avoid real engagement, creating synthetic understanding that looks precise but misses what actually matters. Yet the same tools, used differently, can open more space for human judgment by handling routine cognitive load and revealing where listening is breaking down.

The leaders who will matter in this next phase are not those with the most perfect dashboards, but those who:

- Refuse the shortcut of performative listening, insisting on encounters where their own thinking may be changed by what they hear.
- Design "genuine projects" that require people from different services, generations, cultures, and disciplines to succeed together, so that empathy is built in shared work, not in abstract training.
- Balance empathetic understanding with clear authority, making decisions that some will dislike but many can accept because their perspectives were genuinely engaged.

In such leadership, empathy does not replace authority; it makes authority more effective and more legitimate under conditions of uncertainty.

There is a deeper test embedded in this approach, one that separates leaders who truly listen from those who merely process inputs. It is the willingness to be surprised, to encounter information, perspectives, or realities that do not fit your existing mental models and to let that surprise reshape your understanding rather than dismissing it as noise.

In military transformation, I have watched this capacity determine which organizations adapt and which calcify. The services that thrived through the shift from platform-centric to network-centric warfare were not those with the best technology, but those whose leaders created space for junior officers, enlisted personnel, and civilians to challenge assumptions about how wars would be fought. They built "thinking organizations" not through doctrine alone, but through systematic practice in taking seriously what did not fit.

The same dynamic appears in corporate strategy, policy design, and family systems. Organizations that can be collectively surprised that can absorb disconfirming evidence without fragmenting possess a strategic advantage that no amount of forecasting or scenario planning can replicate. They learn faster because they have built the relational infrastructure that allows uncomfortable truths to travel upward and inward rather than being filtered out by layers of defensive reasoning.

This capacity is not innate; it is constructed through deliberate design. It requires leaders who model intellectual humility, systems that reward people for surfacing problems rather than hiding them, and rhythms of interaction that create space for reflection rather than constant reaction. Most critically, it demands that listening be understood not as information gathering but as a practice that changes the listener.

The framework I have developed around "chaos management" rather than crisis management captures something essential about the leadership challenge you face. Crises have beginnings and ends; chaos is the operating environment. Crises are temporary deviations from normal; chaos reveals that what we called normal was a brief historical anomaly.

Managing chaos requires different muscle memory than managing crises. Crisis management assumes you can restore equilibrium through decisive action. Chaos management assumes that equilibrium itself may be gone, and the task is to build organizations capable of continuous adaptation while maintaining coherence around shared purpose.

This distinction matters because leaders trained for crisis management often accelerate organizational breakdown when they try to apply those skills to chaotic conditions. They seek control when what is needed is coordination. They impose clarity when what is needed is the capacity to hold ambiguity while acting. They centralize authority when what is needed is distributed sense-making across the organization.

The practices explored in this book, disciplined listening, generative conversation, operational empathy, are the fundamental capabilities of chaos management. They allow organizations to remain coherent without becoming rigid, to act decisively without premature closure, and to maintain human connection in circumstances that fragment and isolate.

If there is a single through line in these pages, it is that listening, conversation, and empathy are crafts that are only learned in use. They are not personality traits to be admired from afar, but repeatable disciplines that can be strengthened the way a pilot builds pattern recognition or a joint force builds interoperability through sustained, structured practice under real conditions.

Consider how fighter pilots develop. They do not simply study aerodynamics and then fly. They spend thousands of hours in simulators, in basic flight training, in advanced tactical exercises, building neural pathways and cognitive frameworks that allow them to process information and make decisions at speeds that conscious thought cannot match. When they finally enter combat, their training allows them to operate in chaotic circumstances while maintaining situational awareness and mission focus.

The same investment is required for the leadership capabilities this book describes. You cannot become genuinely empathetic by reading about empathy. You cannot learn to facilitate generative conversation by studying meeting design. You cannot build the capacity to listen in ways that change your thinking without repeatedly entering conversations where you do not know the answer and accepting the discomfort of having your assumptions challenged.

Yet most organizations provide no equivalent to flight training for these capabilities. Leaders are expected to "have good people skills" without systematic development, to "communicate effectively" without practice in facilitation, to "understand different perspectives" without structured experiences that force them beyond their comfort zones.

The organizations that will thrive in the decades ahead will be those that treat these capabilities as trainable, measurable, and essential to operational effectiveness. They will build what I have called "genuine projects" or real work that requires people from different backgrounds, generations, and disciplines to succeed together, creating natural laboratories for developing listening, conversation, and empathy under actual organizational pressures.

The fragmentation we face is not theoretical. It shows up in the breakdown of civil discourse, in organizations where departments cannot coordinate, in families where generations talk past each other, in alliances where partners no longer share strategic assumptions, in military forces where services compete rather than complement.

This fragmentation does not happen because people lack good intentions. It happens because the pressures of speed, complexity, and technological change have outrun our communicative infrastructure. We have built systems optimized for information transmission but not for shared understanding, for decision velocity but not for decision quality, for individual productivity but not for collective intelligence.

The practices this book describes are not about being nicer to each other, though they may have that effect. They are about building the organizational capabilities required to function effectively in an environment where unilateral action fails, where no single perspective captures the whole picture, and where adaptation must happen faster than formal authority structures can keep pace.

For military leaders, this means forces that can operate in distributed fashion while maintaining unity of effort. For corporate leaders, it means organizations that can innovate across boundaries rather than within silos. For public sector leaders, it means institutions that retain legitimacy and effectiveness even when serving populations with fundamentally different worldviews. For all leaders, it means the difference between organizations that fragment under pressure and those that become stronger through it.

The pressures around you will not slow down, and the fragmentation described here will not reverse itself. What remains within your control is how you enter the next interaction, meeting, or negotiation: whether you come to confirm what you already think, or to discover what you and others have not yet seen.

Each time you choose to listen as if you might be changed by what you hear, to convene a conversation as shared inquiry rather than staged debate, and to exercise empathy as disciplined understanding rather than performance, you are quietly re-architecting the systems you inhabit.

These choices compound. A single conversation conducted with genuine listening may seem insignificant, but it creates a precedent and a memory within your organization. Others notice when a leader makes space to be surprised, when authority is exercised with empathy, when decisions emerge from real dialogue rather than predetermined positions. Over time, these moments accumulate into a culture—a set of shared expectations about how work gets done and how people treat each other when the stakes are high.

This book has argued that such choices are now the decisive margin of leadership effectiveness in a chaotic age. Not because empathy replaces expertise, analysis, or authority, but because it is the enabling condition that allows those capabilities to be deployed effectively when circumstances exceed what any individual or any pre-existing plan can handle.

The cauldron is here. The question is whether you will help build organizations and communities capable not simply of enduring it, but of learning and leading within it through the hard, essential work of listening to lead.

Your leadership in this moment matters not because you have all the answers, but because you have the courage to enter conversations where the answers have not yet been discovered.

# BIBLIOGRAPHY


Asana. (n.d.). *Effective active listening: Examples, techniques and exercises.* **https://asana.com/resources/active-listening**

Baird, J., and Sullivan, E. (2021). *Leading with heart: Five conversations that unlock creativity, purpose, and results.* Harper Business.

Brown, B. (2010). *The gifts of imperfection.* Hazelden.

Brown, B. (2018). *Dare to lead: Brave work. Tough conversations. Whole hearts.* Random House.

Cardona, C., and Velazquez, L. (2024). *Cultural competence in ADR: Understanding differences, creating solutions* [Conference paper]. Federal Mediation and Conciliation Service.

Cascade Employers Association. (2024, April 1). *The power of perspective taking: A catalyst for workplace success.* **https://www.cascadeemployers.com**

Choosing Therapy. (n.d.). *Empathy burnout: What it is and how to cope.* **https://www.choosingtherapy.com/empathy-burnout**

Corporate Wellness Magazine. (n.d.). *Mindful communication: How to foster empathy and understanding in the workplace.* **https://www.corporatewellnessmagazine.com**

Cuddy, A. (2015). *Presence: Bringing your boldest self to your biggest challenges.* Little, Brown.

Deloitte. (n.d.). *Working in multicultural teams: A case study.* **https://www.deloitte.com**

Family Resource Home Care. (n.d.). *Understanding empathy: A guide for caregivers.* **https://jobs.familyresourcehomecare.com/empathy-guide-for-caregivers**

Glaser, J. E. (2013). *Conversational intelligence: How great leaders build trust and get extraordinary results.* Bibliomotion.

Goleman, D. (1995). *Emotional intelligence: Why it can matter more than IQ.* Bantam Books.

Goleman, D., Boyatzis, R., and McKee, A. (2013). *Primal leadership: Unleashing the power of emotional intelligence* (Rev. ed.). Harvard Business Review Press.

Groysberg, B., and Slind, M. (2012). Leadership is a conversation. *Harvard Business Review, 90*(6), 76–84.

Harvard Business Publishing. (n.d.). *Empathetic leadership: How to go beyond lip service.* **https://www.harvardbusiness.org**

Heifetz, R. A. (1994). *Leadership without easy answers.* Harvard University Press.

Heifetz, R. A., and Linsky, M. (2002). *Leadership on the line: Staying alive through the dangers of leading.* Harvard Business School Press.

Heifetz, R. A., Linsky, M., and Grashow, A. (2009). *The practice of adaptive leadership: Tools and tactics for changing your organization and the world.* Harvard Business Review Press.

Hooks, B. (2000). *All about love: New visions.* William Morrow.

Horizon. (n.d.). *Unlocking empathy, communication, and leadership through VR training.* **https://horizon.mit.edu**

Kegan, R., and Lahey, L. L. (2016). *An everyone culture: Becoming a deliberately developmental organization.* Harvard Business Review Press.

Klein, C. (2023). The effectiveness of empathy in reducing interpersonal stress. *NousTro.* **https://noustro.com**

Krisco, K. H. (2002). *Leadership and the art of conversation.* Jaico Publishing House.

Laloux, F. (2014). *Reinventing organizations: A guide to creating organizations inspired by the next stage of human consciousness.* Nelson Parker.

Linsky, M., and Heifetz, R. A. (2002). *Leadership on the line: Staying alive through the dangers of leading.* Harvard Business School Press.

Medium. (n.d.). *Redefining connectivity: How tech transforms empathy in the modern world* (D. Hallmon, Author). **https://medium.com**

Mosaic Minds Counseling. (n.d.). *Empathy and mental health: How are they connected?* **https://mosaicmindscounseling.com**

Mu Sigma. (n.d.). *Empathy-driven business decision making with the iceberg model.* **https://www.linkedin.com**

Neff, K. (2011). *Self-compassion: The proven power of being kind to yourself.* William Morrow.

One Eighty. (n.d.). *The role of empathy in conflict management.* **https://www.oneeighty.io**

Pallapa, G. (2021). *Leading with empathy: Understanding the needs of today's workforce.* Notion Press.

PositivePsychology.com. (n.d.). *Understanding empathy vs. sympathy: What's the difference?* **https://positivepsychology.com/empathy-vs-sympathy**

Red Bear Negotiation. (n.d.). *The role of empathy in negotiation.* **https://www.redbearnegotiation.com**

Rifkin, J. (2010). *The empathic civilization: The race to global consciousness in a world in crisis.* Tarcher/Penguin.

Ross, M. (2019). *The empathy edge: Harnessing the value of compassion as an engine for success.* Page Two Books.

Schein, E. H. (2013). *Humble inquiry: The gentle art of asking instead of telling.* Berrett-Koehler.

Senge, P. M. (1990). *The fifth discipline: The art and practice of the learning organization.* Doubleday.

Sue, D. W. (2010). *Microaggressions in everyday life: Race, gender, and sexual orientation.* John Wiley and Sons.

Study.com. (n.d.). *Cultural empathy: Definition and examples.* **https://study.com/academy/lesson/cultural-empathy-definition-examples.html**

Tannen, D. (1995). *Talking from 9 to 5: Women and men at work.* William Morrow.

Turkle, S. (Host). (2020). Is technology killing empathy? [Audio podcast episode]. In *Speaking of psychology.* American Psychological Association. **https://www.apa.org**

Uhl-Bien, M., and Arena, M. (2017). Complexity leadership: Enabling people and organizations for adaptability. *Organizational Dynamics, 46*(1), 9–20. **https://doi.org/10.1016/j.orgdyn.2016.12.001**

Ventura, M. (2018). *Applied empathy: The new language of leadership.* Touchstone.

Weick, K. E., and Sutcliffe, K. M. (2015). *Managing the unexpected: Sustained performance in a complex world* (3rd ed.). John Wiley and Sons.

West, M. A. (2012). *Effective teamwork: Practical lessons from organizational research* (3rd ed.). BPS Blackwell.

Wikipedia. (n.d.). *High-context and low-context cultures.* Retrieved January 11, 2026, from       **https://en.wikipedia.org/wiki/High-context_and_low-context_cul tures**

Winters, M.-F. (2020). *Inclusive conversations: Fostering equity, empathy, and belonging across differences.* Berrett-Koehler.

Writing-Skills.com. (n.d.). *How to show empathy in your customer service emails.* **https://www.writing-skills.com**

Zenger, J., and Folkman, J. (2014). *The inspiring leader: Unlocking the secrets of how extraordinary leaders motivate.* McGraw-Hill.

Zoll, S., et al. (2021). "Taking the empathy to an activist state": Ally engagement and the politics of solidarity. *Journal of Global Ethics, 17*(2), 150–170.

# PUBLISHED BOOKS BY ROBBIN F. LAIRD

## COLD WAR AND SOVIET-ERA WORKS

Robbin F. Laird and Erik P. Hoffmann, *Politics of Economic Modernization in the Soviet Union* (Cornell University Press, 1982). [Co-authored]

Erik P. Hoffmann and Robbin F. Laird, *The Scientific-Technological Revolution and Soviet Foreign Policy* (Pergamon Press, 1982). [Co-authored]

Dale R. Herspring and Robbin F. Laird, *The Soviet Union and Strategic Arms* (Westview, 1984). [Co-authored]

Erik P. Hoffmann and Robbin F. Laird, eds., *The Soviet Polity in the Modern Era* (Aldine, 1984). [Edited]

Erik P. Hoffmann and Robbin F. Laird, *Technocratic Socialism: The Soviet Union in the Advanced Industrial Era* (Duke University Press, 1985). [Co-authored]

Robbin F. Laird, *The Soviet Union, the West, and the Nuclear Arms Race* (Wheatsheaf Books, 1986).

Robbin F. Laird, ed., *Soviet Foreign Policy* (Aldine, 1987). [Edited]

Erik P. Hoffmann, Fred H. Fleron, and Robbin F. Laird, eds., *Soviet Foreign Policy: Classic and Contemporary Issues* (1991).

Erik P. Hoffmann, Fred H. Fleron, and Robbin F. Laird, eds., *Contemporary Issues in Soviet Foreign Policy: From Brezhnev to Gorbachev* (Routledge, 2008).

## EUROPEAN SECURITY AND NATO

Robbin F. Laird, *French Security Policy in Transition: Dynamics of Continuity and Change* (Westview, 1985).

Robbin F. Laird, *France, the Soviet Union, and the Nuclear Weapons Issue* (Westview/Routledge, 1985).

Robbin F. Laird and Jim Lacy, *Perspectives on Defense Futures: National Developments in Europe* (1985).

Robbin F. Laird, *French Security Policy: From Independence to Interdependence* (Westview, 1985).

Robbin F. Laird, Strangers and Friends: *The Franco-German Security Relationship* (Palgrave Macmillan, 1989).

Robbin F. Laird, *West European Arms Control Policy* (Westview, 1989).

Robbin F. Laird and Betsy Jacobs, eds., *The Future of Deterrence: NATO Nuclear Forces after INF* (Westview, 1990). [Edited]

Susan Clark and Robbin F. Laird, eds., *The USSR and the Western Alliance* (Unwin Hyman, 1990). [Edited]

Robbin F. Laird, *The Europeanization of the Alliance* (Westview/Routledge, 1991).

Robbin F. Laird, *The Soviets, Germany, and the New Europe* (Westview, 1992).

Robbin F. Laird and Murielle Delaporte, *The Return of Direct Defense in Europe: Meeting the 21st Century Authoritarian Challenge* (2020).

Robbin Laird, editor, *French Defense Policy Under Macron, 2017-2021* (2023).

## REVOLUTION IN MILITARY AFFARIS, AIR-MARITIME POWER, AND PACIFIC STRATEGY

Robbin F. Laird and Holger H. Mey, *The Revolution in Military Affairs: Allied Perspectives* (NDU, 2012).

Robbin F. Laird, *Three Dimensional Warriors,* 2nd ed. (2013).

Robbin F. Laird, Edward Timperlake, and Richard Weitz, *Rebuilding American Military Power in the Pacific: A 21st-Century Strategy* (Praeger, 2013). [Co-authored]

Robbin F. Laird, *The F-35 and 21st Century Defence: Shaping a Way Ahead* (2016).

Robbin Laird, *The Role of the Osprey in the Pivot to the Pacific* (2023).

Robbin Laird, *Training for the High-End Fight: The Paradigm Shift for Combat Pilot Training* (2025).

Robbin Laird, *My Fifth-Generation Journey: 2004-2018* (Second Edition, 2025).

Robbin Laird, *Remembering the B-17 and Its Role in World War II: Noirmoutier Island, France 2013* (2025).

Robbin Laird, *Italy and the F-35: Shaping 21st Century Coalition-Enabled Airpower* (2025).

# CONTEMPORARY STRATEGY
# AND ALLIED TRANSFORMATION

Robbin F. Laird, *Training for the High-End Fight: The Strategic Shift of the 2020s* (2021).

Robbin F. Laird, ed., *2020: A Pivotal Year? Navigating Strategic Change at a Time of COVID-19 Disruption* (2021).

Robbin F. Laird, *Joint by Design: The Evolution of Australian Defence Strategy* (2021).

Robbin F. Laird, *Australian Defence and Deterrence: A 2023 Update* (2023).

Kenneth Maxwell and Robbin F. Laird, eds., *Kenneth Maxwell on Global Trends: An Historian of the 18th Century Looks at the Contemporary World* (2023).

Robbin Laird, editor, *Assessing Global Change: Strategic Perspectives of Dr. Harald Malmgren* (2025).

Robbin Laird, editor, *America, Global Military Competition, and Opportunities Lost: Reflections on the Work of Michael W. Wynne* (2025.

Robbin Laird, *Australian Defence and Deterrence: A 2024 Update* (2024).

Robbin Laird, *The Australian Defence Force: Meeting the Modernization Challenges* (2025).

Robbin Laird, editor, *The Emergence of the Multi-Polar Authoritarian World: Looking Back from 2024* (2025).

Robbin Laird, editor, *The Obama Administration Confronts Global Change* (2024).

Robbin Laird, *Australian Defence and Deterrence: A 2025 Update* (2025).

Robbin Laird, editor, *The Biden Administration Confronts Global Change: Déjà vu All Over Again* (2025).

## KILL WEB, USMC, AND MARITIME AUTONOMOUS SYSTEMS

Robbin F. Laird, *The U.S. Marine Corps Transformation Path: Preparing for the High-End Fight* (2022).

Robbin F. Laird and Edward Timperlake, *A Maritime Kill Web Force in the Making: Deterrence and Warfighting in the 21st Century* (2024).

Robbin F. Laird, *The Coming of the CH-53K: A New Capability for the Distributed Force* (2023).

Robbin Laird, *Australia and Indo-Pacific Defense: Anchoring a Way Ahead* (2023).

Robbin Laird, *MAWTS-1: The 2023 Visit and Interviews* (2023).

Robbin F. Laird, *The Coming of Maritime Autonomous Systems: Empowering and Integrating the Maritime Kill Web* (2024).

Robbin Laird and Ed Timperlake, *MAWTS-1: An Incubator for Military Transformation* (2024).

Robbin F. Laird, *A Paradigm Shift in Maritime Operations: Autonomous Systems and the Future Maritime Force* (2025).

Robbin Laird, *A Tiltrotor Enterprise: From Iraq to the Future* (2025).

Robbin Laird, *A Tiltrotor Perspective: Exploring the Experience* (2025).

Robbin Laird, *2nd Marine Air Wing: Transforming the 'Fight Tonight Force'* (2025).

Robbin Laird, *Fight Tonight Force: Combat Readiness at the Speed of Relevance* (2026).

## DEFENSE XX SERIES AND RELATED EDITED WORKS

Robbin F. Laird, ed., *Defense XXI: Shaping a Way Ahead for the United States and Its Allies* (2022).

Robbin F. Laird, ed., *Defense XXII: A World in Transition* (2023).

Robbin F. Laird, ed., *Defense XXIII: America Faces a Very Different World* (2024).

## PERSONAL AND PROFESSIONAL DEVELOPMENT SERIES

Robbin Laird, *Public Speaking for Professionals: How to Engage Your Audience* (2025).

## REISSUED BY ROUTLEDGE

*France, the Soviet Union, and the Nuclear Weapons Issue* (Routledge, 2019).

*French Security Policy: From Independence to Interdependence* (Routledge, 2020).

*The Future of Deterrence: NATO Nuclear Forces after INF* (Routledge, 2021).

*The USSR and the Western Alliance* (Routledge, 2022).

What unifies Laird's diverse body of work is his commitment to understanding how things actually work rather than how theories suggest they should work. His extensive interview-based methodology, talking with military leaders, defense officials, pilots, and strategic thinkers, reflects his conviction that transformation happens through human decisions in specific contexts, not through abstract forces operating independently of agency. His description of himself and Kenneth Maxwell as "outliers" navigating different historical "ecosystems" captures this perspective: they observed and analyzed rather than prescribing from theoretical frameworks.

Laird's guidance from General Patton, "if everyone is thinking alike, someone isn't thinking", might serve as his methodological north star. He has consistently questioned consensus views, whether about Soviet stability in the 1980s, the inevitability of European integration in the 1990s, or the nature of 21st-century competition today. This intellectual independence stems not from contrarianism but from his practitioner's focus on operational realities that often diverge from policy rhetoric or academic theory.

Looking across four decades of published work, one sees a practitioner and analyst who has continuously adapted his focus to emerging challenges while maintaining consistent analytical commitments. He has examined how organizations and alliances navigate transformational change, how technology creates opportunities and imperatives that institutions must accommodate, and how strategic competition evolves in response to shifting power distributions and operational concepts. His current work on chaos management and autonomous systems represents not a departure from his earlier Soviet analysis but a continuation of the same fundamental inquiry: how do actors maintain effectiveness when the environments in which they operate undergo fundamental transformation?

This consistency of purpose, combined with flexibility in application, may be Laird's most important intellectual contribution. In an era that increasingly demands we operate within complexity rather than seeking to eliminate it, his career-long examination of transformation provides not answers but a methodology, a way of seeing that privileges adaptation over adherence, operational reality over theoretical elegance, and continuous evolution over arrival at final solutions.

# MASTERING CHAOS

## Shaping a Way Ahead for Chaos Management

You cannot plan your way through genuine chaos. The question facing senior leaders today is not whether you will encounter complex, unpredictable situations where the parameters of the system itself are shifting, but whether you have built the organizational capacity to function effectively within them.

Throughout four decades working with military services, government institutions, and defense organizations, I have studied how organizations navigate what scholars call wicked problems: complex, interconnected challenges that resist traditional solution frameworks. This work has taught me not just how to respond to crises, but how to recognize the fundamental nature of historical transitions and build adaptive capacity before it is urgently needed.[*]

## WHAT THIS BOOK WILL ENABLE YOU TO DO

If you are a flag officer, senior executive, or C-suite leader, this book

_____________

[*] Much of my work on the dynamics of change in military organizations will be summarized in my forthcoming book entitled: *Lessons in Military Transformation: From the RMA to the Drone Wars.* I have provided a summary to the book in the epilogue to this book.

provides you with a practical framework for building organizational capabilities that thrive in chaotic environments. After reading, you will be able to:

- Diagnose whether your organization is optimized for stability or adapted for chaos. Most organizations unconsciously optimize for efficiency in stable conditions, making them dangerously brittle when the environment shifts. You will learn to assess your organization's adaptive capacity across three dimensions: intellectual flexibility, institutional resilience, and social cohesion. This diagnostic capability allows you to identify vulnerabilities before they become crises.
- Reframe strategic planning from scenario prediction to capability building. Traditional planning assumes we can forecast conditions and prepare specific responses. In chaotic environments, this approach fails because the underlying parameters are shifting. You will learn to shift your strategic planning focus from "what will happen" to "what capabilities do we need to adapt to whatever happens." This means making different investment decisions, building different organizational structures, and evaluating success differently.
- Build decision-making processes that function under uncertainty. Many leaders find themselves paralyzed when facing ambiguous situations with incomplete information. You will learn specific approaches for maintaining operational tempo even when you cannot fully understand the situation. This includes understanding when to act on incomplete information, how to create decision frameworks that preserve optionality, and how to maintain organizational coherence when different parts of your organization are seeing different aspects of a complex problem.
- Transform your organizational culture from risk-averse to adaptation-focused. The single greatest barrier to thriving in

chaos is organizational culture that treats uncertainty as a threat rather than as an operational environment. You will learn concrete approaches for creating cultures where questioning assumptions is valued, intellectual diversity is cultivated, and adaptation is treated as a core competence rather than an unfortunate necessity.

- Recognize the difference between complicated and complex problems, and apply appropriate responses to each. Many leadership failures occur because leaders apply linear problem-solving approaches to nonlinear systems. You will develop the judgment to distinguish between situations where traditional planning and control methods work effectively and situations where they make things worse. This distinction is fundamental to avoiding catastrophic misapplication of resources and attention.

- Preserve institutional knowledge and build organizational memory across leadership transitions. Organizations routinely lose critical understanding when key individuals depart. You will learn approaches for capturing, codifying, and transmitting knowledge that transcends any single person. This creates the institutional memory necessary to learn from past adaptations without repeating past mistakes.

- Lead through historical transitions by maintaining social cohesion under pressure. The decisive factor in organizational survival during major transitions is the strength of internal bonds and shared purpose. You will learn specific practices for building the trust necessary for rapid coordination under pressure, creating space for honest disagreement about tactics while maintaining consensus about fundamental values.

These capabilities are not theoretical constructs. They are practical competencies I have observed in organizations that successfully navigate complex, rapidly changing situations. The difference between organizations that break under pressure and those that adapt successfully comes down to whether these capabilities have been deliberately cultivated before they become urgently necessary.

# WHY CHAOS MANAGEMENT MATTERS NOW

We are in a period of fundamental historical transition. The institutions, practices, and assumptions that governed the post-World War II era are breaking down faster than new patterns can form. This is not hyperbole. Consider the markers: the fragmentation of international institutions, the collapse of consensus around democratic norms in many Western nations, technological change accelerating beyond regulatory capacity, the breakdown of shared information environments, and the inability of traditional governance structures to address transnational challenges.

The challenge in this context is not crisis management as traditionally understood. Traditional crisis management assumes disorder is temporary, an aberration that can be resolved through proper planning and execution, allowing return to normal functioning. This approach made sense in stable historical periods where change was incremental and the basic parameters remained constant.

Chaos management recognizes that modern environments are inherently chaotic systems characterized by nonlinear dynamics, emergent behaviors, and unpredictable interactions between multiple variables. Attempting to control these systems through traditional command and control methods creates rigidity that prevents adaptation. You cannot plan your way through genuine chaos because the parameters themselves are shifting.

Organizations trained in chaos management can maintain operational coherence and continue effective execution while adversaries struggle to maintain coordination. They do not need to understand everything happening around them. They need only to be more resilient, more adaptable, and more capable of rapid learning than their competitors or the challenges they face.

# THE FOUNDATION: THREE PILLARS OF ADAPTIVE CAPACITY

While we cannot predict exactly what the next historical period will bring, we can prepare by cultivating three essential capacities: intellectual flexibility, institutional resilience, and social cohesion. These are not abstract virtues but concrete organizational capabilities that determine whether entities survive periods of fundamental transition.

- Intellectual flexibility means developing organizations where people understand that different analytical frameworks illuminate different aspects of complex problems, where questioning established assumptions is valued rather than threatening, and where comfort with change itself is treated as a core competence. This requires educational systems that teach how to think rather than just what to think, exposure to multiple disciplines, genuine intellectual diversity, and training to recognize the limits of mental models.

- Institutional resilience means building organizations that can operate effectively under a range of different conditions through redundant capabilities, backup systems, diverse skill sets, and multiple approaches to core functions. Organizations optimized for efficiency in stable environments become dangerously brittle when conditions shift. Resilient institutions accept some inefficiency as the price of survivability, preserve institutional knowledge across leadership transitions, and invest in infrastructure that can support multiple possible futures rather than just the most likely scenario.

- Social cohesion is perhaps the most fundamental requirement for navigating chaos. Organizations fragment under pressure unless they maintain strong bonds of trust, shared purpose, and mutual commitment. History suggests that organizations that successfully navigate major transitions preserve what is essential about their identity

while remaining flexible about implementation. They create
space for honest disagreement about tactics while
maintaining consensus about fundamental values. They
build the trust necessary for rapid coordination under
pressure. In chaotic environments, the ability to coordinate
effectively becomes the decisive advantage, but
coordination requires trust, trust requires relationship, and
relationship requires investment in social infrastructure.

## HOW THIS BOOK IS ORGANIZED

Part One examines the nature of historical transition and why traditional crisis management frameworks fail in genuinely chaotic environments.

Part Two provides detailed frameworks for assessing and building
the three pillars of adaptive capacity in your own organization. Each
chapter includes diagnostic questions, implementation approaches,
and common failure modes. You will learn how to identify where your
organization is most vulnerable and how to prioritize capability-
building efforts given resource constraints.

Part Three addresses the leadership challenges of maintaining organizational coherence during transition. Leading through chaos requires
different skills than leading in stable environments. You will learn
approaches for preserving social cohesion under pressure, maintaining
operational tempo despite uncertainty, and creating organizational
cultures that treat adaptation as a competence rather than a crisis
response.

The anarchy of the moment is real. But it is also generative. From
the dissolution of old orders come the seeds of new ones. The question
is not whether we will face this transition, we are already in it, but
whether we will navigate it with the adaptive capacity necessary to
emerge stronger. This is the work before us: to build organizations
capable not just of surviving chaos, but of thriving within it.

# HOW TO USE THIS BOOK

This book is a practical guide for senior leaders driving organizational transformation over 12–24 months. Read it cover to cover or use each part as a timed playbook for your timeline.

## Part One: Assessment and Diagnosis (Months 1–3)

Use these chapters to build your conceptual foundation and evaluate your current state.

- Run an organizational diagnostic using the three pillars (intellectual flexibility, institutional resilience, social cohesion) to spot stability optimizations that create brittleness.
- Stress-test your strategic planning: are you predicting scenarios or building adaptive capacity?
- Triage vulnerabilities, distinguishing complicated problems (fix with traditional management) from complex ones (requiring new approaches).

## Part Two: Capability Building (Months 4–18)

Apply these implementation frameworks to build the three pillars through structural and cultural changes.

- Months 4–8: Build intellectual flexibility by revising training/education, fostering genuine intellectual diversity, and training comfort with ambiguity (expect resistance from efficiency-optimized cultures).
- Months 9–14: Develop institutional resilience with redundancy in key capabilities, knowledge-transfer systems, and multi-future infrastructure (prioritize survivability over max efficiency).
- Months 15–18: Strengthen social cohesion through trust-

building, shared values, and stress-tested cultural norms (beyond superficial team-building).

## Part Three: Leading Through Transition (Months 19–24 and Beyond)

Use these tools to sustain coherence as basic capacity matures.

- Maintain operational tempo when uncertainty breaks standard metrics and procedures.
- Preserve culture amid growth, contraction, or restructuring to protect social bonds and purpose.
- Institutionalize adaptation as ongoing competence, preventing reversion to pre-chaos optimization.

Return to sections as challenges evolve: this is your extended transformation reference.

This is not a book to read once and shelve. It is a reference guide for an extended transformation process. Different sections will become relevant at different stages of your journey. Return to it as you encounter new challenges, using it to maintain perspective during difficult phases of organizational change.

# SETTING THE STAGE

Part One sets the conceptual foundation for the entire book by explaining why today's environment is structurally chaotic and what that means for how leaders must think and organize. It moves you from experiencing "the anarchy of the moment" as an endless series of emergencies to recognizing the underlying dynamics that make those emergencies inevitable and potentially manageable.

This section has three jobs. First, it clarifies how our era differs from earlier periods of turbulence: not just more crises, but tightly coupled systems, cascading disruptions, and a collapse of temporal slack that compresses decision-making to the breaking point. Second, it shows why legacy crisis-management models fail under these conditions, particularly approaches that assume problems are isolated, linear, and containable. Third, it translates these structural realities into the cognitive demands placed on senior leaders: the mental habits you must deliberately cultivate if you want your organization to operate coherently inside chaos rather than constantly chase it.

Chapter One, "The Anarchy of the Moment," describes the condition of perpetual disruption that defines our time, the speed of events, the ubiquity of crisis triggers, and the paradox of connectivity that turns local disturbances into global shocks. Chapter Two, "Managing in the Age of Chaos," examines how this environment breaks traditional management logic, drawing out patterns like tight coupling, normal accidents, and the transparency paradox that make conventional planning insufficient. Chapter Three, "The Cognitive Skills for Mastering Chaos," then identifies the core mental capabilities leaders must build: adaptive thinking that can shift frames quickly, pattern recognition that sees emerging structures in noise, and metacognitive discipline that keeps judgment from collapsing under pressure.

You can think of Part One as your diagnostic lens. As you engage with the material, the goal is not simply to agree that the world is chaotic, but to see more precisely *how* chaos operates in your domain and where your current assumptions, processes, and leadership habits are mismatched to that reality. The later parts of the book will give you detailed frameworks and tools; Part One ensures you are asking the right questions before you apply them.

# THE ANARCHY OF THE MOMENT

World leaders find themselves lurching from crisis to crisis with little time to catch their breath. This reactive scramble has become the defining characteristic of our era or what might be called the "anarchy of the moment."

Unlike the grand ideological struggles or systematic breakdowns that marked previous periods of global disorder, today's chaos feels fundamentally different. It's not driven solely by competing visions of world order or the collapse of established systems, but rather by an endless succession of urgent, interconnected crises that demand immediate responses. Each moment brings its own emergency, its own imperative for action, leaving little room for the kind of strategic thinking that once shaped international relations.

## THE SPEED OF EVERYTHING

The anarchy of the moment is born from velocity. Information travels instantly, markets react in milliseconds, and social movements can mobilize millions within hours. When a single tweet can trigger a diplomatic incident or a supply chain disruption in one region can cause shortages halfway around the world within days, the traditional tools of governance, deliberation, consultation, careful planning, begin to feel obsolete.

Consider how recent global events have unfolded. Conflicts that might once have simmered for months before drawing international attention now explode into global consciousness within hours, complete with real-time footage, competing narratives, and immediate demands for action from world leaders. Economic disruptions that previous generations might have had weeks to analyze and respond to now require emergency measures implemented over weekends.

This compression of time has fundamentally altered the nature of leadership and decision-making. Rather than chess masters contemplating long-term strategy, today's leaders increasingly resemble emergency room doctors, triaging an endless stream of urgent cases while trying to keep the patient alive.

## THE UBIQUITY OF CRISIS

What makes this anarchy particularly disorienting is its ubiquitous character. In previous eras, global disorder often emanated from great powers or major institutions. Today's chaos emerges from everywhere and anywhere, a single individual with a smartphone can trigger international incidents, small-scale cyber attacks can cascade into major disruptions, and local environmental disasters quickly become global concerns.

This ubiquitous of crisis means that traditional hierarchies and channels of influence are constantly being bypassed. A teenager's climate activism can reshape international negotiations. A regional bank's collapse can threaten global financial stability. A local conflict can draw in major powers through the magnetic pull of social media attention and public pressure.

The result is a world where the next major disruption is as likely to come from an unexpected corner as from the usual suspects, making prediction and preparation extraordinarily difficult.

# THE PARADOX OF CONNECTIVITY

Ironically, the very systems designed to bring order and efficiency to our interconnected world have amplified the anarchy of the moment. Global supply chains that optimize for efficiency prove brittle when disrupted. Financial systems that enable instant capital flows also enable instant contagion. Communication networks that allow unprecedented coordination also facilitate the rapid spread of misinformation and panic.

Our interconnectedness means that local disturbances rarely remain local, while our real-time awareness of these cascading effects creates a constant sense of crisis. We are simultaneously more informed about global events than any previous generation and less able to process that information in ways that lead to coherent action.

# LIVING IN THE ETERNAL PRESENT

Perhaps most fundamentally, the anarchy of the moment reflects a collapse of temporal perspective. When every crisis is immediate and urgent, the distinction between important and unimportant, lasting and temporary, becomes difficult to maintain. Long-term challenges compete for attention with daily emergencies, often losing out to whatever is most visceral and immediate.

This creates a kind of political and social attention deficit disorder, where societies career from one focus to another without ever developing the sustained attention necessary for addressing complex, systemic problems. The urgent consistently drives out the important.

# THE SEARCH FOR PATTERN

Yet even within this apparent chaos, patterns persist. The anarchy of the moment may feel random and unpredictable, but it unfolds within existing structures of power, wealth, and influence. Some actors are better positioned to exploit the chaos than others. Some institutions prove more resilient than expected. Some problems, despite being urgent, never quite rise to the level of demanding immediate action.

Understanding these underlying currents or the persistent forces that shape how moments of anarchy unfold may be key to navigating this new reality. Rather than trying to eliminate the chaos or return to some imagined era of stability, perhaps the task is learning to operate effectively within it.

The challenge is in effect chaos management.

The anarchy of the moment may be the defining condition of our interconnected age. The question is not whether we can restore order in the traditional sense, but whether we can develop new forms of adaptability, resilience, and wisdom that allow us to thrive amid the constant churn of urgent demands and immediate crises.

In a world where the next moment might bring anything, the premium is no longer on predicting the future but on cultivating the capacity to respond thoughtfully when that unpredictable future arrives.

By some sort of cosmic accident, my dissertation at Columbia University was entitled: "On *Historical Change: Order Within Chaos*."

But then again, I took a two-year course when an undergraduate on something called "symbolic logic" and no one including myself understood why I was doing so. I would like to say authoritatively that I was anticipating AI but of course that would be something only a politician could claim concerning personal foresight.

# MANAGING IN THE AGE OF CHAOS

The landscape of organizational management has undergone a seismic shift. What worked for corporate leaders a generation ago now appears painfully inadequate for the complex, interconnected challenges that define the contemporary environment.

From COVID-19 supply-chain collapse to cascading failures in financial systems, from cyber incidents that trigger diplomatic crises to climate events that disrupt entire industries simultaneously, modern crises defy the neat categorizations and linear response strategies that once guided organizational leadership.

This transformation is not one of degree but of kind. Contemporary organizational crises differ fundamentally from those of previous decades in ways that demand a radical rethinking of how organizations prepare for, respond to, and recover from disruption. Understanding these differences is not an academic exercise; it is an existential necessity for organizations that hope to survive and thrive in an increasingly volatile world.

# THE FOUR DIMENSIONS OF MODERN CRISIS COMPLEXITY

## 1. Deep interconnectivity and cascading disruption

The first and perhaps most consequential shift concerns the depth and density of interconnections within and between systems. Unlike the relatively isolated disruptions of the past, contemporary crises are increasingly characterized by tightly coupled networks where a seemingly localized problem in one region or sector rapidly propagates through global systems, triggering second- and third-order effects leaders neither anticipated nor fully understand.

The 2011 Tōhoku earthquake and tsunami in Japan provided an early template. While the immediate devastation was regional, the effects cascaded across the global economy within days: automotive manufacturers in the United States could not complete vehicles because specialized components from Japanese suppliers were unavailable; electronics companies worldwide faced similar constraints; and the Fukushima disaster triggered policy shifts on energy production and nuclear safety far beyond Japan. A geological event on one section of the Pacific Rim became a crisis for organizations with no physical presence in the affected region.[*]

Modern supply chains now represent some of the most complex systems humans have constructed, with dependencies that are simultaneously tight and opaque. A single factory producing a specialized semiconductor can serve as a critical node for dozens of industries; when that node fails, through natural disaster, geopolitical friction, or internal disruption, the effects propagate in ways that defy simple mapping.

The 2021 Suez Canal blockage made this visible to a wider audi-

---

[*] See, for example, C. Freund et al., "Natural Disasters and the Reshaping of Global Value Chains," World Bank, 2022; U.S. Congressional Research Service, *The Motor Vehicle Supply Chain: Effects of the Japanese Earthquake and Tsunami* (R41831), 2011; Reserve Bank of Australia, Box A: *The Japanese Earthquake and Global Supply Chains,* August 2011; and OECD Nuclear Energy Agency, *Impacts of the Fukushima Daiichi Accident on Nuclear Development Policies,* 2017.

ence. When the Ever Given ran aground, it did not simply delay ship-ments; it exposed the fragility of global logistics systems operating at near-maximum efficiency with minimal redundancy. A six-day obstruc-tion created a cascade: delayed raw materials produced delayed production schedules, missed deliveries, inventory shortages, and lost sales for businesses that appeared entirely unconnected to maritime shipping.[*]

Crucially, these cascading crises rarely emerge from a single point of failure. They arise from collisions between multiple systems oper-ating at different scales and speeds. A pandemic is not just a public-health crisis; it intersects simultaneously with healthcare systems, economic structures, social norms, political institutions, and technological capacities. The resulting effects are not additive but multiplicative, producing emergent phenomena that cannot be predicted by examining individual components in isolation.

Organizations increasingly find themselves confronting what complexity theorists call tight coupling: components are so interde-pendent that a failure in one immediately affects others, leaving little time for intervention.

This tight coupling has become a defining characteristic of contemporary systems, military operations, supply chains, financial networks, alliance structures alike. In loosely coupled systems there is slack; leaders can observe, assess, and respond before a local failure cascades. In tightly coupled systems, propagation occurs faster than human decision cycles. Failure is not merely transmitted; it is amplified through interconnections before anyone can intervene.

I have seen this repeatedly in military contexts. Integration of sensors, shooters, and command systems can create tremendous capa-bility, until one node fails and the force is not just degraded but effec-tively blind or unable to act. The network that was your greatest strength becomes a transmission mechanism for failure. The usual answer, more redundancy, more backup systems, often simply adds

---

[*] PortEconomics, "Blockage of the Suez Canal, March 2021," *Port Economics,* May 1, 2025; FreightAmigo, "The Suez Canal Crisis: How the Ever Given Blockage Impacts Global Trade," October 27, 2025; New Zealand Treasury, "Supply Chains to the Last Bus Stop on the Planet," 2024.

more coupling: redundant systems tightly linked to the primary architecture fail in the same way at the same time.

These systems are also characterized by interactive complexity: critical interactions between components are not visible or fully understood, even by experts. The combination of tight coupling and interactive complexity produces what Charles Perrow called "normal accidents": failures that are not anomalous but structurally inevitable.[*]

Traditional crisis assumptions, that crises can be contained, that their effects are predictable, that organizations can develop specific response plans for specific scenarios, no longer hold in a world of deep interconnectivity.

Containment becomes illusory, predictability collapses under emergent behavior, and scenario-specific playbooks prove inadequate when the nature of the crisis itself keeps shifting.

## 2. The dual-edged sword of information flow

The second critical dimension is the speed and character of information flow. Social media, instant communication, and pervasive transparency have fundamentally altered the temporal dynamics of crisis. Information that once took days or weeks to circulate now travels globally in minutes. This acceleration creates a transparency paradox: organizations operate under unprecedented scrutiny while simultaneously drowning in unprecedented noise.

Faster information flow in principle enables faster awareness and response. When a crisis emerges, organizations can mobilize resources quickly, communicate with stakeholders, and coordinate across geographies with an agility previous generations lacked. Real-time data allows for real-time adjustment; digital platforms allow rapid dissemination of critical information to those who need it.

But the same technologies that enable rapid response also accelerate misinformation, amplify stakeholder reaction, and compress decision-making timeframes to the point where careful deliberation

---

[*] Charles Perrow, *Normal Accidents: Living with High Risk Technologies* (Princeton University Press, 2011).

becomes nearly impossible. Leaders must make high-stakes choices with incomplete and often contradictory information under intense public scrutiny, conditions that invite error.

The 2010 Deepwater Horizon spill illustrates this dynamic. BP confronted not only the technical challenge of stopping an underwater blowout but also the communicative challenge of operating in an environment where every statement was instantly scrutinized, every image globally distributed, and every decision subjected to real-time commentary. Initial attempts to control the narrative, including underestimates of the spill's magnitude, backfired as independent sources produced conflicting information and social media amplified criticism. I was consulting to the U.S. Coast Guard at the time and saw first-hand how a force that is very good at chaos management struggled for resourcing and recognition even as its capabilities were demonstrated.[*]

Internally, the speed of information can overwhelm structures designed for a slower age. Leaders receive conflicting reports from multiple sources, each demanding attention. Social media monitoring produces massive data streams, but separating signal from noise becomes increasingly difficult. The pressure for immediate response collides directly with the need for thoughtful analysis.

Stakeholder expectations have also shifted. Silence is interpreted as evasive or incompetent; delayed responses are treated as evidence of failure rather than prudent deliberation. The 24-hour news cycle has been replaced by a continuous, never-sleeping global conversation that demands perpetual engagement. Organizations that once could gather facts, consult experts, and craft measured responses now find themselves expected to react in real time, even when the facts are uncertain and the optimal course of action is unclear.

The result is temporal compression: the collapse of time available for each stage of crisis response. Detection, assessment, decision, implementation, and evaluation, once sequential phases unfolding over days or weeks, now occur almost simultaneously and must often be

---

[*] I describe this in greater detail in my 2026 book published on Amazon and entitled: *Always Ready, Persistently Under-Resourced: The Modern United States Coats Guard Story.*

repeated as new information emerges. Leaders are forced to act while learning, adjusting responses even as they execute them.

Misinformation adds another layer. False or misleading content often spreads faster than accurate information, especially when it aligns with existing beliefs or triggers emotion. Organizations must manage both the actual crisis and competing narratives about the crisis, straining capacity and credibility. Correcting misinformation is far harder than preventing its spread and prevention is often impossible at current speeds.

In this environment, decisions that might once have been revisable become locked in by public commitments and rapid stakeholder reactions. The iterative learning essential for managing complex crises collides with demands for definitive positions and apparent certainty.

## 3. The challenge of contested problems

A third dimension of modern crisis complexity lies in the nature of the problems themselves. Many contemporary challenges are "wicked problems": situations where the problem definition is contested, solutions create new problems, and there is no clear stopping point for declaring success. Climate change, systemic inequality, cybersecurity, and public-health threats all fall into this category. Linear problem-solving, assume clear problem, identify root cause, design solution, implement, measure, simply does not fit.

Wicked problems differ from tame problems in several ways. There is no definitive formulation of the problem; different stakeholders see different problems, and each formulation implies different "solutions." There is no stopping rule; efforts do not end in a clear "victory" but in provisional improvements or trade-offs. Solutions are not right or wrong but better or worse, and evaluation depends on contested values. Every intervention changes the problem itself, as system and context co-evolve.

The COVID-19 pandemic displayed these dynamics on a global scale. Even basic questions, how to balance public health against economic activity, how to allocate scarce resources, how to weigh different forms of harm, lacked consensus answers. Different societies, with different values and institutions, reached very different conclusions. Interventions, lockdowns, school closures, vaccination campaigns, produced complex side-effects that generated new policy dilemmas.

Organizations confronting wicked problems cannot "solve" them in the traditional sense. They must instead engage in continuous experimentation, learning from partial implementations, adapting strategies as new information emerges, and accepting that progress will be nonlinear and contested. This requires a shift in mindset, from solution to stewardship of an ongoing process; from certainty to managed uncertainty; from command-and-control to convening, collaboration, and learning.

Yet structures, incentives, and cultures often push in the opposite direction. Leaders are rewarded for decisiveness and consistency, not for revising course. Organizations invest in particular approaches and defend them despite mounting evidence of inadequacy. Expertise trained on tame problems struggles with the ambiguity and conflict that define wicked ones. Traditional performance metrics, time to "resolution," cost incurred, stakeholder satisfaction, make little sense when there is no resolution, costs and benefits are unevenly distributed, and satisfaction is value-laden.

## 4. The inadequacy of linear problem-solving

These three dimensions, interconnectivity, information velocity, and wickedness, collectively overwhelm traditional crisis-management approaches that assume linearity, control, and clear causation. The mid-20th-century crisis model rests on assumptions that no longer hold: that crises are discrete, containable events; that root causes can be isolated and fixed; that objectives are stable; and that the environment is slow enough for plans to be implemented and evaluated before conditions change again.

Modern crises are often chronic rather than acute, ongoing conditions that require sustained adaptation rather than episodic response. Climate change is a process, not an event. Digital disruption is continuous transformation, not a one-time shock. Inequality is a structural feature, not an aberration. In complex systems with nonlinear interactions, feedback loops, and lagged effects, "root cause" analysis is frequently misleading. Multiple factors interact in ways that defy simple attribution.

Standard crisis management presumes organizations can develop plans, execute them, and achieve predetermined objectives. In complex, contested crises, both objectives and means have to be continuously negotiated.

- What counts as success?
- Whose interests are prioritized?
- How are trade-offs evaluated?

These are not technical questions with "correct" answers; they are political and moral questions requiring ongoing deliberation.

The inadequacy of linear problem-solving now manifests in familiar patterns. Leaders implement solutions that address symptoms while leaving structures untouched, ensuring recurring crises. Organizations optimize for efficiency and short-term performance while sacrificing resilience, increasing vulnerability to shocks. Approaches that work in one context fail when transplanted to another, but the reasons remain obscure. Expertise and "best practices" developed for previous challenges prove irrelevant or counterproductive in new conditions.

## TOWARD AN ITERATIVE, ADAPTIVE APPROACH

If linear problem-solving is insufficient, what should replace it?

The answer is an iterative, adaptive approach that embraces experimentation, continuous learning, and resilience over optimization.

An iterative approach begins with the recognition that in complex environments, understanding often follows action rather than preceding it. Organizations cannot fully analyze a crisis before responding; they must respond in order to better understand it.

This means designing interventions as experiments, actions taken not because they are certain to succeed but because they will generate information regardless of outcome. It means implementing changes in ways that allow rapid feedback and adjustment rather than committing irreversibly to a single pathway.

Adaptation requires both structural flexibility and cultural humility. Structurally, organizations need modular designs that allow different units to try different approaches; distributed decision-making that permits local adjustment; and looser coupling that prevents failures in one area from cascading uncontrollably. Culturally, they must value learning from failure, reward the questioning of assumptions, and support leaders who change course when evidence warrants rather than doubling down on failing strategies.

Continuous learning requires systematic processes for capturing experience, analyzing what works and what does not, and incorporating insights into evolving practice.

This means learning not only from major incidents but from near-misses and from the experiences of others; investing in the capacity to make sense of ambiguous information; scanning for weak signals; and distinguishing pattern from noise.

Several principles follow:

- Embrace plurality rather than forcing premature consensus; wicked problems rarely have single "right" answers.
- Design for resilience rather than maximum efficiency; accept some redundancy and slack as the price of survivability.
- Distribute authority and empower frontline judgment; centralized command-and-control cannot keep pace with rapidly evolving situations.
- Invest in relationships and networks before crises; trust and collaboration cannot be improvised in the moment.
- Address power and inequality explicitly; pretending neutrality in unequal systems produces perverse outcomes.
- Value process as much as outcome; when outcomes are ambiguous, the legitimacy and quality of decision processes become decisive.
- Cultivate organizational humility; acknowledge limits of

foresight, remain open to disconfirming evidence, and treat expertise as provisional.

# BARRIERS AND IMPLICATIONS FOR LEADERSHIP

If adaptive approaches are so clearly needed, why have so few organizations fully embraced them?

Structural inertia, professional cultures built on linear problem-solving, short-term incentives, cognitive biases, risk-averse cultures, and existing power arrangements all work against genuine adaptation. Complexity itself can overwhelm leaders already stretched by day-to-day operations.

The implication is that leadership itself must be reconceived. Command-and-control models, leaders at the top plan and direct, others execute, fit poorly with complex, cascading, contested crises.

More effective models emphasize convening, facilitation, and sense-making: bringing the right people together; enabling honest, informed deliberation; empowering distributed action; and helping the organization interpret what it is experiencing.

Decisiveness does not disappear, but it relocates: from a single heroic leader to a network of empowered actors operating within a shared intent and set of principles. Accountability does not vanish, but it is grounded less in strict adherence to pre-set plans and more in the quality of processes, the integrity of trade-offs, and the willingness to learn.

In short, managing in the age of chaos requires organizations to abandon the comforting illusion that the right plan will restore stability. Instead, they must build the adaptive capacity to operate coherently inside permanent turbulence, turning chaos from a debilitating external force into a medium in which they can still think, decide, and act effectively.

● 3

# THE COGNITIVE SKILLS FOR MASTERING CHAOS

The contemporary organizational landscape is defined by volatility, complexity, and ambiguity. Frameworks built for stable, predictable environments increasingly fail when confronted with cascading uncertainties, tight coupling, and contested problems.

In this context, technical competence and traditional strategic acumen are necessary but no longer sufficient. Leaders must develop a distinct set of cognitive capabilities that allow them to think clearly and act coherently inside chaos.

These cognitive skills enable leaders to process complex information rapidly, maintain emotional equilibrium under pressure, and guide their organizations through uncertainty without succumbing either to paralysis or to reckless overconfidence.

This chapter examines four foundational capabilities: adaptive thinking and cognitive flexibility, pattern recognition under uncertainty, metacognitive awareness and reflective practice, and emotional regulation in high-pressure contexts. They are not optional refinements; they are core competencies for anyone expected to lead in complex adaptive systems.

# ADAPTIVE THINKING AND COGNITIVE FLEXIBILITY

At the foundation of effective chaos management lies cognitive flexibility: the capacity to shift mental frameworks as circumstances evolve. This is more than a general openness to change. It is a disciplined orientation toward reality that treats all interpretations as provisional and keeps multiple hypotheses in play at once.

Leaders with high cognitive flexibility can hold competing explanations of a situation without insisting prematurely on a single, comforting story. They resist the urge to resolve ambiguity simply because it feels uncomfortable.

Instead, they act on the best available understanding while remaining alert to disconfirming evidence and prepared to revise when the situation demands. This combination, willingness to act coupled with willingness to update, is the essence of adaptive thinking.

The poet John Keats called this "negative capability": the ability to remain in uncertainties and doubts without irritably reaching after fact and reason.[*] In leadership terms, it means avoiding two opposite errors: waiting indefinitely for perfect information or locking into a confident narrative too early. Karl Weick's work on sensemaking points in the same direction: leaders must cultivate a bias toward action that treats each move as an experiment rather than a final verdict.[†]

Cognitive flexibility has three practical dimensions.

- First, comfort with ambiguity: the ability to function effectively when key variables are unknown, indicators are conflicting, and outcomes cannot be forecast with precision.
- Second, level shifting: moving quickly between tactical detail and strategic overview, understanding how local

---

[*] John Keats, "Negative Capability," Wikipedia, https://en.wikipedia.org/wiki/Negative_capability

[†] Louis A. Schmidt, "Karl E. Weick and the Dawning Awareness of Organized Cognition," ResearchGate, 2015, https://www.researchgate.net/publication/280034351_Kar l_E_Weick_and_the_dawning_awareness_of_organized_cognition.; Laura McNamara, "Sensemaking in Organizations: Reflections on Karl Weick and Organized Cognition," EPIC People, 2011, https://www.epicpeople.org/sensemaking-in-organizations/.

events connect to the broader system and how high-level
decisions play out on the ground.
- Third, paradox management: holding opposing demands
such as speed and reflection, control and autonomy, stability
and change without forcing false either/or choices.[*]

In chaotic environments, these tensions never fully resolve; they
must be managed continually. Leaders who insist on eliminating
paradox usually end up overcorrecting, swinging between extremes
instead of steering through them. Adaptive thinking accepts that
contradiction is a normal feature of complex systems, not a sign of
personal failure.

## PATTERN RECOGNITION UNDER UNCERTAINTY

If cognitive flexibility keeps leaders from freezing or fixating, pattern
recognition under uncertainty helps them decide what actually
matters. In chaotic environments, organizations are flooded with data,
alerts, opinions, and signals. The challenge is not scarcity of information but discerning signal from noise.

Effective pattern recognition is not simply spotting obvious trends
in clean datasets. It involves detecting weak signals, early, subtle indicators of emerging shifts, while avoiding the temptation to see patterns
where none exist. Leaders must learn to recognize feedback loops,
tipping points, and non-linear effects: how small interventions can
yield outsized consequences, and how apparently large actions can
dissipate without effect.

This capability rests on two intertwined elements.

- First, mental models of system dynamics: an intuitive grasp
of how the relevant system actually behaves over time, not
just how it is supposed to behave on paper. Leaders who

---

[*] Wendy Smith, "Leaders Need Both/And Thinking to Navigate Paradoxical Challenges," *Academy of Management Today*, March 7, 2025, https://today.aom.org/leaders-need-both-and-thinking-to-navigate-paradoxical-challenges/.

understand their operating environment as a living system, economic, political, operational, technological, can better anticipate how interventions might ripple through it.

- Second, disciplined pattern testing: continuously checking emerging interpretations against new evidence, explicitly asking what would disconfirm the current story rather than only what confirms it.

Importantly, pattern recognition is a collective endeavor as much as an individual skill. In complex situations, no single leader sees enough of the picture alone. The organization must develop "distributed cognition": combining the perspectives of operators, analysts, technologists, logisticians, political advisors, and others into a shared, evolving map of the situation. The leader's role is to set up the conditions under which this collective sensemaking can occur fast enough to matter.

My whole experience with my colleague Harald Malmgren, a noted economist, whereby we worked the intersection between the worlds in which we worked, led to significant insights we would not have had individually. In other words, our interactions uncovered new patterns that neither one of us grasped working in our own disciplines but when sharing issues what we thought "different" we often discovered why. These issues were shaping something new that was not captured by either of our analytical worlds. They lay outside those boundaries and we only discovered them by exploring them together with our different backgrounds, experiences and intellectual training.[*]

## METACOGNITIVE AWARENESS AND REFLECTIVE PRACTICE

Metacognition or thinking about one's own thinking is the control system for all the other cognitive skills. It is the ability to observe how

---

[*] Robbin Laird, *Assessing Global Change: Strategic Perspectives of Dr. Harald Malmgren* (2025).

you are making sense of a situation, recognize the limits and biases of your own judgment, and deliberately adjust your approach.[*]

Under pressure, leaders naturally fall back on familiar patterns. Sometimes those patterns are appropriate; often they are not. Metacognitive awareness allows a leader to notice, in real time, "I am defaulting to a template that does not fit this situation" or "I am ignoring inconvenient data because it contradicts a position I have already defended." Without that awareness, even highly intelligent leaders simply become more efficient at making the same mistakes.[†]

Reflective practice operationalizes metacognition. It means building routines, individually and collectively, for stepping back to examine how decisions are being made, not just what decisions are being made. This includes structured after-action reviews that ask not only "What happened?" but "What did we expect? Why? How did our mental models help or hinder?" It also includes short, in-stride pauses during ongoing operations to check whether current assumptions still fit the evidence.

Learning organizations embed these practices into daily life rather than reserving them for major crises. They treat each significant decision as an opportunity to refine their thinking tools. They encourage constructive dissent about interpretations, not only about tactics. Over time, this builds a culture in which leaders at all levels feel responsible not just for acting, but for improving how the organization thinks.

## EMOTIONAL REGULATION IN HIGH-PRESSURE CONTEXTS

None of the cognitive skills described above can be reliably exercised if emotional responses overwhelm the system. Emotional regulation is therefore not a soft add-on; it is the enabling condition for clear thinking under pressure.

---

[*] "Sensemaking in Organizations," *OER Commons*, accessed January 25, 2026, https://oercommons.org/courseware/lesson/73880/overview?section=9.

[†] "The Schön Reflection Model: In Action and On Action," *Locus Assignments* (blog), accessed January 25, 2026, https://www.locusassignments.com/blog/schon-reflection-in-action-vs-reflection-on-action-difference.

In chaotic situations, leaders experience fear, frustration, anger, and exhaustion as do their teams. Attempts to suppress these emotions outright usually fail and often backfire, consuming mental energy and distorting judgment.[*] Emotional regulation instead involves acknowledging emotional responses, processing them appropriately, and preventing them from hijacking decision-making.[†]

Practically, this includes simple but powerful disciplines: recognizing physiological signs of escalation (tightness, shallow breathing, narrowing attention), using brief resets to restore cognitive bandwidth, and deliberately slowing key decisions when emotional charge is highest and time genuinely permits. It also includes anticipating emotional dynamics in the wider organization: how fear of blame might distort reporting, how loyalty might inhibit speaking up, how pride might block course correction.[‡]

Leaders who regulate their own responses create psychological safety for others. When bad news is met with curiosity rather than anger, people keep bringing hard truths forward. When mistakes are treated as material for learning rather than immediate punishment provided there was no negligence, teams remain willing to experiment and adapt. In chaotic environments, that openness is a strategic asset: it keeps information flowing and preserves the conditions for honest sensemaking.

## INTEGRATION: TOWARD CHAOS LITERACY

Adaptive thinking, pattern recognition, metacognitive awareness, and emotional regulation are deeply interdependent. Cognitive flexibility

---

[*] Brett S. Torrence and Shane Connelly, "Emotion Regulation Tendencies and Leadership Performance: An Examination of Cognitive and Behavioral Regulation Strategies," *Frontiers in Psychology* 10 (2019): 1486, https://pmc.ncbi.nlm.nih.gov/articles/PMC6614202/.

[†] Melrona Kirrane, Deirdre O'Shea, Finian Buckley, Adele Grazi, and Joanne Prout, "Investigating the Role of Discrete Emotions in Silence versus Speaking Up," *Journal of Occupational and Organizational Psychology* 90, no. 3 (2017): 354–378, https://www.dcu.ie/sites/default/files/leadership-talent/melrona_article1.pdf.

[‡] Michael Serwa, "What Is Decision Fatigue: A Leader's Guide to Finding Decision Clarity," *MichaelSerwa.com*, updated January 7, 2026, https://michaelserwa.com/articles/decision-fatigue/.

helps leaders update their understanding as new patterns emerge; pattern recognition gives them something substantive to update toward; metacognition ensures they notice when their own habits are becoming liabilities; emotional regulation keeps the whole system functioning under stress.

Developing these capabilities is not a one-off training event. It requires deliberate practice over time: structured exposure to complex scenarios, opportunities to make and correct judgment calls in low-risk environments, coaching that surfaces blind spots, and organizational norms that reward learning as much as performance.

Simulation-based exercises where leaders must act under time pressure with incomplete information and then debrief how they thought are particularly powerful tools for building this form of "chaos literacy."

Ultimately, the central leadership question in the age of chaos is not "Do you know the right answers?" but "Can you and your organization keep thinking when the situation will not sit still?" The cognitive skills in this chapter are how leaders build that capacity in themselves and in those they lead.

# SHAPING AN APPROACH
# FOR CHAOS MANAGEMENT

Part One diagnosed the anarchy of the moment and why traditional management frameworks collapse under its weight. You now understand the structural realities of tight coupling, temporal compression, and wicked problems that make linear planning obsolete. The cognitive skills required to recognize these dynamics have been identified.

Part Two shifts from diagnosis to action. This section provides concrete frameworks for building the three pillars of adaptive capacity, intellectual flexibility, institutional resilience, and social cohesion, across organizational architecture, leader development, playbook design, and navigator training. These are not theoretical constructs but implementation roadmaps drawn from decades observing organizations that actually adapted successfully during fundamental transitions.

The four chapters form a deliberate sequence, each addressing a distinct capability layer.

Chapter 1: Leading Through Chaos begins at the apex, showing how senior leaders must model adaptive decision-making under uncertainty. Traditional command-and-control fails when parameters shift faster than planning cycles. This chapter provides diagnostic questions to assess your personal and command-team readiness, then outlines specific practices, maintaining operational tempo with incomplete information, preserving optionality in early moves, creating decision frameworks that tolerate ambiguity. You'll learn how to distinguish situations requiring immediate action from those demanding experimentation, and how to maintain organizational coherence when different units see different aspects of the same complex problem. Leadership sets the pace; without it, structural changes later in Part Two become impossible.

Chapter 2: Shaping Chaos-Ready Organizations moves to institutional design. Organizations optimized for efficiency in stable environments become brittle when conditions shift. This chapter provides the architecture for resilience: modular structures that allow distributed adaptation, redundant capabilities that accept inefficiency as the price of survivability, and knowledge-transfer systems that preserve institutional memory across leadership transitions. You'll get concrete implementation steps, rewriting resource allocation for multi-future scenarios, building cross-functional teams that span traditional silos, creating stress-testing protocols that reveal hidden dependencies. The goal is organizations that can maintain coherence while different components experiment with different approaches to the same challenge.

Chapter 3: Designing Your Chaos Management Playbook translates the previous chapters into a 12–24 month transformation roadmap. Strategic planning must shift from scenario prediction to capability sequencing. This chapter provides archetype playbooks for different institutional types, military commands, corporate divisions, government agencies, each with diagnostic tools, implementation sequences, and common failure modes. You'll learn how to triage vulnerabilities (distinguishing complicated problems addressable by traditional management from complex ones requiring new approaches), prioritize capability builds within resource constraints, and create feedback loops that allow continuous adjustment. The playbook is your operational core: a living document that evolves as you learn.

Chapter 4: The Chaos Navigator culminates Part Two by forging the leaders required to execute these frameworks in real time. Even perfect playbooks fail without leaders who treat chaos as baseline operating condition rather than aberration. This chapter details a developmental program, the Chaos Navigator, that operationalizes the cognitive skills from Part One into institutionalized training: simulations that compress years of uncertainty into days, red-teaming that breaks mental models, evaluation metrics that track growth in adaptive thinking rather than rote execution. You'll get the full program architecture, from selection criteria to after-action reviews that build metacognitive discipline. These are not traits leaders are born with; they are competencies built through deliberate stress exposure and reflection.

Together, these chapters fulfill the Introduction's promise: detailed frameworks for assessing vulnerabilities, building capabilities, and avoiding failure modes. Months 1–3: diagnose using Chapter 1 leadership practices and Chapter 2 organizational stress tests. Months 4–18: sequence playbook execution from Chapter 3 while standing up Navigator training in Chapter 4. The result is not an organization that predicts chaos that remains impossible but one that thrives within it.

This sequence matters. Leadership alignment (Ch. 1) enables organizational redesign (Ch. 2), which informs playbook development (Ch.

3), which requires leader development (Ch. 4) to execute. Skip a step, and the others collapse. Implement them as a unified campaign, and you build what history shows separates organizations that break from those that emerge stronger: deliberate adaptive capacity before the next transition hits.

Part Two is your workbench. The tools here have been field-tested in military transformations, corporate restructurings, and government adaptations I have directly observed. Use them to build what cannot be planned: organizational capacity that functions when planning fails.

**4**

## LEADING THROUGH CHAOS

In today's volatile strategic environment, organizations face an unprecedented convergence of disruptions. From global pandemics and geopolitical instability to rapid technological transformation and climate-related crises, the pace and complexity of change have fundamentally altered what it means to lead effectively.

This challenge faces political leaders, military commanders, business leaders or government organizations navigating the ubiquitous security challenges.

Traditional management approaches, built on assumptions of stability and predictability, are increasingly inadequate for navigating the turbulent waters of modern organizational life. The question is no longer whether leaders will face crisis situations, but rather how well-equipped they are to manage them when they inevitably arise.

This reality demands a fundamental reconceptualization of leadership development. Organizations must move beyond conventional crisis management training that focuses primarily on protocols, procedures, and communication plans. While these elements remain important, they represent only the surface level of effective chaos management.

The deeper challenge lies in cultivating the cognitive capabilities that enable leaders to think clearly, act decisively, and adapt continuously in the face of radical uncertainty.

This chapter explores the essential cognitive skills required for chaos management and presents evidence-based approaches to developing these capabilities through sophisticated simulation-based training methodologies.

## THE CHANGING NATURE OF ORGANIZATIONAL CRISES

Contemporary organizational crises differ fundamentally from those of previous decades in several critical dimensions.

- First, they are increasingly characterized by deep interconnectivity and cascading effects. A supply chain disruption in one region can rapidly propagate through global networks, triggering second and third-order consequences that leaders could not have anticipated.
- Second, modern crises often emerge from the collision of multiple systems operating at different scales and speeds, creating what complexity theorists call emergent phenomena that cannot be understood by analyzing individual components in isolation.
- Third, the speed of information flow both enables and complicates crisis response. Social media and digital communication platforms allow for unprecedented coordination and transparency, but they also accelerate the spread of misinformation, amplify stakeholder reactions, and compress decision-making timeframes. Leaders must make high-stakes choices with incomplete information while under intense public scrutiny, often within hours rather than days or weeks.
- Finally, many contemporary challenges are characterized by what organizational theorists call wicked problems: situations where the nature of the problem itself is contested, where solutions create new problems, and where there are no clear

stopping points or measures of success. Climate change, cybersecurity threats, and systemic inequality all exemplify this category. Traditional linear problem-solving approaches prove inadequate for such challenges, demanding instead an iterative, adaptive approach that embraces experimentation and continuous learning.

# ESSENTIAL COGNITIVE SKILLS FOR CHAOS MANAGEMENT

Effective leadership in chaotic environments requires a distinctive set of cognitive capabilities that extend well beyond traditional management competencies. These skills enable leaders to process complex information rapidly, maintain emotional equilibrium under pressure, and guide their organizations through uncertainty without succumbing to either paralysis or reckless action.

## Adaptive Thinking and Cognitive Flexibility

Leaders must master adaptive thinking to survive chaos. Traditional command-and-control logic fails when threats evolve faster than planning cycles and information arrives in contradictory fragments. Adaptive leaders don't cling to initial assessments; they pivot as reality shifts beneath them.

What it looks like in practice: A Joint Task Force commander facing a hybrid threat in the South China Sea receives satellite imagery showing merchant ships massing near disputed reefs. Initial intel suggests fishing militia. Two hours later, ELINT confirms active radar emitters and encrypted comms consistent with PLAN corvettes operating in merchant guise. The adaptive leader immediately shelves the "fishing boat" working assumption, reconvenes the battle staff with a new question set ("What must be true for this to be merchant traffic vs. naval deception?"), and adjusts the rules of engagement brief for the strike group.

Core practices:

- Hold multiple hypotheses simultaneously. Train your staff to maintain three competing explanations for any significant development, retiring the weakest only when contradicted by hard evidence.
- Seek disconfirming data aggressively. Assign a designated "friction officer" whose sole job during crisis deliberations is to attack the emerging consensus with alternative interpretations.
- Self-check question: When did you last publicly reverse a decision based on new information and reward a staffer who challenged your initial judgment?

This isn't theoretical. In Steel Knight 25, an exercise which I attended, I MEF used hub-and-spoke and distributed node concepts to rehearse sustaining forces and logistics under long-range drone and missile threat, including extensive contested-logistics and counter-UAS training.[*]

Simulation training method: Build "Hypothesis Stress Tests" into your next command post exercise. At T+90 minutes, inject deliberately ambiguous information that contradicts the base plan. Force decision-makers to articulate their top three working hypotheses and assign betting odds to each. Score not on who guesses right, but on who maintains cognitive flexibility longest under uncertainty.

## Pattern Recognition Under Uncertainty

Pattern recognition is the ability to discern structure in what initially appears as noise. In stable environments, this often means matching what you see to familiar templates: "We have seen this before; it is that kind of problem; here is the corresponding response." In chaotic environments, this habit becomes dangerous, because the surface resem-

---

[*] U.S. Marine Corps, 2ndLt Lorenzo Meigs, "U.S. Marines Conclude Exercise Steel Knight 25, Strengthening Joint Readiness Across Southern California and Arizona," 1st Marine Division, 15 December 2025, https://www.1stmardiv.marines.mil/News/Article/Article/4361450/us-marines-conclude-exercise-steel-knight-25-strengthening-joint-readiness-acro/

blance of events can conceal fundamentally different dynamics underneath.

In the air traffic control tower, this shift from matching patterns to testing them is not a theory, it is a way of staying alive to what might go wrong next. A controller may be watching an evening push that looks utterly routine when a few small anomalies begin to appear: a slight wobble in an approach path, an unexpected speed reduction, a hesitation in a pilot's voice. None of these, in isolation, proves anything.

The seasoned controller starts instead with a tentative story: "This feels like the start of a weather-driven compression," or "This looks like the kind of vectoring confusion that once led to a loss of separation on this approach." Then comes the crucial inner question: "If that story is true, what should I see in the next sweep or the next two calls?"

They watch for the confirming tell, another aircraft slowing earlier than expected, a pilot asking for a deviation, a track edging a little too close on the scope, and are just as ready to abandon the story if the expected cues do not arrive. In that quiet loop of hypothesis, expectation, and correction, I have seen controllers turn uncertainty from a source of paralysis into a disciplined form of anticipation, using their mental models not as static templates but as probes they push against reality to see where it will bend.

I observed this when working on a study with regard to shaping an air traffic control system built on satellite systems and how AI can be used in such a re-crafted system architecture.

This pattern recognition approach requires a tolerance for incomplete and conflicting signals. The early stages of a crisis rarely present a clean picture. Data streams arrive at different speeds and levels of reliability. Political pressure and media narratives create strong incentives to seize on the first recognizable pattern, declare that you understand what is happening, and act decisively. The discipline of chaos management is to slow that impulse just enough to test whether the pattern you think you see is actually there.

Pattern recognition in this environment is also a team sport. No single leader, regardless of experience, can see the full pattern of a complex, fast-moving situation alone. Different parts of the organization occupy different vantage points. The logistics officer, the cyber cell, the public affairs team, the legal advisor, and the political liaison all see different slices of the same unfolding reality. The leader's task is to create structures and habits that bring these partial views into contact, so that a more accurate pattern can emerge from their interaction.

This means designing the decision-making room as much as designing the plan. Who sits at the table when you conduct your first crisis huddle? Whose information feeds are given priority? How do you prevent one dominant narrative from silencing less dramatic but more accurate signals coming from the edge of the organization? In a chaotic environment, the pattern is often first visible at the periphery, not at the center. Organizations that cannot hear their edges will consistently misread what is happening to them.

Finally, pattern recognition under uncertainty demands a capacity for revision that mirrors adaptive thinking. Sometimes the pattern you thought you saw is simply wrong. Sometimes the adversary is deliberately creating a false pattern to draw you into a trap. Sometimes the pattern itself mutates as your own actions change the environment.

In such cases, the leader must be willing to say: "The pattern has shifted; the map we were using no longer fits the terrain; we need to redraw it and adjust our behavior accordingly." This is not an admission of defeat. It is an acknowledgment that in a world of moving targets, the real failure is not misidentifying a pattern once, but insisting on that pattern long after it has ceased to exist.

## Training Pattern Recognition in Simulations

If pattern recognition under uncertainty is a core leadership skill, it must be treated as a trainable capability rather than a personality trait. The most effective way to do this is to design exercises and simulations that deliberately stress leaders' pattern-forming habits and make those habits visible in the debrief. The goal is not to produce the "right" answer in the scenario, but to surface how quickly, on what basis, and with what degree of confidence leaders commit to a particular pattern reading.

One straightforward method is to build time-phased injects that initially mimic a familiar pattern and then diverge. In the opening phase of a simulation, the indicators look like a conventional cyber intrusion, a routine supply chain disruption, or a localized protest movement. As the scenario unfolds, the data begin to contradict that initial reading. Some teams will cling to the first pattern; others will hesitate to commit to any interpretation. In the hot wash, you do not simply ask, "What did you do?" You ask, "At what moment did you decide what this was, and what made you hold to or revise that judgment?"

A second approach is to assign explicit "pattern roles" inside the exercise. One cell is tasked with articulating the dominant narrative, how the situation appears to the main decision-maker. A second cell is tasked with generating alternative interpretations, however unwelcome. A third monitors specific indicators that would confirm or disconfirm each narrative. This structure forces leaders to hear competing pattern claims in real time and to practice the discipline of testing stories against evidence rather than against their preferences.

Micro-simulations can serve the same purpose without elaborate preparation. In a 20–30 minute drill at the start of a staff meeting, you can present three short incident reports that arrive over a notional 24-hour period. Each report is incomplete, noisy, and slightly misleading. The team must decide when they have enough of a pattern to act. Do they wait for one more report? Do they move on the basis of a fragile pattern? Do they set up monitoring to test whether their early reading is correct? The value lies less in the scenario itself than in the conversation about why the team moved when it did.

Over time, these exercises help shift the culture. Leaders and staff become more comfortable saying, "This is our current pattern read; here are two alternatives; here is what we are watching to see which one is right." They learn to treat patterns as living hypotheses rather than static labels. In a world where adversaries manipulate signals, where crises bleed into one another, and where the first story is rarely the whole story, this habit of trained, collective pattern testing becomes one of the most important safeguards against strategic misjudgment.

## Emotional Regulation and Stress Tolerance

Emotional regulation is not a soft add-on to leadership; it is a core operational capability in an age of chaos. Under severe pressure, the nervous system pushes leaders toward fight, flight, or freeze. In a cockpit, a command center, or a crisis cabinet, those reactions translate into impulsive action, panicked retreat, or paralysis precisely when others most need clear headed direction. Stress tolerance is the capacity to absorb this physiological and psychological shock without letting it dictate your behavior.

In more predictable eras, leaders could often mask their inner state behind institutional routines. The organization could carry them through periods of pressure. In chaotic environments, there are extended periods when no routine fits the situation and everyone in the room is watching the leader for cues. If you transmit panic, the organization will amplify it. If you transmit numbness or denial, the organization will drift. Emotional regulation under these conditions is the ability to acknowledge the gravity of the situation without being consumed by it.

This does not mean suppressing emotion or pretending to be unaffected. On the contrary, leaders who act as if they are untouched by events often lose credibility. People know when the stakes are high. What they need to see is a leader who can name the pressure, take a breath, and then return to deliberate thought and deliberate action. A leader who can say, "This is serious; we are going to feel this; here is the next decision we need to make," provides a form of psychological ballast that no formal plan can substitute for.

Emotional regulation also has a contagious dimension. In a crisis, stress cascades through networks. Staff absorb the leader's tone, and their teams in turn absorb theirs. Small signals, a tightened voice on a conference call, visible agitation when challenged, sarcasm directed at a subordinate, can travel quickly and shape the emotional climate in ways leaders rarely intend. Stress-tolerant leaders pay attention to these signals. They recognize that their own self-management is not a private matter; it is a shared asset or a shared liability.

Developing this capacity requires practice, not slogans. It means exposing leaders to controlled doses of pressure in simulations and exercises, then making the emotional component explicit in the debrief. How did your body react when the inject arrived? What happened to the quality of your listening when the scenario turned against you? At what point did you find yourself reaching for reassurance rather than information? Over time, this kind of reflective practice builds a realistic self-knowledge that is the foundation of genuine stress tolerance.

Ultimately, emotional regulation and stress tolerance are about preserving freedom of action when the situation is trying to take it away. Chaos compresses time, overwhelms attention, and floods the system with signals. The leader who can remain present, keep thinking, and keep others thinking in that environment provides something more than calm. They provide the conditions under which sound judgment is still possible, even when everything in the environment is pushing in the opposite direction.

## Collaborative Sensemaking and Distributed Cognition

No individual, however experienced, can see the full shape of a complex crisis alone. Collaborative sensemaking is the process by which a group builds, tests, and revises a shared understanding of what is happening and what might happen next. Distributed cognition recognizes that the "mind" doing this work is not just the leader's brain, but the combined perception, memory, and judgment of the entire network, people, tools, and information systems working together.

In linear planning cultures, information typically flows upward for a single decision-maker to process. The staff's job is to prepare options; the leader's job is to choose. In chaotic environments, this model breaks down. Information arrives too fast, from too many directions, and with too much ambiguity for one person to integrate alone. The task of the leader shifts from being the sole analyst to being the architect of a process in which diverse perspectives can interact quickly enough to matter.

Collaborative sensemaking begins with who is invited into the conversation and how. A room filled only with people who share the same background, incentives, and blind spots will produce a very coherent but potentially very wrong picture. A chaos-ready organization deliberately brings together operational commanders, technical specialists, political advisers, logisticians, legal counsel, and front-line representatives, not as a courtesy but because the pattern is only visible when their partial views overlap. The leader's role is to ensure that each of these vantage points is heard before the group settles on a story about what is happening.

This requires designing interaction, not just attendance. If the same voices dominate every crisis huddle, if junior officers or specialists are present but silent, the organization will still think with only a fraction of its available brain. Simple structural devices, rounds where each participant must offer a brief assessment, explicit time reserved for "minority views," or a rotating role responsible for challenging the emerging consensus, can keep the group from collapsing too quickly into a single narrative.

Distributed cognition also involves the way tools and systems are used. Dashboards, chat channels, sensor feeds, and analytic platforms are not neutral. They highlight some signals and obscure others. A leadership team that treats these tools as passive background will unconsciously allow the design of the system to shape what they see as real. A team that understands distributed cognition asks: "What is not on this screen? Whose data is not represented here? Which parts of the organization are effectively invisible to us right now?"

True collaborative sensemaking is not endless discussion. It is a disciplined cycle: gather diverse inputs, articulate competing interpretations, identify critical uncertainties, and then act while remaining ready to revise the shared picture as new information appears. The point is not to reach perfect agreement before moving, but to ensure that action is informed by the best composite understanding the system can generate at that moment and that this understanding remains open to update.

In an era where crises cross domains and borders, the organizations that learn to think this way, collectively, reflexively, and with full use of their distributed cognition, will be better positioned to navigate chaos. They will make mistakes, as all human systems do, but they will detect and correct those mistakes faster. In chaotic environments, that speed of collective learning is often the difference between a crisis that is merely costly and one that becomes existential.

# SIMULATION-BASED TRAINING METHODOLOGIES

While the cognitive skills described above sound abstract, they can be developed through carefully designed training experiences. The most effective approaches utilize simulation-based learning: immersive exercises that create realistic psychological and cognitive demands without the consequences of actual crises. Research across multiple domains, from aviation to military operations to emergency medicine, demonstrates that well-designed simulations accelerate skill development and improve performance under pressure.

## Scenario-Based Crisis Simulations

The foundation of effective chaos management training lies in realistic scenario-based exercises that immerse leaders in the uncertainty, time pressure, and complexity of actual crises. Unlike case study discussions or tabletop exercises, high-fidelity simulations create authentic emotional and cognitive demands that trigger the same mental processes required in real situations.

Effective scenario design incorporates several key elements:

- Incomplete information that requires active intelligence gathering rather than passive consumption of provided data.
- Time pressure that forces prioritization and prevents overthinking.
- Unexpected complications and plot twists that disrupt initial plans and require adaptation.

- Competing stakeholder demands that create dilemmas
  without clear right answers.
- Resource constraints that force difficult trade-offs between
  important objectives.
- Ambiguous causality where the relationship between
  actions and outcomes remains uncertain.

The value of simulations comes not only from the experience itself but from structured reflection afterward. After-action reviews provide opportunities for participants to analyze their decision-making processes, identify patterns in their responses to pressure, and develop strategies for improvement.

Effective debriefs focus not on whether participants made the right decisions but on the quality of their thinking: Did they gather diverse perspectives? Did they test their assumptions? Did they consider second-order effects? Did they create conditions for others to contribute?

## Red Team and Blue Team Exercises

Red team exercises, borrowed from military and intelligence communities, involve designated participants actively trying to disrupt plans or identify vulnerabilities in organizational systems. This adversarial approach serves multiple training functions.

- First, it helps leaders develop mental models for how
  systems can fail, expanding their repertoire of possible
  scenarios beyond those they would naturally consider.
- Second, it builds comfort with being challenged and proven
  wrong, reducing the defensiveness that often undermines
  learning in less structured environments.

In red team exercises, one group develops a strategy or plan while another group actively seeks to exploit weaknesses or identify flaws. The adversarial dynamic forces the blue team to defend their thinking rigorously and consider alternative perspectives they might otherwise dismiss. Meanwhile, the red team develops skills in creative problem-finding and systematic analysis of complex systems.

The psychological benefit of red teaming extends beyond specific scenarios. Leaders who regularly engage in structured adversarial thinking develop what psychologists call intellectual humility: awareness of the limitations of their own knowledge and openness to evidence that contradicts their beliefs. This mindset proves invaluable in actual crises, where initial interpretations frequently prove incorrect and success depends on rapid updating based on new information.

## Complexity Gaming and Systems Thinking

Many organizational crises stem from unintended consequences of well-intentioned actions: solutions that work in the short term but create larger problems later, interventions that address symptoms while exacerbating root causes, or policies that optimize one part of a system at the expense of overall performance. Complexity gaming provides a methodology for developing intuition about system dynamics and feedback loops.

These exercises typically involve simplified models of complex systems where participants make sequential decisions and observe how their choices propagate through interconnected variables over time. Unlike traditional business simulations focused on competitive strategy or financial performance, complexity games emphasize understanding relationships between system elements and recognizing patterns that emerge from interaction effects.

Particularly valuable are scenarios where obvious solutions backfire. For example, a simulation might show how aggressive cost-cutting improves short-term financial metrics while degrading organizational capabilities needed for long-term sustainability.

Or how efforts to improve efficiency through standardization reduce the diversity that enables adaptation to unexpected challenges. Such exercises build intuition about leverage points in complex systems: places where small interventions can produce disproportionate effects, for better or worse.

Through repeated exposure to different system configurations, participants develop mental models that help them recognize similar patterns in real organizational contexts. They learn to ask questions about feedback loops, time delays, and unintended consequences that might not occur to those without systems thinking training. This metacognitive awareness proves particularly valuable when facing novel situations where domain-specific expertise provides limited guidance.

## Micro-Simulations and Distributed Practice

While intensive multi-day simulations provide powerful learning experiences, research on skill acquisition demonstrates that frequent, shorter practice sessions often prove more effective than occasional intensive training. Micro-simulations, lasting 15 to 30 minutes, can be integrated into regular management routines to provide ongoing skill development without major disruption to operational responsibilities.

These brief exercises might involve rapid decision-making drills where leaders must process limited information quickly, ethical dilemma discussions that surface value conflicts and trade-offs, or quick diagnostic exercises where participants identify patterns in complex data sets. The key is creating authentic cognitive demand in compressed timeframes, allowing for repeated practice of specific skills with immediate feedback.

Micro-simulations work best when paired with reflection protocols that help participants extract learning from experience. Simple structures like keep-start-stop reflections or before-after-action reviews build metacognitive awareness: the ability to observe one's own thinking and decision-making processes.

Over time, this self-awareness enables leaders to notice when they are falling into unproductive patterns and consciously deploy alternative approaches.

The distributed practice principle suggests that spacing learning over time produces better retention and transfer than massed practice. Organizations might therefore implement regular monthly micro-simulations rather than annual intensive training programs.

This approach also allows for progressive skill building, where each exercise builds on previous ones to develop increasingly sophisticated capabilities.

# BUILDING REQUISITE VARIETY IN MANAGEMENT TEAMS

The concept of requisite variety, drawn from cybernetics, states that a system's ability to respond to environmental complexity depends on having internal variety that matches external variety. For organizations facing chaotic environments, this means management teams must possess cognitive repertoires as diverse and flexible as the challenges they encounter.[*]

Building requisite variety operates on multiple levels. At the individual level, it requires developing broad capabilities across the cognitive skills discussed earlier. Leaders need both analytical and intuitive thinking, both confidence and humility, both decisiveness and patience. Overspecialization in any particular cognitive style creates vulnerabilities when situations demand different approaches.

At the team level, requisite variety involves assembling groups with complementary cognitive styles, diverse backgrounds, and different forms of expertise. Homogeneous teams perform well on routine tasks but struggle with novel challenges that require perspectives outside their shared mental models. Cognitive diversity creates productive friction that surfaces assumptions and generates creative solutions, though it also demands more skillful facilitation to prevent disagreement from becoming dysfunctional conflict.

At the organizational level, building requisite variety requires creating structures and cultures that value exploration alongside exploitation, maintain loose coupling that allows for local adaptation while preserving overall coherence, and cultivate internal networks that enable rapid information flow and resource mobilization during crises. Organizations that optimize too heavily for efficiency in stable

---

[*] W. Ross Ashby, "Cybernetics and Requisite Variety," in *An Introduction to Cybernetics* (London: Chapman & Hall, 1956), extracts reproduced at Panarchy.org, https://www.panarchy.org/ashby/variety.1956.html.; Graham Berrisford, "Ashby's Law of Requisite Variety," in *[Book vol. 2]*, last updated July 22, 2021, https://grahamberrisford.com/Bookvol2/1%20Ashbys%20olaw.htm

conditions typically lack the redundancy and flexibility needed to respond effectively when conditions change.

Training programs contribute to requisite variety by exposing leaders to situations outside their direct experience, challenging them to develop new capabilities, and helping them recognize the limits of their existing mental models.

The goal is not to eliminate specialized expertise but to ensure that specialists can also think systemically, that experts remain open to evidence that contradicts their theories, and that technically trained leaders also develop the interpersonal and emotional capabilities required for effective leadership under pressure.

## IMPLEMENTATION CONSIDERATIONS

Translating these principles into practical training programs requires careful attention to several implementation factors.

- First, simulations must be calibrated appropriately for participants' experience levels. Exercises that are too simple fail to create meaningful learning opportunities, while those that are overwhelmingly complex can induce learned helplessness rather than building confidence and capability.[*]
- Second, organizational culture significantly influences training effectiveness. In cultures characterized by blame and defensiveness, participants may focus more on avoiding mistakes than on genuine learning. Creating psychological safety where failure in training contexts is valued as a learning opportunity rather than penalized requires sustained leadership commitment and careful facilitation.[†]

---

[*] E. Salas and C. S. Burke, "Simulation for Training Is Effective When...," *Quality and Safety in Health Care* 11, no. 2 (2002): 119–20, PMC1743617, https://pmc.ncbi.nlm.nih.gov/articles/PMC1743617/pdf/v011p00119.pdf

[†] Amy C. Edmondson, "Psychological Safety and Learning Behavior in Work Teams," *Administrative Science Quarterly* 44, no. 2 (1999): 350–383; see also R. Patil et al., "Psychological Safety and Team Learning," *The Open Psychology Journal* 16 (2023); and recent studies on blame culture showing that fear of punishment drives defensiveness, suppresses risk-taking, and obstructs learning from errors.

- Third, the transfer of learning from training contexts to actual practice cannot be assumed. Organizations must create opportunities for participants to apply new skills in progressively higher-stakes situations, provide coaching and feedback during real operations, and recognize and reward the behaviors they seek to cultivate. Training represents a necessary but insufficient condition for organizational capability development.[*]

- Fourth, measurement and evaluation of training effectiveness requires looking beyond immediate participant satisfaction to longer-term behavioral change and organizational outcomes. This might include tracking decision quality during actual crises, assessing how quickly organizations detect and respond to emerging threats, or measuring psychological indicators like stress resilience and emotional regulation in high-pressure situations.[†]

# CONCLUSION

The chaotic environment facing contemporary organizations shows no signs of moderating. If anything, increasing interconnection, acceler-

---

[*] Baldwin, T. T., & Ford, J. K. "Transfer of Training: A Review and Directions for Future Research." *Human Resource Development Quarterly* 1, no. 1 (1988): 63–105. Pidd, K. *Organisational Barriers to Training Transfer.* Adelaide: National Centre for Education and Training on Addiction, 2004. Burke, L. A., & Hutchins, H. M. "Training Transfer: An Integrative Literature Review." *Human Resource Development Review* 6, no. 3 (2007): 263–296. Grossman, R., & Salas, E. "The Transfer of Training: What Really Matters." *International Journal of Training and Development* 15, no. 2 (2011): 103–120. Xiao, J., & Tsang, E. W. K. "From Training to Organizational Behavior: A Mediation Model of Perceived Training Adequacy and Organizational Commitment." *International Journal of Training and Development* 21, no. 2 (2017): 125–139.

[†] Kirkpatrick, D. L., & Kirkpatrick, J. D. *Evaluating Training Programs: The Four Levels.* 3rd ed. San Francisco: Berrett-Koehler, 2006. (Levels 3–4: behavior and results.). Tamkin, P., Yarnall, J., & Kerrin, M. *A Review of Models of Training Evaluation.* Brighton: Institute for Employment Studies, 2002.Faisal-E-Alam, M., et al. "Training Effectiveness Evaluation: Advancing a Kirkpatrick Model Based Composite Framework." *Educational Research Review* (2024). Bryghtpath. "The Practice Plan: Why Intention and Evaluation Matter in Crisis Management Training." 2025.

ating change, and growing complexity suggest that leaders will face even more demanding challenges in coming years.

Traditional approaches to leadership development, focused primarily on technical knowledge and routine decision-making, prove inadequate for this reality.

The cognitive skills required for effective chaos management can be systematically developed through well-designed training programs. Adaptive thinking, pattern recognition, emotional regulation, and collaborative sensemaking represent learnable capabilities rather than innate talents. Simulation-based methodologies provide powerful tools for building these skills in safe environments that nonetheless create authentic psychological and cognitive demands.

Success requires more than occasional training events. Organizations must embed continuous learning into leadership development systems, create cultures that value experimentation and learning from failure, and ensure that management teams possess the requisite variety to match the complexity they face. The investment required is substantial, but the costs of inadequate preparation are far higher.

Ultimately, chaos management represents not a technical challenge but a human one. Technology, data analytics, and formal procedures all play important roles, but they cannot substitute for leaders who can think clearly under pressure, maintain relationships amid conflict, make sound judgments with incomplete information, and guide organizations through uncertainty without losing sight of core purposes and values.

Developing such leaders represents one of the most important investments organizations can make in their long-term resilience and effectiveness.

**5**

# SHAPING CHAOS-READY ORGANIZATIONS

Understanding the principles of chaos management is one challenge; building organizations capable of operating within chaos is quite another.

This chapter provides a systematic framework for designing and building organizations that can not merely survive chaos but leverage it as a strategic advantage. The approach is deliberately practical, focusing on concrete organizational elements that leaders can implement, measure, and refine. These are not abstract principles but actionable design choices that determine whether an organization will fracture or thrive when confronted with the unexpected.

The framework addresses five critical organizational dimensions: information architecture, team structures, physical and digital environments, resource allocation systems, and talent acquisition and development.

Each dimension represents a lever that leaders can pull to increase organizational adaptive capacity. Individually, these elements provide incremental improvements. Together, they create emergent properties, organizational capabilities that exceed the sum of their parts.

# INFORMATION ARCHITECTURE FOR RAPID SENSE-MAKING

In chaotic environments, the organization that makes sense of the situation fastest gains decisive advantage. This is not about having more information. In fact, information overload often paralyzes decision-making. Rather, it concerns the architecture through which information flows, is filtered, is integrated, and is made actionable. The design of these information systems fundamentally determines an organization's sense-making velocity.

## Signal Versus Noise Filtering Systems

Traditional organizational hierarchies were designed to filter information as it flows upward, with each layer abstracting and summarizing for the layer above. This architecture made sense in stable environments where senior leaders needed to focus on long-term strategic questions while remaining insulated from operational detail. In chaos, this architecture becomes a liability. Critical weak signals get filtered out as noise, and by the time patterns become obvious enough to survive the filtering process, the window for effective action has closed.

Chaos-ready organizations invert this model. Rather than filtering information before it reaches decision-makers, they build systems that bring raw signals to those with pattern recognition capabilities while providing tools to manage attention and prevent overload. This requires several design elements:

- Direct sensor feeds: Create channels that allow decision-makers to access unfiltered information from organizational sensors, front-line employees, customers, suppliers, market signals, without waiting for reports to percolate through hierarchical layers. This might include daily briefings from customer service representatives, real-time dashboards of operational metrics, or direct channels for field personnel to flag anomalies.

- Pattern detection algorithms: Implement systems that flag deviations from expected patterns rather than simply reporting aggregate statistics. These systems should be tuned to detect weak signals, small changes that might herald larger shifts, rather than only obvious trends. This requires baseline pattern libraries and anomaly detection capabilities that adapt as patterns evolve.

- Attention management protocols: Provide decision-makers with frameworks for allocating attention across multiple information streams without becoming overwhelmed. This includes clear protocols for prioritization, designated deep-work periods free from interruption, and structured routines for scanning across different time horizons (tactical, operational, strategic).

- Contextual delivery systems: Ensure information reaches decision-makers with sufficient context to be actionable. This means attaching relevant background, highlighting connections to other signals, and indicating confidence levels. Raw data without context creates confusion rather than clarity.

The goal is not to eliminate filtering entirely for that would be impossible and counterproductive but to design filtering systems that preserve weak signals while managing information volume. This requires ongoing calibration as the organization learns which signals matter most for its specific challenges.

## Cross-Functional Integration Mechanisms

Most organizations are structured around functional specialization, with separate departments for operations, finance, technology, human resources, and so forth. This structure creates efficiency in stable environments by allowing deep expertise within domains.

However, chaos rarely respects departmental boundaries. Understanding what is actually happening requires integrating information across functional silos, such as connecting financial signals with operational patterns, technological changes with market dynamics, human resource trends with strategic risks.

Building effective integration mechanisms requires several architectural elements:

- Shared sense-making forums: Establish regular cross-functional sessions where leaders from different domains collectively interpret signals and develop integrated understanding. These are not status meetings but active sense-making exercises where participants challenge assumptions, identify connections across domains, and build coherent narratives about what is happening and why.
- Common operating pictures: Create visual representations that integrate information from multiple functional areas into coherent displays. These might include dashboard systems that overlay operational metrics with financial indicators and market signals, or network visualizations that show relationships between different types of events. The goal is to make cross-domain patterns visible rather than leaving each function with its own isolated view.
- Boundary-spanning roles: Designate specific individuals or teams responsible for translating across functional languages and identifying cross-domain implications. These boundary spanners need sufficient expertise in multiple domains to recognize patterns that specialized experts might miss, along with credibility to engage effectively with each functional area.
- Integrated data architectures: Build technical systems that allow data from different sources to be queried and analyzed together. This requires common data standards, interoperable systems, and analytical tools that can work across different data types. Without this technical foundation, cross-functional integration remains superficial.

The challenge is maintaining functional expertise while building integration capacity. Organizations need both deep domain knowledge and cross-domain synthesis. The architecture must support both without allowing either to atrophy.

## Distributed Cognition Systems

No individual, regardless of capability, can process all the information relevant to navigating organizational chaos. Effective sense-making in complex environments necessarily involves distributed cognition or cognitive processes that span multiple individuals, tools, and artifacts rather than residing in any single mind. The quality of these distributed systems largely determines organizational sense-making capacity.

Building effective distributed cognition requires attention to several elements:

- Cognitive artifacts: Develop tools and representations that extend human cognitive capacity. These might include decision frameworks that structure complex choices, visualization tools that make patterns visible, or simulation systems that allow exploration of scenarios. The key is that these artifacts do not simply store information but actively support reasoning processes.
- Complementary expertise networks: Deliberately construct teams with diverse but complementary forms of expertise. Rather than seeking consensus among similar thinkers, create systems where different perspectives constructively challenge each other. This requires both diversity in viewpoints and protocols for productive disagreement.
- Institutional memory systems: Build mechanisms that capture organizational learning over time. This goes beyond simple documentation to include structured debriefs after significant events, pattern libraries that codify recognized signatures, and narrative histories that preserve context. Without these systems, organizations continually relearn lessons at great cost.

- Transparent reasoning processes: Make organizational reasoning visible rather than opaque. Document key assumptions, record decision logic, and maintain clear chains of reasoning. This allows others to build on previous thinking, identify flawed assumptions, and maintain cognitive continuity even as individuals change roles.

The most sophisticated information architecture remains ineffective if the organization lacks the culture and practices to use it well. Technology enables distributed cognition, but culture and process determine whether that potential is realized.

# TEAM STRUCTURES: BALANCING STABILITY AND FLEXIBILITY

Traditional organizational structures optimize for either stability or flexibility, rarely both. Hierarchical bureaucracies provide clear authority and coordination but struggle to adapt quickly. Flat, fluid structures enable rapid reconfiguration but can dissolve into chaos without clear accountability. Chaos-ready organizations must somehow achieve both: Maintaining enough structural stability to preserve organizational capability while retaining enough flexibility to reconfigure as conditions demand.

## Core and Surge Architecture

One effective approach distinguishes between core capabilities that must remain stable and surge capabilities that can be rapidly mobilized and reconfigured. The core comprises those functions that define organizational identity and provide essential continuity. The minimum viable organization that must persist regardless of circumstances. Surge capacity represents additional capabilities that can be activated and directed toward emerging challenges as needed.

Implementing this architecture requires several design choices:

- Clear core definition: Explicitly identify which capabilities and functions constitute the organizational core. This requires discipline. The tendency is to declare everything essential. A useful test is asking what the organization absolutely must preserve to maintain its fundamental identity and mission. Everything else becomes potential surge capacity.

- Modular surge teams: Design surge capacity as relatively self-contained modules that can be assembled into different configurations. Each module should have clear interfaces, defined inputs, outputs, and integration requirements, that allow rapid connection with other modules and core functions. This modularity enables reconfiguration without requiring wholesale reorganization.

- Activation protocols: Establish clear processes for mobilizing surge capacity. This includes decision criteria for when to activate additional resources, procedures for rapidly forming and deploying teams, and coordination mechanisms to integrate surge efforts with core operations. Without clear protocols, surge activation becomes ad hoc and inefficient.

- Reserve capacity maintenance: Maintain surge capacity even when not actively deployed. This requires investing in capabilities that may sit idle during normal operations but become critical during crisis. Organizations often cut reserve capacity during periods of apparent stability, only to discover its absence when conditions deteriorate. Building reserve capacity into baseline planning prevents this short-sighted optimization.

The core and surge architecture provides stability where needed while preserving flexibility for adaptation. It acknowledges that not everything can or should be fluid while ensuring the organization is not rigidly locked into a single configuration.

## Mission Command Principles

Military organizations have long grappled with the challenge of coordination under conditions of uncertainty and rapid change. The concept of mission command, developed particularly within German and later U.S. military doctrine, offers valuable insights for civilian organizations facing similar challenges. Mission command decentralizes execution while maintaining strategic coherence through clearly communicated intent and empowered subordinate leaders.

Adapting mission command principles to civilian organizations requires several elements:

- Clear commander's intent: Senior leaders articulate the purpose and desired end-state of initiatives without prescribing detailed execution plans. This intent provides the reference point for decentralized decision-making, allowing subordinate teams to adapt methods to circumstances while maintaining alignment with overall objectives. Effective intent statements explain both what must be accomplished and why it matters within the broader organizational context.
- Disciplined initiative: Empower teams to take action within their areas of responsibility without waiting for detailed guidance. This requires both authority and capability for teams must have genuine decision rights and the competence to exercise them wisely. The organization accepts that some initiatives will fail but trusts that overall effectiveness increases when teams can respond rapidly to local conditions.
- Mutual trust and accountability: Build relationships where leaders trust subordinate teams to exercise judgment while those teams remain accountable for outcomes. This is not a free pass for poor performance but rather a recognition that micromanagement is incompatible with rapid adaptation. Trust develops through demonstrated competence,

transparent communication, and shared understanding of objectives.
- Understanding over compliance: Emphasize understanding why actions are taken rather than simply following orders. When team members understand the logic behind decisions and the broader strategic context, they can adapt intelligently as circumstances change. This requires investment in communication and education but pays dividends when script-following becomes impossible.

Mission command is not simply delegation or empowerment. It is a disciplined approach to decentralized execution that maintains coherence through shared understanding rather than detailed control. This makes it particularly effective in chaotic environments where centralized control becomes impossible.

## Network-Enabled Coordination

Traditional organizational structures assume that coordination requires hierarchy that someone must be in charge to prevent chaos. Network-enabled coordination offers an alternative model where teams coordinate laterally through peer-to-peer connections rather than vertical command chains. This approach leverages modern communication technology to enable forms of coordination that were previously impossible at scale.

Implementing network-enabled coordination requires several elements:

- Transparent information sharing: Make relevant information visible across the organization rather than routing it through hierarchical channels. This includes operational status, resource availability, emerging challenges, and lessons learned. When teams can see what others are doing and what they need, coordination can occur without central direction.

- Direct communication channels: Establish tools and norms that allow teams to communicate directly rather than requiring messages to flow up and down hierarchical chains. This might include collaboration platforms, regular cross-team meetings, or liaison roles that facilitate direct connection. The key is reducing friction in peer-to-peer communication.
- Shared situational awareness: Build systems that give all teams visibility into the broader operational picture. When everyone can see the same situation, they can make locally appropriate decisions that remain coherent with what others are doing. This is not simply information broadcasting but active cultivation of shared understanding.
- Self-synchronization protocols: Develop norms and procedures through which teams coordinate their actions without central direction. This might include standardized communication formats, shared planning rhythms, or explicit coordination responsibilities. Self-synchronization is not spontaneous but rather emerges from deliberate protocol design.

Network-enabled coordination does not eliminate hierarchy entirely for strategic decisions still require centralized authority, and someone must ultimately be accountable for outcomes. However, it shifts the locus of tactical coordination from hierarchical approval processes to distributed peer networks. This dramatically increases coordination speed while reducing bottlenecks at hierarchical pinch points.

## PHYSICAL AND DIGITAL ENVIRONMENT DESIGN

The environments where people work profoundly shape how they think, communicate, and collaborate. Physical and digital workspace design represents a powerful but often underutilized lever for building adaptive capacity. Thoughtful environment design can facilitate the kinds of interactions, information flows, and cognitive processes that chaos management requires. Conversely, poorly designed environments can inadvertently prevent exactly the behaviors organizations claim to value.

## Collaboration Space Architecture

Effective collaboration in chaotic environments requires spaces that support different modes of interaction from focused individual work to intensive team problem-solving. The trend toward open office plans, while motivated by legitimate desires to increase interaction, often creates environments that support neither focused work nor substantive collaboration. Chaos-ready organizations need more sophisticated spatial strategies.

Key elements of effective collaboration space design include:

- Diverse space types: Provide a range of space types suited to different activities, private spaces for concentration, small meeting rooms for team work, larger spaces for group collaboration, and casual areas for informal interaction. The specific mix depends on organizational needs, but the principle is matching space characteristics to activity requirements rather than forcing all work into identical environments.
- Flexible reconfiguration: Design spaces that can be quickly reconfigured as needs change. This includes movable furniture, modular wall systems, and flexible technology infrastructure. During crisis periods, organizations may need to rapidly establish war rooms, stand up new teams, or reorganize existing spaces. Spaces that resist reconfiguration become constraints rather than enablers.
- Visual information displays: Incorporate surfaces and systems for making information visible, whiteboards, digital displays, pin-up walls. The ability to externalize thinking and work with visual representations supports collaborative problem-solving. Spaces without adequate display

capabilities force teams to work with information in purely abstract forms, reducing cognitive effectiveness.

- Proximity without intrusion: Balance the benefits of physical proximity with the need for focused work. This might mean clustering teams that need to interact frequently while providing adequate acoustic separation, or creating neighborhoods where teams can maintain awareness of each other without constant interruption. The goal is supporting both chance encounter and deep concentration.

Physical space is particularly important for distributed organizations. While remote work provides flexibility, it can impair the rich, spontaneous interactions that facilitate sense-making and innovation. Organizations that maintain primarily remote operations must compensate through more intensive periodic in-person collaboration and more sophisticated digital collaboration tools.

## Digital Workspace Design

Most organizations accumulated their digital tools opportunistically, adopting whatever seemed useful at the time without coherent architectural principles. The result is typically a bewildering array of platforms, applications, and systems that do not integrate well, create duplicate information in multiple locations, and require constant context-switching that degrades cognitive performance. Chaos-ready organizations need more intentional digital workspace architecture.

Key principles for digital workspace design include:

- Integration over proliferation: Resist the temptation to adopt every new tool that promises productivity gains. Instead, focus on creating an integrated ecosystem of core tools that work well together. This requires saying no to many individually attractive tools in favor of maintaining a coherent, interoperable digital environment. Integration enables workflows that span multiple tools without constant manual data transfer.

- Single source of truth: Eliminate information duplication across multiple systems. Each category of information should have one authoritative source with other systems accessing or referencing that source rather than maintaining separate copies. This prevents the version control nightmares and information inconsistency that plague organizations with fragmented data architectures.
- Context preservation: Design systems that maintain context across different activities. When switching between communication tools, document repositories, and analytical platforms, relevant context should move with the user. This might mean integration layers that surface related information automatically or unified interfaces that reduce the need for context switching.
- Collaboration scaffolding: Build in structures that guide effective collaboration rather than leaving teams to figure out their own ad hoc approaches. This includes templates for common activities, workflow automation for routine processes, and integration of communication channels with work artifacts. The goal is reducing the overhead of collaboration so teams can focus on substantive work.

Digital workspace design is never finished, new tools emerge, organizational needs evolve, and continuous refinement is necessary. However, maintaining architectural discipline prevents the drift toward tool chaos that plagues many organizations.

## DECISION SUPPORT SYSTEMS

Decision-making under uncertainty requires both intuitive judgment and systematic analysis. Effective decision support systems augment human judgment without attempting to replace it. These systems help structure complex decisions, surface relevant information, identify assumptions, and facilitate learning from outcomes—but ultimately support rather than automate judgment.

Key elements of effective decision support include:

- Structured decision frameworks: Provide templates and processes for different decision types: strategic choices, resource allocations, risk assessments, and operational trade-offs. These frameworks should prompt consideration of critical factors without imposing rigid analysis requirements. The goal is reducing cognitive load while ensuring systematic thinking.
- Assumption tracking: Build systems that explicitly capture and track key assumptions underlying decisions. This makes it possible to revisit decisions as new information emerges, identify which assumptions proved correct or incorrect, and develop more calibrated judgment over time. Without explicit assumption tracking, organizations struggle to learn effectively from experience.
- Scenario exploration tools: Provide capabilities for exploring different scenarios and their implications before committing to action. This might include simulation models, scenario planning frameworks, or structured what-if analysis. The goal is not predicting the future but developing mental models of how different factors might interact.
- Post-decision learning: Create systems for structured reflection after significant decisions. This includes documenting what was decided and why, tracking outcomes against expectations, and conducting systematic analysis of what worked and what did not. Organizations that fail to build learning systems repeat mistakes unnecessarily.

The most sophisticated decision support systems remain useless if organizational culture does not support their use. Leaders must model thoughtful decision-making, reward careful analysis even when it reaches unpopular conclusions, and maintain realistic expectations about what decision support can achieve.

# RESOURCE ALLOCATION IN VOLATILE ENVIRONMENTS

Traditional resource allocation follows annual planning cycles whereby organizations develop budgets, allocate resources to specific initiatives, and execute according to plan. This approach works reasonably well in stable environments where next year looks similar to this year. It fails dramatically in chaotic environments where circumstances change faster than planning cycles. Chaos-ready organizations need fundamentally different approaches to resource allocation.

## Dynamic Resource Reallocation

Rather than locking resources into annual allocations, chaos-ready organizations maintain the capacity to reallocate resources rapidly as conditions change. This does not mean abandoning all planning for some baseline resource commitments remain necessary but it does mean preserving flexibility to redirect resources toward emerging priorities.

Implementing dynamic reallocation requires several elements:

- Reserve capacity: Maintain a portion of organizational resources uncommitted to specific initiatives. This might be 10-20% of budget, personnel time, or other critical resources held in reserve for emerging needs. The specific percentage depends on environmental volatility, but organizations without meaningful reserves cannot respond effectively to the unexpected.
- Rapid reallocation protocols: Establish clear processes for reallocating resources outside normal planning cycles. This includes decision criteria for triggering reallocation, approval authorities for different reallocation scales, and procedures for rapidly standing up or standing down

initiatives. Without clear protocols, reallocation becomes politically fraught and painfully slow.

- Portfolio management approach: Treat resource allocation as managing a portfolio of bets rather than a set of commitments. This means explicitly accepting that some initiatives will fail, maintaining a mix of different risk profiles, and continuously rebalancing the portfolio based on results. Organizations that cannot abandon failing initiatives cannot reallocate resources effectively.
- Transparent reallocation criteria: Make explicit the factors that drive reallocation decisions. This might include changing strategic priorities, emerging threats or opportunities, performance metrics, or external conditions. Transparency reduces political gaming and allows teams to anticipate potential reallocation rather than being blindsided.

Dynamic reallocation is psychologically difficult. It means admitting plans were wrong, disappointing people whose initiatives are defunded, and accepting the discomfort of continuous adjustment. Organizations that cannot embrace this discomfort cannot allocate resources effectively in chaotic environments.

## Investment in Adaptive Capacity

Traditional resource allocation focuses on delivering specific outputs such as product features, service improvements, operational targets. These remain important, but chaos-ready organizations also invest explicitly in building adaptive capacity: Organizational capabilities that enable effective response regardless of specific challenges encountered. These investments often appear inefficient by traditional metrics because they do not directly produce immediate outputs, yet they determine long-term organizational resilience.

Key categories of adaptive capacity investment include:

- Learning infrastructure: Invest in systems and processes that enable organizational learning, after-action reviews, knowledge management systems, deliberate practice opportunities, and structured reflection. These investments do not produce immediate deliverables but build the organizational capability to learn from experience and improve over time.
- Redundancy and resilience: Maintain backup systems, alternative suppliers, cross-trained personnel, and other forms of redundancy that enable continued operation when primary systems fail. Efficiency-focused organizations eliminate this redundancy as waste, only to discover its value when disruptions occur. Deliberate redundancy is insurance, not inefficiency.
- Exploratory capacity: Allocate resources to exploration and experimentation even when immediate returns are uncertain. This includes research and development, pilot programs, and exploratory partnerships. Organizations that invest only in activities with clear ROI cannot discover new possibilities or adapt to fundamental shifts in their environment.
- Relationship capital: Invest in building and maintaining relationships with partners, suppliers, customers, and other stakeholders. Strong relationships provide flexibility during crisis, partners are more willing to accommodate unusual requests, suppliers extend credit or expedite deliveries, customers remain loyal despite service disruptions. These relationships do not appear on balance sheets but represent crucial adaptive capacity.

The challenge is that investments in adaptive capacity must be made before they are needed, when their value is hardest to demonstrate. Organizations under financial pressure tend to cut exactly these investments, optimizing for short-term efficiency at the cost of long-term adaptability.

# TALENT ACQUISITION AND DEVELOPMENT

All the organizational architecture discussed thus far means nothing without people capable of operating within it. Building chaos-ready organizations ultimately depends on acquiring and developing talent with specific characteristics, specifically cognitive flexibility, emotional resilience, collaborative capability, and adaptive expertise. This requires fundamentally different approaches to both hiring and development than most organizations currently employ.

## Hiring for Adaptive Potential

Traditional hiring focuses on matching candidates to specific role requirements, do they have the necessary experience, skills, and credentials?

This approach makes sense for stable roles but becomes problematic when roles themselves are fluid and future requirements unknown. Chaos-ready organizations must hire for adaptive potential or the capacity to learn, grow, and thrive amid uncertainty as much as for current capabilities.

Key elements of hiring for adaptive potential include:

- Learning agility assessment: Evaluate candidates' capacity to learn from experience and apply lessons to new situations. This includes assessing how they have navigated past uncertainty, what they learned from setbacks, and how they approach unfamiliar challenges. Past learning agility predicts future adaptability better than any specific skill set.
- Cognitive flexibility evaluation: Test candidates' ability to shift between different perspectives, tolerate ambiguity, and work with incomplete information. This might include case studies requiring multi-dimensional analysis, simulations involving changing conditions, or discussions of complex problems without clear solutions. Cognitive rigidity is a disqualifier regardless of technical expertise.

- Collaborative capability: Assess candidates' ability to work effectively in diverse teams, integrate different perspectives, and build productive working relationships. Technical brilliance that comes with interpersonal toxicity undermines organizational adaptive capacity. The ability to collaborate effectively under stress is non-negotiable.
- Values alignment: Evaluate whether candidates share core organizational values around learning, transparency, accountability, and service. Skills can be developed but fundamental values orientations are difficult to change. Hiring people who do not share organizational values creates friction that becomes acute during crisis.

This does not mean ignoring domain expertise for obviously technical competence remains important. However, adaptive potential becomes the primary filter, with technical skills serving as secondary qualifications. Better to hire someone with moderate technical skills and high adaptive potential than someone with deep expertise but cognitive rigidity.

## Deliberate Development Systems

Most organizations approach development opportunistically, providing training when requested, offering stretch assignments when available, and hoping that experience alone produces growth. This approach yields uneven results at best. Chaos-ready organizations need more systematic development approaches that deliberately build adaptive capacity.

Effective development systems include several key elements:

- Progressive challenge sequencing: Design career progressions that systematically increase complexity and ambiguity. This means deliberately moving people through assignments with escalating adaptive demands rather than simply promoting based on performance in previous roles.

Each assignment should stretch capabilities just beyond current comfort zones while providing adequate support.

- Structured reflection practices: Build in regular opportunities for structured reflection on experience. This includes after-action reviews, developmental coaching, peer learning groups, and guided self-assessment. Experience alone teaches nothing, rather learning requires deliberate reflection on experience to extract lessons and integrate them into practice.
- Simulation-based training: Provide opportunities to practice adaptive skills in simulated environments before applying them in high-stakes situations. Well-designed simulations allow people to experience realistic pressure, make mistakes, receive feedback, and develop intuitions without risking actual organizational consequences. This is particularly valuable for developing crisis leadership capabilities.
- Mentorship and coaching: Connect developing leaders with experienced mentors who can provide guidance, feedback, and perspective. Effective mentorship relationships accelerate development by helping people make sense of experiences, recognize patterns, and develop judgment. This requires both formal mentorship programs and cultural norms that encourage informal mentoring relationships.

Development systems must be sustained over years to produce meaningful results. Organizations that approach development as an occasional intervention rather than a sustained system will not build the depth of adaptive capacity that chaos requires.

## Retention of Adaptive Expertise

Adaptive expertise is hard-won and easily lost. Organizations invest significant resources developing people with the cognitive flexibility, emotional resilience, and judgment that chaos management requires. When these people leave, their adaptive capacity leaves with them, and the organization must begin development from scratch with their replacements. Chaos-ready organizations must therefore prioritize retention of adaptively capable people.

Retention strategies include:

- Meaningful challenge: Provide ongoing opportunities for people to work on genuinely difficult problems that stretch their capabilities. Adaptively capable people become bored and disengaged when work becomes routine. Retention requires ensuring they always have access to challenges worthy of their abilities.
- Autonomy and influence: Grant significant autonomy in how work is accomplished and genuine influence over organizational direction. People with adaptive capacity want to shape outcomes, not simply execute others' plans. Organizations that micromanage or ignore their input will lose them to environments offering more agency.
- Growth opportunities: Maintain clear pathways for continued development and advancement. This includes both vertical promotion opportunities and lateral moves into new domains. Stagnation is the enemy of retention for adaptively capable people for they need to see paths forward.
- Cultural fit: Cultivate organizational cultures where adaptively capable people want to work. This means valuing learning over ego protection, rewarding thoughtful risk-taking, maintaining high standards without toxicity, and fostering genuine collegiality. Culture fit increasingly determines retention as material compensation becomes more standardized across competitive employers.

No retention strategy is perfect. Some turnover is inevitable and even healthy. However, organizations that systematically lose their most adaptively capable people face compounding disadvantages in chaotic environments. Retention must be a strategic priority, not an afterthought.

# FROM DESIGN TO IMPLEMENTATION

The organizational architecture described in this chapter represents an integrated system rather than a menu of independent options. Information architecture enables effective sense-making, but only if teams have the structure and autonomy to act on what they learn. Team structures provide flexibility, but only if supported by appropriate physical and digital environments. Resource allocation enables rapid response, but only if the organization has acquired and developed people capable of effective execution. These elements must work together to create emergent organizational capabilities.

The question facing leaders is not whether to implement all elements simultaneously that is typically impossible given resource constraints and organizational capacity for change.

Rather, leaders must identify which elements represent the most binding constraints on their organization's adaptive capacity and address those systematically. For some organizations, information architecture is the primary limitation. For others, team structures or talent development represents the critical bottleneck. Effective implementation requires honest assessment of current state and strategic sequencing of improvements.

Several principles guide effective implementation:

- Start with pilots: Rather than attempting organization-wide transformation, begin with targeted pilots in specific units or functions. This allows learning about what works in your particular context before scaling successful approaches. Pilots also create proof points that help build organizational confidence in new approaches.
- Iterate based on feedback: Treat implementation as an experimental process requiring ongoing adjustment. Monitor results, gather feedback from participants, identify problems quickly, and refine approaches continuously. No architectural design survives first contact with organizational reality unchanged.

- Build internal capability: Develop internal expertise in chaos management rather than relying exclusively on external consultants. External expertise can help jumpstart change, but lasting transformation requires that organizational members develop their own understanding and capability. This typically means investing in training, creating internal communities of practice, and ensuring knowledge transfer from any external partners.
- Maintain persistence: Building chaos-ready organizations takes years, not months. Results often lag investment significantly, creating periods where costs are visible but benefits remain unclear. Leaders must maintain commitment through this difficult middle period when abandoning the effort becomes tempting. Persistence distinguishes organizations that successfully transform from those that cycle through abandoned initiatives.

The urgency of implementation depends on environmental volatility and organizational vulnerability. Organizations operating in highly volatile environments with low current adaptive capacity face existential risk if they defer investment. Those in more stable environments or with stronger existing capabilities can approach transformation more deliberately. However, waiting until crisis strikes to begin building adaptive capacity is invariably too late. The time to build organizational resilience is before it becomes desperately needed.

The architecture described in this chapter provides a framework for systematic organizational development. It does not prescribe a single optimal design. Different organizations will emphasize different elements based on their specific contexts and constraints.

However, the principles remain constant: build information systems that enable rapid sense-making, create team structures that balance stability and flexibility, design environments that facilitate productive work, maintain resource allocation flexibility, and acquire and develop people with adaptive capacity. Organizations that attend systematically to these elements position themselves to navigate whatever chaos the future holds.

● 6

# DESIGNING YOUR CHAOS MANAGEMENT PLAYBOOK

The preceding chapters have traced how the anarchy of the moment emerged, why traditional crisis management has failed, and how organizations can begin to build the adaptive capacity required to survive and thrive in this new operating environment.

This chapter is about translation. It is written for the hybrid leader: the flag or general officer, the senior civil servant, and the corporate executive who must steer complex institutions through conditions that will not "settle down." Its purpose is to help you turn the conceptual framework of chaos management into a practical agenda for the next 12 to 24 months inside your own organization, whether that organization wears uniforms, holds elections, or reports quarterly earnings.

The playbook that follows does not offer a template to be applied mechanically. Instead, it provides a structured way to interrogate your current posture, identify where you are optimized for a world that no longer exists, and choose a small number of high-impact moves that build the intellectual flexibility, institutional resilience, and social cohesion you will need in the years ahead.

# A SHORT DIAGNOSTIC: HOW CHAOS-READY ARE YOU?

The first step is not action but awareness. Before you rewire your organization, you need an honest picture of how it behaves under stress, where it fractures, and where it surprises you with resilience. The questions that follow are not a survey for the staff to complete and file. They are prompts for candid conversations among the people who actually carry authority in your system.

You can use them in a small senior seminar, a command off-site, a board strategy session, or a ministerial retreat. Pick three or four areas where your answers are most uncomfortable. Those are your starting points.

## Intellectual flexibility

- When the environment shifts in ways that invalidate existing plans, do we treat that as a planning failure to be concealed, or as a learning opportunity to be surfaced and examined?
- Do our senior leaders regularly encounter disconfirming evidence and alternative conceptual frameworks, or does staff work mainly refine and justify existing assumptions and concepts of operations?
- In practice, are our strategic documents treated as living hypotheses that can be adapted, or as sacred texts that must be defended?

## Institutional resilience

- Where are we most dangerously optimized for efficiency, single suppliers, single exquisite platforms, single information hubs, rather than for survivability?
- If one or two key nodes in our organization (a headquarters, a data center, a port, a plant) were degraded or cut off, what

decisions could still be made and executed effectively within 24 hours?
- How much critical institutional memory resides in a handful of individuals, and what would we lose if they were suddenly absent?

## Social cohesion

- In our last major disruption, did trust across echelons and functions deepen or erode? What did we learn about who we really are under pressure?
- Do we have shared stories and values strong enough to sustain support when some units, departments, or business lines must bear disproportionate risk or sacrifice?
- Information architecture and decision-making
- How quickly can frontline observations and weak signals reach decision-makers who can act on them, without being filtered into unreality along the way?
- To what extent can decision-making be distributed, as in a mesh or kill-web architecture, when central nodes are saturated, misinformed, or cut off?

## Leadership development

- Where, concretely, are we building the cognitive skills for mastering chaos, ambiguity tolerance, pattern recognition, emotional regulation, and collaborative sense-making, rather than assuming they appear automatically with seniority?
- How often do we expose future leaders to synthetic but realistic environments that replicate the anarchy of the moment: incomplete information, hostile narratives, compressed time, and political cross-pressures?

If you find yourself answering "not often," "not really," or "only in theory" to a majority of these questions, you are in the same position as most institutions I have worked with. The point is not to generate guilt; it is to identify where you must now move.

# THREE ARCHETYPE PLAYBOOKS

Different institutions face different constraints. A joint force command cannot behave exactly like a tech firm, and a critical-infrastructure operator cannot simply emulate a Marine Corps task force or a special operations unit. But there are family resemblances in how chaos-ready organizations behave. The following mini-playbooks are built from the cases already explored in this book, from the war in Ukraine to the evolution of the Marine Corps and the MISR experience.

They are not exhaustive. They are meant to be provocations or starting points you can adapt to your particular legal, political, and cultural context.

## 1. A military service or major command

For a military organization, chaos management begins with the recognition that the traditional force-structure planning cycle has broken down. You cannot specify in detail the force you will need three decades from now in an environment of software-defined systems, autonomous platforms, and adversaries learning in real time from current conflicts. You can, however, build a force that learns faster than its competitors.

Key moves over the next 12–24 months might include:

- Create a standing "chaos cell" close to the commander. Its job is not to produce glossy concepts but to run short, iterative experiments that test assumptions about distributed operations, command and control, logistics resilience, and alliance integration.

- Reframe major exercises as laboratories rather than examinations. Instead of using large-scale events to validate predetermined plans, deliberately design them to break those plans, expose vulnerabilities, and explore alternative ways of organizing sensors, shooters, and decision-makers.
- Institutionalize rapid learning loops. Require that insights from operations and exercises be captured quickly, shared horizontally across units and allies, and fed directly into doctrine, training, and acquisition discussions. The goal is to prevent your organization from repeatedly learning the same painful lesson at high cost.
- Integrate Chaos Navigator-style training into professional military education. Use simulations, red-teaming, and wargames not only to teach tactics and campaign design but to train the cognitive skills senior leaders will need when the information environment collapses around them.

If you do these things seriously, you will not have eliminated chaos. You will have positioned your force to treat chaos as an environment it understands and can exploit rather than as a one-time emergency to be survived.

## 2. A civil ministry or critical-infrastructure operator

Ministries of health, energy, interior, and finance; national emergency management agencies; and private or public operators of critical infrastructure face a double bind. They must preserve essential services under stress, yet they operate inside legal and political frameworks designed for more stable times. They cannot choose their crises, but they can choose how prepared they are when those crises arrive.

For such institutions, a chaos-management playbook could focus on:

- Mapping your real system of systems. Go beyond organizational charts and jurisdictional maps to understand how energy, transport, digital networks, finance, and public health actually interact in practice, in your country or region. Identify the nodes whose failure would cascade across systems.

- Building cross-ministry and cross-operator crisis cells. Instead of treating cyber attacks, pandemics, or supply-chain disruptions as isolated technical problems, bring operators, regulators, intelligence officers, and political principals together for regular scenario work and simulations.

- Creating controlled redundancy in critical processes. Accept some inefficiency now so that you can continue to function when your primary channels, legal, logistical, or informational, are degraded. This might mean backup authorization pathways, alternative communications systems, or pre-agreed emergency procurement mechanisms.

- Exposing ministers and senior officials to realistic chaos simulations. It is not enough for staff to run table-top exercises while principals are briefed afterwards. The political decision-makers themselves must experience what it feels like to make consequential choices under pressure, incomplete information, and hostile narratives.

These moves will not spare you from hard political choices. They will, however, allow your system to act more coherently when those choices can no longer be deferred.

## 3. A large private firm in a disrupted market

In the private sector, the anarchy of the moment shows up as volatile demand, sudden regulatory shifts, fragile supply chains, and competitors who emerge seemingly from nowhere. Here too, the traditional strategic planning cycle has become part of the problem. Firms are still writing five-year plans for industries that can be transformed in eighteen months.

A practical playbook for the C-suite might emphasize:

- Replacing annual strategy with rolling "chaos sprints." Use 90-day cycles in which small, cross-functional teams stress-test your assumptions about markets, technology, and regulation; prototype responses; and feed back results to the executive team in time to matter.
- Building a portfolio of options rather than a single bet. Commit a modest but protected fraction of capital and talent to a series of exploratory projects, new products, new markets, new partnerships, that can be scaled up quickly if conditions warrant.
- Aligning incentives with enterprise resilience. Ensure that business units and functional leaders are rewarded not only for local efficiency but also for their contribution to overall adaptability and risk reduction across the firm.
- Adapting Chaos Navigator principles for corporate leadership development. Design leadership programs around complex scenarios that integrate geopolitical risk, technological disruption, social media dynamics, and regulatory shock, instead of treating each domain as a separate specialist concern.

The goal is to make your firm a learning organism in a turbulent ecosystem, not a fortress hoping the storm will pass.

## FROM PLAYBOOK TO PRACTICE

Every institution will answer the diagnostic questions differently and will pick different moves from these archetype playbooks. That is as it should be. Chaos management is not a doctrine to be imposed from above; it is a discipline of continual adaptation grounded in a clear understanding of your own operating reality.

What does matter is that you choose. In an era defined by the speed of everything, by ubiquitous crises, and by the collapse of traditional temporal perspective, drifting is itself a decision with predictable results. You can continue to optimize for a world of episodic disruptions and stable baselines, or you can begin the slower, harder work of building organizations that can absorb shock, learn quickly, and act coherently when the parameters of the system shift beneath their feet.

The chapters that follow turn from institutional design to the demands placed on individual leaders. They explore the imperatives, skills, and developmental pathways that will allow you and those you lead to become true navigators of chaos rather than its victims.

Even the most carefully constructed chaos management playbook is only as effective as the leaders entrusted to apply it under real-world pressure. The ability to think, decide, and adapt inside turbulence is not an optional enhancement to this framework; it is the decisive variable. Chapter Four turns from system design to leader design, outlining the developmental pathway for the chaos navigators your organization will need, the men and women trained to operate at tempo, preserve coherence under stress, and turn perpetual disruption into a working environment rather than a debilitating shock.

# THE CHAOS NAVIGATOR: FORGING LEADERS FOR AN ERA OF PERPETUAL DISRUPTION

The previous chapters have focused on designing organizations that can function inside chaos, not merely brace against it. You now have the tools to build a chaos management playbook, redesign structures, and tune information flows so your institution does not shatter under pressure.

But even the most carefully engineered system fails if the people running it cannot think, decide, and coordinate at the speed and ambiguity of the environment. A chaos-ready organization still breaks if key leaders revert to linear planning, cling to first interpretations, or freeze when the playbook collides with reality. This is the gap Chapter Four is designed to close. It turns from system design to leader design: how you deliberately forge the people who can inhabit, interpret, and adapt the architecture you have just built.

The central claim is straightforward. In a world of perpetual disruption, leadership is no longer primarily about having better plans; it is about having better minds at the controls. The question is not whether you can identify the next crisis, but whether you have developed leaders who can learn faster than conditions are changing, hold their teams together when the map no longer fits the terrain, and treat chaos as a working environment rather than a temporary aberration.

# WHAT IS A CHAOS NAVIGATOR?

A Chaos Navigator is not a heroic individual who single-handedly restores order. That image belongs to an earlier age, when disruptions were episodic and systems were loosely coupled enough that one person's judgment could dominate.

Chaos Navigators are leaders who can do four things reliably under pressure:

- Hold multiple, conflicting interpretations of a situation without demanding premature closure.
- Detect weak patterns early and revise those patterns quickly when the evidence shifts.
- Regulate their own emotional state well enough to keep thinking and keep others thinking when the nervous system wants to fight, flee, or freeze.
- Turn leadership from a solo act into a collaborative sensemaking process, using the distributed cognition of the team and the wider system.

They are not defined by rank, although senior leaders must embody these traits if the organization is to move. They can sit in a joint operations center, a corporate risk committee, a cabinet office, or a logistics operations room. What marks them out is not their position on the chart but their behavior in the moment: how they frame problems, how they invite or suppress dissent, how they hold the tension between action and learning.

The critical point is that Chaos Navigators are made, not born. There is nothing mystical about these capacities. They can be developed through repeated exposure to structured stress, well-designed simulations, disciplined reflection, and organizational cultures that reward learning under pressure rather than punishing every misstep. The Chaos Navigator program is simply a way to institutionalize that development rather than leaving it to chance.

# THE COGNITIVE CORE: FOUR TRAINABLE CAPABILITIES

Part One introduced the cognitive skills required for mastering chaos: adaptive thinking, pattern recognition under uncertainty, emotional regulation, and collaborative sensemaking. The Navigator program takes those same pillars and turns them into a practical training architecture.

## 1. Adaptive thinking: acting on provisional maps

Adaptive thinking is the ability to act on an incomplete understanding without pretending that understanding is final. In practice, this means holding multiple working hypotheses about what is happening, choosing a course of action based on the best current hypothesis, and being willing to revise both the hypothesis and the action as new information appears. The opposite is premature certainty: locking onto a story early because ambiguity is uncomfortable, then defending that story long after the environment has moved on.

In chaotic environments, adaptive thinking shows up in small, observable behaviors. Navigators ask "What else could this be?" before committing to an interpretation. They articulate their level of confidence explicitly, so their teams know where there is room to challenge. They build options that preserve room to maneuver rather than committing all resources to a single, brittle path. These are not personality traits; they are habits that can be trained and reinforced.

## 2. Pattern recognition under uncertainty

Chaos overwhelms leaders not because there is no information, but because there is too much. Raw data, social media noise, sensor feeds, and fragmentary reports swamp attention. Navigators develop the capacity to see emerging patterns without waiting for perfect clarity and to abandon those patterns when they stop fitting. They distinguish signal from noise, but they also understand that today's noise may become tomorrow's signal as conditions shift.

The practical test is simple. When new reports arrive that contradict the dominant narrative, does the leader suppress them as anomalies or treat them as possible hints that the pattern is changing? Do they have explicit "tripwires" that tell them when their working model needs to be re-examined? Navigator training makes these questions explicit, then rehearses them in simulations until they become reflex.

## 3. Emotional regulation and stress tolerance

Under genuine pressure, the nervous system pushes toward fight, flight, or freeze. In a command center or C-suite, that translates into impulsive action, panicked retreat, or paralysis at precisely the moment when others look to the leader for orientation. Emotional regulation is not about suppression; it is about acknowledging the gravity of the situation without letting physiology dictate behavior.

Chaos Navigators learn to name what is happening ("this is serious; we are going to feel this") and then return the team to the next concrete decision. They understand that their tone, body language, and micro-signals propagate through the organization as quickly as any formal directive. Training therefore treats emotional regulation as an operational skill: something to be practiced in realistic simulations and examined explicitly in debriefs, not left to chance or personality.

## 4. Collaborative sensemaking and distributed cognition

No individual can see the full shape of a complex crisis. Different parts of the organization occupy different vantage points: cyber, logistics, public affairs, operations, legal, political. The leader's job is to turn those partial views into a coherent, evolving picture, not to out-think every specialist in the room.

Chaos Navigators design the conversation, not just the plan. They deliberately bring in divergent perspectives before the group settles on a story, create space for minority views, and structure meetings so that the same voices do not dominate every time. They understand tools and dashboards as part of the cognitive system, asking "What is missing from this picture?" as often as "What does it show?" The result is a form of collective intelligence that updates faster than any individual mind.

# TRAINING CHAOS NAVIGATORS: DESIGNING THE FORGE

If Chaos Navigators are made rather than born, the critical question becomes: what does the forge look like?

Traditional leadership programs are rarely sufficient. Classroom instruction, generic case studies, and occasional offsites do not recreate the time compression, ambiguity, and emotional pressure that define genuine chaos. They also tend to reward performance in retrospect, what people say they would have done, rather than how they actually behave when the situation unfolds in real time.

A Navigator program has to reverse that logic. It must bring leaders into contact with controlled turbulence, observe their cognitive and emotional patterns under stress, and make those patterns visible enough that they can be deliberately reshaped. This requires three elements working together: realistic simulation, structured reflection, and organizational follow-through.

## Realistic Simulation

The most effective training environments share a common feature: they compress the essential features of chaos, information overload, ambiguous intent, cascading second-order effects, into a time-bounded exercise where leaders must make real decisions with incomplete data. The goal is not to mimic a specific scenario with perfect fidelity but to stress the same cognitive muscles they will need when the real thing arrives.

Useful simulations often have the following characteristics:

- They start with a pattern that looks familiar, then deviate. The early injects resemble a known crisis type: a routine cyber intrusion, a localized protest, a weather-related supply disruption. Halfway through, the data begin to contradict that reading. Leaders must decide whether to cling to the initial pattern or revise under pressure.

- They are multi-domain. Injects arrive simultaneously from operational, political, information, and economic channels. Participants are forced to prioritize limited attention, not just limited resources.
- They include moral and reputational dimensions. Leaders must weigh tradeoffs between speed and accuracy, transparency and containment, short-term operational gains and long-term trust. This mirrors the wicked nature of real problems, where there is no clean solution that satisfies every stakeholder.

Crucially, simulations should be short and frequent as well as large and elaborate. A full-scale crisis exercise once a year is useful, but so are 30-minute micro-drills embedded into existing routines. In a staff meeting, you can run a three-inject scenario that forces a quick pattern call, a decision, and a reassessment. Over time, this repetition normalizes the experience of acting under uncertainty and revising course in public.

## Structured Reflection

Without deliberate reflection, even the best simulation becomes a one-off experience. The debrief is where navigation skills are actually forged. The focus should be less on the outcome of the scenario and more on the cognitive and emotional process.

Useful questions include:

- At what moment did you decide what kind of problem this was?
- What evidence pushed you toward that interpretation? What evidence did you ignore?
- When did you feel your stress level spike? How did that change the way you listened, asked questions, or gave direction?

- Whose voice shifted your thinking the most? Whose voice
  did you fail to hear?

Making these questions routine does two things. First, it builds metacognition or the ability of leaders to notice their own thinking as it happens, not just in hindsight. Second, it normalizes the idea that revising judgments is a mark of professionalism rather than a sign of weakness. Over time, this creates leaders who can say, "Here is my current read; here is how I could be wrong," even in front of their peers and subordinates.

## Organizational Follow-through

Navigator development cannot be a detached training experience that ends when people return to "real work." If the operating environment punishes the very behaviors you are trying to cultivate, open acknowledgment of uncertainty, deliberate revision, collaborative sensemaking, the program will fail.

This means aligning three elements of the broader system:

- Incentives. Promotion and evaluation criteria must
  explicitly value adaptive thinking, cross-boundary
  collaboration, and intelligent risk-taking. Leaders who
  change course in light of new evidence should not be
  penalized for inconsistency when their decisions are
  grounded in transparent reasoning.
- Rituals. Regular after-action reviews, cross-functional
  debriefs, and "near miss" discussions signal that learning
  from turbulence is part of the job, not a distraction from it.
- Signal protection. Leaders who raise early concerns,
  challenge emerging narratives, or surface uncomfortable
  data must be protected, not marginalized. A Navigators'
  effectiveness depends on a flow of honest information from
  the edges; if whistleblowers and dissenters are punished,
  that flow will dry up.

In short, the forge extends beyond the training facility. It is built into the way the organization works every day.

# BUILDING A NAVIGATOR PIPELINE

Most institutions already have people who approximate Chaos Navigators. They are the officers, executives, or managers others gravitate toward when things go sideways, the ones whose phones ring first when ambiguity spikes. Building a Navigator pipeline means doing three things: identifying these people more systematically, broadening the pool, and routing them through developmental experiences that compound their capabilities.

## Identification

Traditional selection processes often prioritize technical expertise, tenure, and performance in stable conditions. Those variables matter, but they are not reliable predictors of how someone will function in chaos. You need additional lenses.

Indicators of Navigator potential include:

- A track record of volunteering for complex, ill-defined problems rather than only well-specified tasks.
- Evidence of cross-boundary work: roles that bridge departments, cultures, or domains.
- Feedback from peers that the individual is someone they trust to keep thinking clearly under pressure.

Assessment centers and simulations can be used not just for training but for selection. Observing how candidates handle conflicting information, time pressure, and criticism provides a more accurate picture of their navigation capacity than interviews alone.

# Developmental Pathways

Once you have identified potential Navigators, you can design accelerated pathways that deliberately expose them to the kinds of experiences that build their capabilities.

Typical elements include:

- Rotational assignments that move them across functional or geographic boundaries, increasing their ability to see patterns across systems rather than within a single silo.
- Shadow roles in crisis cells or operational centers, where they can watch experienced Navigators work in real time and debrief decisions afterward.
- Lead roles in controlled simulations, where the stakes are high enough to feel real but low enough that mistakes become learning rather than catastrophe.

The goal is to ensure that by the time someone arrives in a senior position, they have not only read about chaos but lived through structured approximations of it.

# Deployment and Leverage

Navigator talent is too valuable to scatter randomly. Once you know who your Navigators are, you should think about their placement as a strategic asset.

Questions to consider:

- Where in your organization does turbulence concentrate?
- What units or functions routinely sit at the intersection of multiple systems?
- Which teams are responsible for first response when events break?
- Where are the seams between organizations. alliances, joint ventures, public-private interfaces, where misalignment can quickly become crisis?

Those are the places where Navigators should be concentrated. At the same time, you can use Navigators as force multipliers by pairing them with less experienced leaders in high-risk roles, creating dyads or triads where navigation skills are shared and diffused rather than hoarded.

# MAKING THE CASE: WHY NAVIGATOR DEVELOPMENT IS NOT OPTIONAL

In resource-constrained environments, any new program invites skepticism. Leaders understandably ask: why invest in another leadership initiative when we are already stretched? The answer lies in the nature of the environment described in Part One and the organizational investments outlined earlier in Part Two.

You have already committed to building a chaos management playbook, redesigning structures, and accepting some inefficiency as the price of resilience. Those moves are necessary, but they are not sufficient. Without leaders who can operate inside that new architecture, leaders who can interpret weak signals, keep teams aligned under pressure, and adapt the playbook in real time, you will have built a sophisticated instrument with no one able to play it.

Three arguments make the Navigator program more than a luxury.

### 1. Risk mitigation

In tightly coupled systems, a single catastrophic decision at the wrong moment can propagate across the entire network. Training navigators is a way of reducing the variance of your worst decisions under stress. You are not just trying to raise the ceiling of brilliance; you are trying to raise the floor of competence in the worst hour. That is a form of risk management as concrete as any redundancy in hardware or infrastructure.

### 2. Return on existing investments

Every structural and technological enhancement you make from new information systems to redesigned command arrangements relies on human judgment to be used effectively. Navigators are the interface between your investments and the environment. If that interface is weak, the return on your other expenditures will be correspondingly low. Navigator development is a relatively modest investment that amplifies the value of everything else.

3. Talent retention and culture

Paradoxically, building a Navigator program can help you retain your best emerging leaders. Many of them already sense that the environment has changed and are hungry for ways to make sense of it. Offering a coherent development path that acknowledges the realities of chaos, rather than pretending we still live in a predictable world, signals that your institution is serious about preparing them for the future they will actually face. That sense of seriousness can be a powerful cultural adhesive.

# TRANSITION: FROM NAVIGATORS TO LEADERSHIP IMPERATIVES

This chapter has focused on a particular kind of leader, the Chaos Navigator, and on the programmatic steps necessary to forge and deploy such people. It has argued that in an era of perpetual disruption, leader development is not an add-on to structural reform but its essential complement. You can design all the playbooks you like; without leaders who can run them inside turbulence, the architecture collapses at first contact.

The next part of the book widens the lens again. Where this chapter has been about a specific cadre of leaders and the skills they need, Part Three distills the broader leadership imperatives that must shape your behavior and your institution over time. It will translate the Navigator's capabilities into enduring practices: how you preserve social cohesion under sustained pressure, how you maintain operational tempo when metrics fail, and how you institutionalize adaptation so that chaos management becomes a permanent competence rather than a temporary campaign.

Even the most carefully constructed chaos management playbook is only as effective as the leaders entrusted to apply it under real-world pressure. The ability to think, decide, and adapt inside turbulence is not an optional enhancement to this framework; it is the decisive variable. The work of forging Chaos Navigators is therefore not a side project. It is the human core of your entire approach to mastering chaos.

# FURTHER THOUGHTS ON LEADERSHIP FOR MASTERING CHAOS

Part Three deepens the leadership focus of the book by translating the structural argument about chaos into concrete imperatives for how senior leaders must think, decide, and behave over the next 12–24 months. It assumes the reader has accepted that disruption is now the enduring operating environment, not a temporary deviation, and asks what kind of leadership stance can build and sustain organizations that function coherently when "normal" keeps moving.

Part Three, "Further Thoughts on Leadership for Mastering Chaos," is organized around three chapters: "Five Leadership Imperatives for Mastering the Age of Chaos," "Round Up and Final Thoughts," and the "Chaos Management Cheat Sheet." Together, they move from sharpening the leadership mindset to consolidating the book's argument into a portable, practice-oriented guide for ongoing use.

The first chapter distills the earlier analysis into five imperatives: managing chaos as a continuous condition rather than discrete crises, prioritizing resilience over brittle efficiency, normalizing action under ambiguity, treating wicked problems as enduring terrain, and making leaders' own thinking patterns a primary object of attention. These imperatives describe a shift away from the heroic, crisis-fixing leader toward an architect of adaptive capacity, someone who shapes conditions so that others can keep thinking and acting effectively under pressure.

The "Round Up and Final Thoughts" chapter pulls the book's threads together and frames chaos management explicitly as a 12–24 month agenda rather than a one-off initiative. It revisits the three pillars of adaptive capacity, intellectual flexibility, institutional resilience, and social cohesion, and emphasizes that real progress comes from sequenced moves: diagnosing brittle optimizations, redesigning structures and information flows, and investing in leader development that embeds the cognitive skills needed for chaos navigation. The chapter underlines that the goal is not to eliminate surprise or prevent all crises but to reduce self-inflicted blindness, speed and align responses, and cultivate a workforce that can learn its way through unprecedented situations.

The "Chaos Management Cheat Sheet" functions as a compact field reference for leaders before crises, exercises, or strategy sessions. It summarizes the three pillars and translates them into crisp prompts and reminders, for example, teaching people how to think rather than what to think, trading some efficiency for redundancy and optionality, and deliberately investing in trust and shared purpose as strategic assets rather than afterthoughts. The cheat sheet reinforces that chaos management is a permanent competence: something to be rehearsed, refreshed, and returned to as conditions evolve, not a conceptual framework to be read once and shelved.

Across Part Three, the emphasis is on leadership as the continuous design and stewardship of adaptive capacity rather than episodic crisis heroics. Leaders are urged to see themselves less as the ones who personally solve each disruption and more as the builders of systems, cultures, and decision architectures that can absorb shocks, learn quickly, and adapt faster than the environment is changing.

This requires a conscious time horizon: using the next 24 months to re-balance away from single points of failure and efficiency-only optimization, to institutionalize distributed decision-making, and to normalize acting on provisional maps while revising them in public as new information emerges.

Part Three explicitly links back to the earlier sections: Part One's diagnosis of the "anarchy of the moment" and Part Two's frameworks for building chaos-ready organizations and forging Chaos Navigators.

It recasts those structural and developmental arguments as ongoing leadership practice, insisting that your "real work" is to shape the conditions under which everyone else can keep thinking in turbulence.

In this sense, Part Three serves as both a capstone and an operational bridge: it ensures that the conceptual and organizational architecture developed earlier is translated into a lived leadership posture, supported by a practical "cheat sheet" that leaders can carry into the next crisis, exercise, or major decision cycle.

# FIVE LEADERSHIP IMPERATIVES
# FOR MASTERING THE AGE OF CHAOS

We now live in a world where disruption is not an interruption to normal life but the environment in which leadership actually occurs. Crises no longer arrive as isolated events with clean beginnings and endings. They cascade, overlap, and recombine, creating a continuous operating condition that feels like permanent turbulence. The familiar move from "crisis back to stability" has become the exception, not the rule.

Parts One and Two of this book explained why this is happening and how to build organizations with the adaptive capacity to survive and thrive in such conditions.

This chapter turns directly to you as a senior leader. It distills those arguments into five practical imperatives that should shape how you think, where you spend your time, and how you structure your leadership team over the next 12 to 24 months. These imperatives apply whether you wear a uniform, lead a ministry, or run a global enterprise.

## 1. STOP MANAGING CRISES. START MANAGING CHAOS.

Traditional crisis management assumes that disorder is temporary, bounded, and containable. The goal is to identify a discrete problem, fix it, and restore a previous steady state as quickly as possible. That logic still has its place for localized, well-understood events, but it fails catastrophically when the system itself is shifting under your feet.

Chaos management starts from a different premise: continuous volatility is the baseline, not the exception. Instead of trying to restore an old equilibrium, your strategic task is to build adaptive capacity so your organization can operate coherently across a range of unpredictable conditions. In practice, this means investing in capabilities that increase your ability to absorb shock, learn quickly, and reconfigure operations as the environment changes, even when you cannot define the next crisis in advance.

A useful test is to examine your calendar, budget, and promotion system. If most of your leadership energy and resources are still organized around "solving" named crises one by one, you are optimizing for a world of episodic disruption that no longer exists. If, instead, you deliberately allocate time and resources to building the three pillars of adaptive capacity, intellectual flexibility, institutional resilience, and social cohesion, you are beginning to lead for chaos rather than trying to out-run it.

## 2. BUILD FOR RESILIENCE, NOT BRITTLE EFFICIENCY.

Modern management has trained leaders to prize efficiency above almost everything else. In stable environments with predictable demand and long planning horizons, squeezing out redundancy and slack made obvious sense. In chaotic environments, those same optimizations produce fragility. Systems built for maximum efficiency under assumed conditions tend to fail abruptly when those assumptions no longer hold.

Leading through the age of chaos requires a conscious rebalancing. You still care about efficiency, but you treat resilience as a primary design objective rather than a nice-to-have. That means accepting what will look, in the short term, like "waste": multiple suppliers for critical components, overlapping communication channels, backup decision paths, leadership depth beyond immediate needs, and infrastructure that can support several futures rather than one forecast.

This is not an abstract virtue. Resilience shows up in concrete questions: If you lose a key node, a data center, a headquarters, a key port, a senior leader, what can still function effectively within 24 hours? Where are you dangerously dependent on single points of failure? Which areas have just enough redundancy to bend rather than break under stress? Leaders who treat those questions as central, rather than technical details to be delegated away, are the ones actually preparing their organizations for the world they now inhabit.

# 3. NORMALIZE OPERATING IN SUSTAINED AMBIGUITY.

In the age of chaos, you will often have to act before you fully understand what is happening. Waiting for clarity is itself a high-risk decision, because clarity frequently arrives only after windows of opportunity have closed and damage has compounded. At the same time, lunging at the first plausible interpretation of events is equally dangerous; it locks you into a narrative that may rapidly become false.

Your job is to make operating in sustained ambiguity feel normal for your organization. That begins with your own posture. Do you insist on complete information before moving, or can you act on partial, contested, and evolving data? Do you frame early decisions as experiments designed to generate information, or as irreversible commitments that must be defended?

Leaders who are comfortable saying "this is our best working hypothesis for now, and here is what we will watch to prove it right or wrong" signal that adaptation is expected and legitimate rather than a sign of initial failure.

Practically, this means institutionalizing living plans and provisional narratives rather than static strategies. It means teaching your team to hold multiple possible explanations in mind at once, to surface disconfirming evidence, and to revise the story together as new signals appear. The goal is not to eliminate uncertainty for that is impossible but to prevent uncertainty from paralyzing action or driving your organization into premature closure.

# 4. TREAT WICKED PROBLEMS AS ONGOING TERRAIN, NOT SOLVABLE TASKS.

Many of the challenges that define this era, geopolitical rivalry, climate disruption, digital fragmentation, societal polarization, are not "problems" in the classical sense. They are wicked problems: open-ended, interconnected conditions that cannot be definitively solved, only navigated more or less skillfully over time. Attempts to treat them as conventional projects with clear endpoints typically produce frustration and unintended consequences.

Leading in this context requires a shift in mental model. Instead of promising to "fix" wicked problems, you frame them as enduring terrain in which you and your organization must learn to operate. Your responsibility becomes to improve your positioning, reduce your vulnerabilities, and exploit openings as they arise, not to deliver a final resolution.

For example, you cannot eliminate cyber risk, information disorder, or supply chain fragility. You can, however, change your exposure, improve your detection and recovery speed, and adjust your dependencies so that failures are painful but not existential.

This mindset change affects how you communicate with your board, your workforce, and your stakeholders. Honest leaders in the age of chaos do not offer false certainty. They offer a credible path to becoming harder to break and faster to learn in the face of conditions no one controls.

# 5. MAKE YOUR MOST IMPORTANT JOB THINKING ABOUT YOUR THINKING.

In more stable periods, a leader's primary value often lay in accumulated experience and mastery of established playbooks. In chaotic environments, those playbooks can become liabilities as quickly as assets, because they tempt you to impose familiar patterns on fundamentally new situations. The currency that matters most is no longer what you know, but how you think—especially under pressure.

This is why your most important job is to attend to your own and your team's cognitive habits. The four cognitive capabilities developed earlier in the book, adaptive thinking, pattern recognition under uncertainty, emotional regulation, and collaborative sensemaking, are not abstract ideals. They are practical tools that determine whether you can maintain judgment when your nervous system, your organization, and the wider environment are all pulling you toward panic, denial, or rigid overconfidence.

You cannot outsource this work. You need to expose yourself and your senior team to realistic simulations, red-team challenges, and after-action reviews that surface how you actually reason and decide when the stakes feel real. You need to notice when you cling to a failing narrative, when you ignore weak signals because they do not fit your expectations, and when your emotional state is driving decisions you later rationalize as purely analytical. Leaders who build this kind of metacognitive discipline create organizations that can learn in real time rather than only in post-mortems.

## BRINGING THE IMPERATIVES TOGETHER

These five imperatives are mutually reinforcing. Committing to chaos management over serial crisis management pushes you toward investing in resilience rather than brittle efficiency. Resilience, in turn, makes it safer to act in ambiguity because your organization can survive missteps.

Treating wicked problems as enduring terrain keeps you from wasting energy on false finish lines and instead focuses you on continuous navigation. Attending deliberately to your own and your team's thinking patterns ensures that these choices are grounded in genuine cognitive capacity, not slogans.

In the chapters that follow, we move from the level of imperatives to the practical stance and behaviors required to live them. The "Round Up and Final Thoughts" chapter will help you translate these ideas into concrete moves over the next two years, and the Chaos Management Cheat Sheet will give you a compact reference you can keep at hand when the next wave of disruption arrives.

**9**

# ROUND UP AND FINAL THOUGHTS

This book began from a simple observation: you can no longer plan your way through genuine chaos. The challenge for senior leaders is not to predict the next crisis, but to build organizations that can keep thinking, deciding, and acting coherently when the parameters of the system itself are shifting. The question is no longer "How do we get back to normal?" but "How do we become the kind of institution that can function effectively when normal keeps moving?"

Part One explained why this shift is structural, not cyclical. The anarchy of the moment is driven by tightly coupled systems, cascading disruptions, compressed decision timelines, and overlapping crises that never fully resolve. Under these conditions, classic crisis-management logic, contain, fix, restore equilibrium—, repeatedly fails.

Part Two offered a practical answer: build intellectual flexibility, institutional resilience, and social cohesion as deliberate capabilities, and organize your information flows, team structures, environments, resources, and people around that purpose. Part Three has translated those insights into concrete leadership imperatives.

## FROM DIAGNOSIS TO LEADERSHIP STANCE

If you take nothing else from this book, take this: in the age of chaos, your real work is to shape the conditions under which everyone else can think and act effectively under pressure. That begins with diagnosis. You need a clear picture of where your organization is dangerously optimized for stability and efficiency, and where it already shows signs of adaptive capacity. The diagnostic questions in Part Two are designed to anchor that conversation: where do you see brittle single points of failure, where is information trapped in silos, where does culture punish rather than reward thoughtful dissent and experimentation?

But diagnosis is only useful if it leads to a different leadership stance. Chapter One in this part outlined five imperatives for leading in this environment: managing chaos rather than discrete crises, privileging resilience over brittle efficiency, normalizing action under ambiguity, treating wicked problems as enduring terrain, and making your own thinking patterns a primary object of attention. Together, they describe a leader who is less a heroic crisis-solver and more an architect of adaptive capacity. You are designing a system that can keep learning and adjusting faster than the shocks hitting it.

## A 24-MONTH AGENDA, NOT A ONE-TIME INITIATIVE

It is tempting to treat chaos management as one more initiative: a program to be launched, branded, and reported on. That instinct is understandable and dangerous. The capabilities described in this book develop over years, not quarters. They also rarely produce immediate, headline-grabbing wins. In the early phases, they can look like cost, friction, or unnecessary redundancy to those who are not seeing the whole board.

A more realistic framing is to see chaos management as a 12–24 month agenda embedded inside your existing responsibilities. You do not stop running your organization to do chaos management; you change how you run it. Over the first six months, you might focus on honest diagnostics and a handful of visible moves: changing how you run crisis huddles, adjusting who is in the room, creating space for alternative pattern reads, or piloting new training that builds ambiguity tolerance and collaborative sensemaking. Over the next year, you begin to hardwire what you learn into structures, processes, and incentives.

The Chaos Management Cheat Sheet that follows this chapter is designed as a practical bridge between these ideas and your calendar. It is not meant to be read once and filed away, but kept visible in your workspace, used to frame leadership team discussions, and revisited as new shocks expose fresh vulnerabilities. If the main text gives you the logic of chaos management, the cheat sheet is your compact operating guide.

# LINKING TRANSFORMATION LESSONS TO YOUR OWN CONTEXT

Throughout this book, I have drawn on military experience because armed forces have long had to operate in conditions of extreme uncertainty and high consequence. The epilogue includes summaries to two of my most recent books that highlight this dynamic of military transformation and learning.

The first is "Lessons in Military Transformation: From the RMA to the Drone Wars" and provides a condensed synthesis of how real organizations attempted to transform under pressure, from early precision-strike concepts to kill webs and contemporary drone warfare. Those cases are not here as war stories for their own sake. They show, in practice, what happens when institutions do or do not build the three pillars of adaptive capacity.

You do not need to command a Marine air wing, a NATO base, or a joint task force to use those lessons. The patterns are portable. Practitioner-led innovation that outpaces central planning, the dangers of exquisite but brittle systems, the importance of training for cognitive demands rather than just technical skills, the gap between transformation rhetoric and actual capability, these are dynamics that appear in ministries, corporations, universities, and civil society organizations as readily as they do in defense establishments.

The second is my 2026 book entitled, *From Crisis Response to Chaos Management: USMC Air as a Key Enabler*, which provides a case study of many of the concepts introduced and discussed in this book.

The USMC's evolution from crisis response to chaos management illustrates the book's core argument in action. Marine aviation enables this shift by powering the operational trinity of speed, connectivity, and distribution in environments of persistent disruption.

The epilogue is there as an evidence base for the argument of this book and as a resource when you need concrete examples to persuade others that change is not optional.

# WHAT YOU CAN REASONABLY EXPECT

Leading through the age of chaos does not mean eliminating surprise, preventing all crises, or insulating your organization from loss. Those promises would be dishonest. What you can reasonably expect, if you take this work seriously, is different.

You can expect fewer catastrophic surprises that come from self-inflicted blindness, because you have built information architectures and cultures that surface weak signals earlier.

You can expect faster, more coherent responses when shocks arrive, because you have invested in distributed decision-making and rehearsed operating in ambiguity.

You can expect a workforce that is less brittle and more capable of learning its way through unprecedented situations, because you have treated cognitive skills and social cohesion as core strategic assets rather than soft add-ons.

Above all, you can expect to feel less like an exhausted fire chief racing from blaze to blaze, and more like a steward of your institution's long-term survivability and purpose.

The anarchy of the moment will not relent. But leaders and organizations that treat chaos as the environment to be mastered, rather than an aberration to be endured, will have disproportionate influence over what comes next. Your task is to make sure your organization is among them.

# CHAOS MANAGEMENT CHEAT SHEET

Use this page as a fast refresher before a crisis, exercise, or strategy session.

## 1. THREE PILLARS OF ADAPTIVE CAPACITY

### Intellectual Flexibility

- Teach people how to think, not what to think.
- Hold multiple interpretations at once; avoid premature closure.
- Build routines that actively seek disconfirming evidence.
- Institutional resilience
- Trade some efficiency for redundancy, buffers, and optionality.
- Preserve institutional memory across rotations and leadership changes.
- Design infrastructure (physical and intellectual) to support multiple futures, not one forecast.

## Social Cohesion

- Invest intentionally in trust, shared purpose, and mutual commitment.
- Normalize honest dissent on tactics while protecting core values and identity.
- Build the relationships and habits that allow fast coordination when formal systems strain.

# 2. FOUR CORE COGNITIVE SKILLS

## Adaptive Thinking

- Keep several working hypotheses open; update quickly as reality shifts.
- Treat early decisions as tests, not final commitments.
- Practice "negative capability": stay with ambiguity long enough to learn.

## Pattern Recognition Under Uncertainty

- Look for weak signals at the edges, not just in formal reports.
- Ask: "If this pattern is real, what should we see next?" and watch for confirmation or contradiction.
- Use diverse vantage points (ops, intel, logistics, comms, legal) to build the picture.

## Emotional Regulation and Stress Tolerance

- Under pressure, name the stakes, then return the team to deliberate thinking.
- Notice your own stress signals and how they propagate through the organization.

- Use simulations and hot-wash discussions to practice staying effective under load.

## Collaborative sensemaking & distributed cognition

- Design the room: who must be in the conversation for the pattern to emerge?
- Structure interaction so minority views and edge data are heard before closure.
- Iterate: gather inputs → articulate competing interpretations → identify key uncertainties → act and revisit.

# 3. CORE VS SURGE: YOUR CHAOS ARCHITECTURE

## Core Capacity (What Must Endure)

- Essential missions and minimum viable services.
- Protected people, processes, and systems that keep the organization coherent.
- Surge capacity (what flexes)
- Pre-identified people, partners, and platforms you can rapidly re-task or scale.
- Standing mechanisms to shift resources between lines of effort as conditions change.

Quick check: Can you describe your core and surge in one page? If not, you have work to do before the next disruption.

# 4. SIX QUICK QUESTIONS BEFORE YOU ACT

- What are our three best current hypotheses about what is happening?
- What would disprove each?

- Where might our information be incomplete or systematically biased?
- What is the smallest reversible step we can take now to learn more, without locking into a bad path?
- Who is not in this room whose perspective could change our understanding?
- If this disruption lasts much longer than we expect, what breaks first and how do we build slack there now?

## 5. YOUR NEXT 90 DAYS

- Run one simulation or tabletop explicitly designed to break your current playbook.
- Map your three biggest areas of brittleness and identify at least one resilience investment in each.
- Establish a recurring forum (monthly or quarterly) for cross-boundary sensemaking about emerging weak signals.

# EPILOGUE

This epilogue highlights the operational experience that sits behind much of the analysis in the current book on the challenges facing chaos management.

These experiences are provided in detail in my 2026 books *Lessons in Military Transformation: From the RMA to the Drone Wars* and *From Crisis Response to Chaos Management: USMC Air as a Key Enabler*.

## LESSONS IN MILITARY TRANSFORMATION: FROM THE RMA TO THE DRONE WARS

Across four decades of fieldwork with militaries and defense institutions, I have watched transformation unfold not in briefing charts or strategy documents, but on flight decks, in maintenance hangars, and across evolving command-and-control architectures.

The cases examined in the book show how real organizations built (or failed to build) intellectual flexibility, institutional resilience, and social cohesion long before those terms appeared explicitly in their doctrine.

Conventional accounts of the Revolution in Military Affairs (RMA) and subsequent transformation programs tend to emphasize declared revolutions, elegant PowerPoint concepts, and centrally managed change. The lived reality was different.

What actually moved the needle were practitioners solving concrete operational problems under constraint, improvising with imperfect tools, and gradually reshaping concepts of operations as they learned.

From early precision-strike experiments to today's drone-saturated battlefields, meaningful change emerged through continuous adaptation inside complex systems rather than through single decisive breaks.

The journey from the RMA to network-centric warfare and onward to contemporary kill webs and drone wars thus provides more than a technology story. It is a record of how organizations learned to operate inside what this book calls the age of chaos while still speaking the language of crisis management. The integration of dispersed sensors and shooters, the compression of sensor-to-shooter timelines, the reconceptualization of platforms like the F-35 and MV-22 as network nodes rather than standalone assets, and the emergence of kill web operations all illustrate the same underlying pattern.

Transformation proved durable when it cultivated the three pillars of adaptive capacity highlighted in this book; it stalled or failed when institutions clung to linear, platform-centric, and centrally controlled models better suited to a more predictable era.

The book reconsiders the RMA, examines practitioner-led innovation in programs such as the F-35, MV-22, and CH-53K, traces the shift from kill chains to kill webs, explores training revolutions at places like MAWTS-1 and the International Flight Training School, and analyzes both successful and failed attempts at modernization from the U.S. services to key allies.

Taken together, these cases provide the empirical backbone for the chaos management approach highlighted in the current book. They show, in practice, how organizations either learned to navigate an environment of perpetual disruption or paid the price for assuming they were still managing discrete crises.

# *FROM CRISIS RESPONSE TO CHAOS MANAGEMENT: USMC AIR AS A KEY ENABLER*

My 2026 book entitled, *From Crisis Response to Chaos Management: USMC Air as a Key Enabler*, provides a case study of many of the concepts introduced and discussed in this book as well.

The USMC's evolution from crisis response to chaos management illustrates chaos management argument in action. Marine aviation enables this shift by powering the operational trinity of speed, connectivity, and distribution in environments of persistent disruption.

## Chaos as Baseline Environment

Traditional crisis response treated disruptions as temporary aberrations to be resolved linearly. Deploy rapidly, restore order, withdraw. Chaos management accepts perpetual volatility, gray zone pressures, hybrid threats, adaptive adversaries, as the norm. USMC air platforms like the F-35, MV-22, and CH-53K now integrate into kill webs, generating effects through network resilience rather than platform dominance.

This mirrors the book's three pillars of adaptive capacity. Marines build intellectual flexibility by treating doctrine as provisional, revising tactics mid-operation via digital links. Institutional resilience emerges from distributed logistics and attritable assets that survive contested access. Social cohesion sustains through alliance nodes, like Australian forward supplies, ensuring rapid reconfiguration under stress.

## Aviation's Role in the Trinity

Speed: MV-22s tiltrotor range lets dispersed units reposition faster than adversaries react, compressing decision cycles.

Connectivity: F-35s sensors create shared awareness, turning helicopters and tankers into kill web nodes.

Distribution: CH-53K and KC-130J sustain forward units without vulnerable hubs, embodying resilience over efficiency.

Steel Knight 2025 tested this live: HMLA-267 helicopters

networked effects across expeditionary C2, exposing gaps in contested comms while proving tempo in ambiguity.

## Building Chaos Navigators

USMC leaders must embody the book's Chaos Navigator traits: hold multiple hypotheses, regulate stress, sense-make collaboratively. Steel Knight rehearsed this as expeditionary hubs shifted as threats evolved, forcing adaptive thinking over rigid plans.

Challenges persist: institutionalizing adaptation against standardization biases, developing talent for ambiguity over rote execution. Politically, explaining resilience (not decisive victories) demands the book's honest communication imperative.

This case grounds the book's abstractions: chaos-ready organizations prioritize learning loops, like MAWTS-1 training, over perfect forecasts. USMC air shows how military services, one of the book's archetypes, trade efficiency for survivability, turning perpetual disruption into competitive edge.

# BIBLIOGRAPHY

Argyris, Chris. 1991. "Teaching Smart People How to Learn." *Harvard Business Review* 69 (3): 99–109.

Argyris, Chris, and Donald A. Schön. 1978. *Organizational Learning: A Theory of Action Perspective*. Reading, MA: Addison-Wesley.

Ashby, W. Ross. 1956. *An Introduction to Cybernetics*. London: Chapman & Hall.

Freund, C., et al. 2022. "Natural Disasters and the Reshaping of Global Value Chains." World Bank Report.

Heifetz, Ronald A., 1994. *Leadership Without Easy Answers*. Cambridge, MA: Harvard University Press.

Heifetz, Ronald A., Alexander Grashow, and Marty Linsky. 2009. *The Practice of Adaptive Leadership: Tools and Tactics for Changing Your Organization and the World*. Boston: Harvard Business Press.

Kahneman, Daniel, 2011. *Thinking, Fast and Slow*. New York: Farrar, Straus and Giroux.

Klein, Gary. 1998. *Sources of Power: How People Make Decisions*. Cambridge, MA: MIT Press.

Klein, Gary, 2007. "Performing a Project Premortem." *Harvard Business Review* 85 (9): 18–19.

Klein, Gary, 2009. *Streetlights and Shadows: Searching for the Keys to Adaptive Decision Making*. Cambridge, MA: MIT Press.

Laird, Robbin, 2025. *Assessing Global Change: Strategic Perspectives of Dr. Harald Malmgren*. Arlington, VA: Second Line of Defense.

Laird, Robbin, 2026. *Always Ready, Persistently Under-Resourced: The Modern United States Coast Guard Story*. Amazon.

Laird, Robbin, and Edward Timperlake. 2022. *A Maritime Kill Web Force in the Making: Deterrence and Warfighting in the 21st Century*. [

March, James G. 1991. "Exploration and Exploitation in Organizational Learning." *Organization Science* 2 (1): 71–87.

March, James G., and Herbert A. Simon, 1958. *Organizations*. New York: Wiley.

Perrow, Charles, 1999. *Normal Accidents: Living with High-Risk Technologies*. Updated ed. Princeton, NJ: Princeton University Press.

PortEconomics. 2025. "Blockage of the Suez Canal, March 2021." Port Economics, May 1.

Rittel, Horst W. J., and Melvin M. Webber, 1973. "Dilemmas in a General Theory of Planning." *Policy Sciences* 4 (2): 155–169.

Schön, Donald A., 1983. *The Reflective Practitioner: How Professionals Think in Action*. New York: Basic Books.

Senge, Peter M., 1990. *The Fifth Discipline: The Art and Practice of the Learning Organization*. New York: Doubleday.

Simon, Herbert A., 1955. "A Behavioral Model of Rational Choice." *Quarterly Journal of Economics* 69 (1): 99–118.

Snowden, David J., and Mary E. Boone, 2007. "A Leader's Framework for Decision Making." *Harvard Business Review*, November.

Taleb, Nassim Nicholas. 2007. *The Black Swan: The Impact of the Highly Improbable*. New York: Random House.

Taleb, Nassim Nicholas, 2012. *Antifragile: Things That Gain from Disorder*. New York: Random House.

Taleb, Nassim Nicholas, 2018. *Skin in the Game: Hidden Asymmetries in Daily Life*. New York: Random House.

Weick, Karl E., 1993. "The Collapse of Sensemaking in Organizations: The Mann Gulch Disaster." *Administrative Science Quarterly* 38 (4): 628–652.

Weick, Karl E., 1995. *Sensemaking in Organizations*. Thousand Oaks, CA: Sage Publications.

Weick, Karl E., and Kathleen M. Sutcliffe. 2007. *Managing the Unexpected: Resilient Performance in an Age of Uncertainty*. San Francisco: Jossey-Bass.

Vanderberg, Frank, et al. 2023. "Kill Webs: The Future of Integrated Operations." U.S. Marine Corps.

Dr. Robbin F. Laird is a strategic defense analyst whose four-decade career has been defined by a singular methodological principle: operational reality takes precedence over theoretical frameworks. As Editor and Co-Founder of *Second Line of Defense* and *Defense.info*, and a Board of Contributors member for Breaking Defense, he has built his analytical reputation not through Washington conference rooms but through sustained field research with military practitioners across Europe, Australia, Canada, and allied nations.

Laird's approach follows the maxim attributed to General Patton: "If everyone is thinking alike, someone isn't thinking." This principle shapes his contrarian methodology, challenging conventional defense establishment thinking through extensive interviews with operational commanders, combat pilots, defense officials, and strategic practitioners who understand transformation from the cockpit and the deck plate rather than the briefing room.

His academic foundation began at Columbia University, where he earned his Ph.D. under Zbigniew Brzezinski, studying the strategic transitions that would define the post-Cold War era. He has taught at Queens College Johns Hopkins, and other institutions, but his intellectual development has been shaped equally by decades of field research documenting how military organizations actually adapt to strategic competition, technological change, and operational demands.

Laird's analytical work spans the full arc of post-Cold War military transformation. His early career focused on Soviet studies and European security, including direct analysis of post-Soviet nuclear security challenges and European integration dynamics. He experienced the September 11 Pentagon attack firsthand, an event that shifted his focus toward homeland security and defense transformation. Throughout this period, he developed what would become his signature approach: prioritizing practitioner knowledge over policy theory, emphasizing how technological capabilities must be matched with organizational adaptation, and documenting the gap between acquisition programs and operational reality.

His recent work has concentrated on several interconnected themes that define modern military transformation. He has documented the U.S. Marine Corps' evolution from counterterrorism operations to strategic competition readiness, particularly the Second Marine Aircraft Wing's transformation through platforms like the MV-22 Osprey, CH-53K King Stallion, and F-35 Lightning II. His research on combat pilot training transformation examines how aviation education has shifted from traditional stick-and-rudder skills to cognitive decision-making and information management in fifth-generation warfare.

Working with Ed Timperlake, Laird developed the "kill web" concept as an alternative to traditional "kill chain" thinking, arguing for networked operations that reflect the distributed nature of modern combat. This framework has influenced naval doctrine development and represents his broader analytical emphasis on how operational concepts must evolve to match technological capabilities and strategic demands.

His theoretical contributions center on the evolution from "crisis management" to "chaos management" as a framework for understanding modern military operations. This concept challenges traditional planning assumptions, arguing that contemporary strategic environments require organizations capable of functioning effectively when the parameters of the system itself are shifting, not merely responding to crises within stable frameworks.

Laird's methodology remains consistent across all his work: extensive international travel for face-to-face interviews, emphasis on how operators actually employ systems rather than how they were designed to be used, and sustained attention to organizational culture and adaptation patterns. His analysis of Coast Guard modernization, NATO transformation, Australian defense integration, and European security challenges all reflect this practitioner-focused approach.

Currently based in Arlington, Virginia and Paris, France, Laird continues his field research while collaborating with Kenneth Maxwell on a co-autobiography examining strategic transitions across decades.

Laird's contribution to defense analysis lies in rigorously documenting how practitioners adapt to operational realities, how organizations develop or fail to develop the cognitive flexibility required for strategic competition, and how technological capabilities translate into operational advantages only when matched with appropriate organizational structures and strategic thinking. His work provides essential insight for senior leaders navigating the gap between policy aspirations and operational effectiveness.